AVIONICS FOR THE PILOT

An introduction to navigational and radio systems for aircraft

JOE JOHNSTON A.M.E.

Airlife

First published in 1998 by
Airlife Publishing, an imprint of
The Crowood Press Ltd
Ramsbury, Marlborough
Wiltshire SN8 2HR

www.crowood.com

This impression 2007

British Library Cataloguing-in-Publication Data
A catalogue record for this book is available from the British Library.

ISBN   978 1 86126 896 9

Typeset by Phoenix Typesetting, Auldgirth, Dumfriesshire

Printed and bound in Great Britain by Biddles Ltd, King's Lynn

Dedicated to my grandchildren
Aoife, Maeve and Shane

ACKNOWLEDGEMENTS

For permission to use copyright material and illustrations thanks are due to Boeing Commercial Airplane Group, British Aerospace Systems and Equipment Limited, Honeywell Air Transport Systems, Airbus Industries, Rockwell, and Collins Corporation.

I should like to thank Liam Hynan, Captain Roy Gordon and Johanna Johnston who read and criticised the book during its preparation; I am also much indebted to Matt Johnston for the illustrations. And one last specific acknowledgement is due to Mr Charles Kilroy of Kilroy's College who suggested I should write this book.

CONTENTS

CHAPTER ONE
RADIO SYSTEMS

Radio and aircraft are children of the twentieth century. On 22 September 1902, the first engine-powered balloon flight to take place in England took off from Crystal Palace, London. The balloon flew over Chelsea and finished the flight over thirty miles away having taken three hours to do it. The pilot of the balloon was Stan Spencer and his airship was powered by a 30hp petrol engine. Londoners of all ages were amazed at the new way of travelling. In many European countries experiments in flying using airships and balloons were taking place by the beginning of 1900; fig. 1–1 shows the different methods of flying which were used in the early years. The same experiments were taking place in America. In 1903 at a place called Kitty Hawk in the state of North Carolina the era of engine-powered aircraft began. At 10.35 on 17 December the American Wright brothers made their historic flight over the sand dunes of the village in a biplane called *The Flyer*.

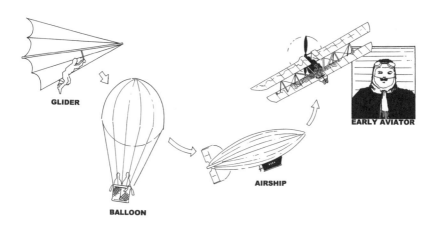

Figure 1–1   Early Methods of Flying

Two years before that event another great first had taken place. In 1901 the Italian physicist, Guglielmo Marconi, had successfully transmitted radio waves across the Atlantic. Three years later John Fleming invented the thermionic valve (diode) in England. In 1906 the American Lee De Forest invented the triode valve which made it possible for radio transmitter receivers to be given more power. Radio moved forward hand in hand with aviation and the rate of development was rapid. During 1958 many of the people who had watched the Spencer Airship in their childhood had the experience of seeing the first transatlantic jet flying across the London sky. The first communication satellite was launched into space that same year. The surge in the capabilities of aviation and radio was mainly due to the demands of the military establishments in the First and Second World Wars. Governments invested a lot of money and manpower into research and development. Radio and aircraft, even though they transport totally different matter, both use the same medium in which to travel, and they complement each other as a result; it did not take long for many industrial and government leaders to realise this fact. Shortly after the end of the Second World War the flying machines that had been working for the military were transferred into civilian airline hands. The aviation work was the same but the freight and passengers had changed and a new industry was born. The marriage of the two new industries was a success, and avionics as we know it today is a product of that partnership.

Before 1920 air traffic control used visual signalling, as shown in fig. 1–2. This method – semaphore – consisted of ground personnel using lights as well as red and green flags to signal instructions to pilots. When airborne, communication was non-existent and this was a grave disadvantage for pilots. Experiments in transmitting messages from air balloons using new radio equipment had been taking place in Britain with increasing success from 1908 to 1912. In the United States serious air-to-ground experiments using aerial-equipped wireless transmitters (in those days it was called a wireless: the use of the name radio came later) were taking place during 1912. In October of 1931 at Langley Field, Virginia, during experiments between two aircraft in flight, clear signals were received over a distance of twenty-five miles and air-to-ground signal transmission and reception signals were heard undistorted over forty miles away from the ground station. Military interest immediately increased the number of men and the amount of money put into research and development.

Figure 1–2   Landing Without Radio

The same process was happening in the building and designing of aircraft. Radio telegraphy was used on aircraft up to the 1930s and a radio operator was part of the flight crew. The radio operator transmitted and received in Morse code. In the following years better radio equipment made it possible for air traffic control to communicate with aircraft on a regular basis. Airports also saw some improvement; light beacons were set up on runways as landing and take-off aids. The utilisation of radio beams to guide aircraft along navigation paths was becoming more advanced and acceptable. At that time radio beam transmitters were set up to give the 100-mile navigation path that an aircraft could follow. When flying along the beam the pilot would hear in his headphones an A (dit dah) Morse signal on one side of the centre line and an N (dah dit) signal on the other. Down the centre the signals combined to give one long continuous note or whistle, as shown in fig. 1–3. On hearing the continuous note in his headphones the pilot knew he was on the centre of the radio beam. The new radio transmitter/receivers also gave pilots the ability to communicate on the ground and in the air.

In 1936 British scientists had already made advances in developing another new method of using radio waves. The invention of radar (radio direction and ranging) in 1940, combined with a faster, more efficient aircraft, the Spitfire, was pivotal to the success of the

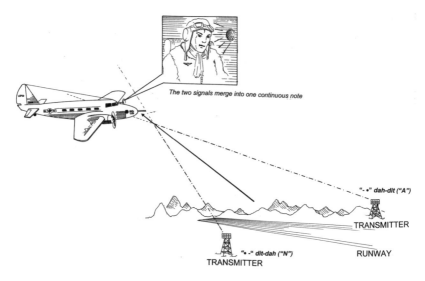

The two signals merge into one continuous note

"- •" dah-dit ("A")

TRANSMITTER

"• -" dit-dah ("N")

TRANSMITTER

RUNWAY

Figure 1–3   Early Radio-Aided Landings

Royal Air Force in the Battle of Britain. Spurred on by this the radio communications and aviation industries made rapid progress in the 1950s. Radar was also operated by air traffic control to make the business of flying safer for the general public. Radio receivers were the first electronic navigation aid used by aircraft. Direction finding (DF) was employed in the 1920s for position-fixing and tuning in to a specific ground radio station. For many years it was called the radio compass.

Radio and avionic navigation systems have come a long way from their humble start in the early days of flying. In the beginning navigation was carried out by pilots looking down for known landmarks. A pilot would follow a railroad, a river or canal, and journey from village or town to his destination. Good eyesight was essential for a pilot. Flying in the early days was carried out at low altitudes for obvious reasons, but that did not stop aircraft flying into church steeples and the pilot, if he survived, pleading temporary blindness. Pilots had to have great courage in the early days of flying. When aviation progressed to a level at which they could operate above the clouds at different times of the day and night, new methods of navigating became necessary. Pilots do and always will look out of cockpit windows, but in the new, fast, all-weather machines navigating by the old method of ground landmarks became redundant. New equipment and techniques were needed to operate the more complex faster-flying machines. Today, radio and avionic navigation systems make it possible for pilots to fly around the world at altitude and speed and at the same time keep in contact with the ground in a style which their ancestors in aviation could only dream about; they are able to land at airports in bad weather and poor visibility with safety. In this section of the book the reader will learn about radio communication systems in use on today's civil transport aircraft. In later chapters avionic navigation systems will be reviewed.

Electromagnetic and radio frequency waves

James Maxwell, a Professor of Physics at Cambridge University, England, proved during experiments that an electrical interruption would cause an effect at another point far away from the place at which it occurred. In 1864 he forecast that electromagnetic waves of energy travel outwards from a source at the speed of light. Four years later a physicist in Germany, Heinrich Hertz, was able within laboratory conditions to prove that Professor Maxwell was correct. Many years later Marconi made use of electromagnetic waves to transmit and receive signals; radio electromagnetic waves had arrived.

Briefly, radio waves are the basic building blocks of all radio communications and navigation systems. Even though they are unseen their effects make modern aviation radio and navigation operations possible. Radio waves have an important purpose in communications, navigation, air traffic control and weather warning systems. The three types of radio waves are space waves, sky waves and ground waves. Each of the radio waves is used for different operations in avionics. Space waves are used when transmitting or receiving radio signals above thirty megahertz. The very high frequency omnidirectional radio range navigation system and very high frequency radio communications avail themselves of space waves. Sky waves are used when transmitting and receiving radio signals from 2 to 30 megahertz; the high frequency radio systems operate in this range. Ground waves are effective in very low frequency and low frequency operations. Omega navigation systems use very low frequency (VLF) radio frequencies. Automatic direction finding (ADF) navigation systems use low and medium frequencies.

When discussing radio waves it helps to remember that electricity and magnetism are linked. For example, magnetism is a directional force and magnets when moved can induce electric current. It is also possible for electric current to produce a magnetic effect. Radio waves have both electricity and magnetism in their make-up. When a heavy magnetic storm takes place in the sky all telecommunications, power supply lines, radar and radio navigation and television broadcast systems can be badly affected. One such storm in Canada in 1989 damaged power lines and a nuclear power station and left six million people without basic electricity. It is also useful to know the following facts about radio waves. Firstly they travel at 186,000 miles per second. Secondly the radio wave is composed of two fields: one is an electrostatic field which is made up of electrons going through an energy change, and the second is a magnetic field. The electrostatic field, or electric field as it is better known, can be polarised. How a radio wave is polarised is resolved by the direction of the lines of force in this field. The direction of the lines of force will be decided by the type of radiating antenna: if it is a vertical antenna the radio wave will be transmitted vertically, and a horizontal antenna will transmit horizontally. This polarisation factor is utilised by radio broadcasting stations. Different radio transmitting and receiving combination antennae are designed depending on what polarisation method is being used.

As well as the type of radio wave and the method by which it is transmitted, another big factor to consider for good radio signals is the effect of the ionosphere (the layer of air molecules located in the earth's atmosphere). In the ionosphere the molecules are affected by the energy of the sun. At certain periods during the day or night and depending on conditions in the ionosphere, radio waves can travel thousands of miles and be received very clear and undistorted. At other times when the ultra-ray radiation from the sun is affecting the earth's atmosphere the transmission and reception of radio signals is not good. The earth's ionosphere is constantly changing, depending on the period of day or night. At night the different layers move closer to the earth. This movement of the earth's ionosphere can affect radio signals. When a radio signal is transmitted at night, instead of passing into space it bounces off the lower layers of the earth's atmosphere. When the signal is reflected in this manner it normally travels a longer distance, and in many cases can be received thousands of miles away from its transmitting point. The radio system which benefits from this method of communicating is the high frequency system.

Radio frequencies are measured in Hertz (named after the physicist

Heinrich Hertz who showed radio waves were like heat and light waves); 1 cycle = 1 hertz, 1,000 cycles = 1 kilohertz, 1,000,000 cycles = 1 megahertz, and 1,000,000,000 cycles =1 gigahertz. The measurements are abbreviated to read 1Hz, 1kHz, 1 MHz, 1GHz.The frequencies are organised in different bands or ranges as follows:

(a) Very low frequency (VLF). Frequency 3–30 kilohertz. The Omega navigation system uses this frequency band.
(b) Low frequency (LF). 30–300 kilohertz. The automatic direction finding and Loran navigation systems make use of this frequency band.
(c) Medium frequency (MF). 300–3,000 kilohertz. Commercial broadcast radio stations operate in the medium frequency band. Automatic direction finding systems operate from 190 to 1,750 kilohertz which is within this band.
(d) High frequency (HF). 2–30 megahertz. The long-range high frequency radio system utilises this range.
(e) Very high frequency (VHF). 30–300 megahertz. This frequency band is used for short-range radio communications by the aircraft very high frequency system. The localiser section of an aircraft navigation radio receiver during an instrument landing system (ILS) landing approach is included in this frequency band. The very high frequency omnidirectional radio range (VOR) system and the marker beacon system utilise this band.
(f) Ultra-high frequency (UHF). 300–3,000 megahertz. The glideslope section of the aircraft navigation receiver would employ this frequency band during an instrument landing system (ILS) runway approach. This band is also put to work by the distance measuring equipment (DME) and air traffic control systems.
(g) Super-high frequency (SHF). 3–30 gigahertz. This band serves the radio altimeter transmitter receiver (RAD-ALT) system.
(h) Extremely high frequency (EHF). 30–300 gigahertz.

Aircraft communication – VHF and HF

Very high frequency radio is used for short-range operations. A typical very high frequency transmitter receiver range is from 0 to 130 miles. High frequency radio is used for long-range communications, and can transmit and receive signals over thousands of miles depending on operating conditions. Both of these radio systems are used by the flight crew to communicate with air traffic control, airport ground service stations and other aircraft. A typical transmit and receive operation is shown in fig. 1–4. Internal communications between flight crew, cabin crew and ground maintenance personnel are taken care of by the flight and service interphone system. The flight and service interphone systems have different functions (see Chapter Two). When flight crews and service personnel are using radio systems to communicate a certain procedure must be followed. The basic radio rules and microphone technique when communicating with short- and long-range airborne systems is as follows:

(a) Before transmitting LISTEN for any conversations already going on and WAIT for a break in transmission.

(b) When beginning a conversation, always transmit the DESTI-NATION of your transmission, followed by your own identification and location. For example: 'Ground Control – from – Echo India Foxtrot Charlie.' Wait for an acknowledgement of your transmission. The reply would be, 'Echo India Foxtrot Charlie.'

(c) Finally, when ending a conversation (not a transmission) use a word or phrase to inform the station to which you are transmitting that the conversation is ended. This could be 'Out', 'Thank you', or any such phrase.

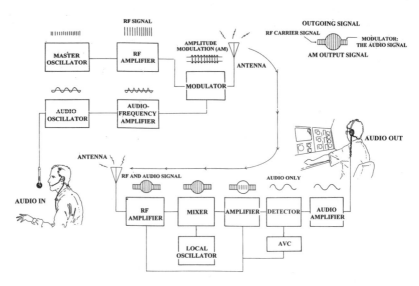

Figure 1–4   Simple Radio Transmitter/Receiver

18

Very high frequency radio

The very high frequency communication system will be discussed first. It is normally employed for voice air-to-ground communications between pilots and air traffic control. Pilots use very high frequency radio to communicate with ground service stations and other aircraft. Very high frequency radio operates in a line-of-sight (LOS) method, which means the transmitting antenna needs to see the receiving antenna for best results, as shown in fig. 1–5. When the signal is radiated the radio waves have to reach and strike a receiving antenna to induce a voltage. This signal voltage is passed into the radio receiver circuits which amplify, demodulate and filter the signal to reproduce the signal intelligence which was contained in the original transmitted radio wave. Some factors affecting a line-of-sight method of transmitting and receiving radio waves are:

(a) the transmitting power of the radio transmitter

(b) the height of the transmitting antenna plus type of radio propagation used

(c) the height of the receiving antenna and the direction the receiving antenna is in with respect to the transmitting station

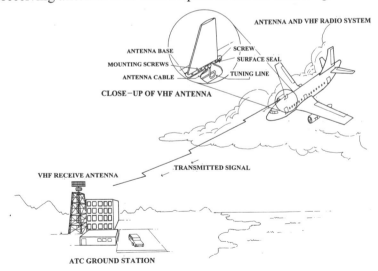

Figure 1–5   Line-of-Sight (LOS) Transmission

(d) the general condition and type of very high frequency radio being used at the receiving station.

A signal path between transmitter and receiving antennae free from obstructions gives the best results. When signals are blocked by high buildings or natural barriers like mountains the radio signals drift in and out and the received message is broken up and distorted. Look at the following examples of a very high frequency radio system operating at different altitudes; an aircraft flying at an altitude of 1,000 feet can communicate for a distance of about thirty miles using very high frequency radio; the same aircraft transmitting at an altitude of 10,000 feet can communicate up to a distance of 130 miles.

The frequency band employed by very high frequency radio in aviation goes from 118 to 135.975 megahertz. Amplitude-modulated (AM) voice signals is the mode of operation in aviation radio. Normally two or three radio systems are installed so that if a system breaks down the crew have a backup communication radio. On an aircraft the basic procedure before operating a very high frequency radio system is as follows. Check that the power is being supplied to the system. Select a transmission frequency on the VHF control panel. Select the microphone switch on the audio select panel. Adjust the audio volume control knob to a comfortable level on the audio select panel. Switch the radio on and if needed adjust the cockpit loudspeaker volume control (if a pilot is using his headphones and boom microphone the cockpit loudspeaker is normally not on). Finally prepare to transmit with either hand or boom microphone. Before transmitting flight crews will observe the correct radio procedure previously described on p. 20.

A very high frequency system consists of a transmitter/receiver, control panel, and an antenna. The basic system is shown in fig. 1–6 The radio control panel is mounted on the pedestal (a dividing panel between the pilot and co-pilot; it normally contains control panels). The transmitter/receiver is secured on a radio rack located in the electronic equipment storage bay. Access to the electronic equipment storage bay is via a flush hatch door located on the bottom of the fuselage. Very high frequency radio antennae are mounted on the top and bottom of the fuselage. The number one system transmits and receives using the top antenna. Normally the captain operates the number one system; the number two antenna serves the co-pilot's transmitter/receiver. The design of the radio systems is

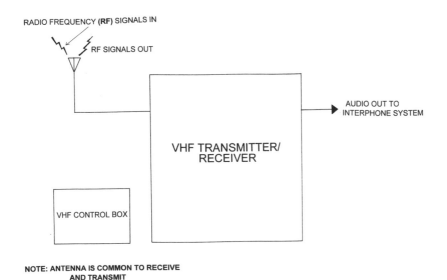

Figure 1–6   VHF Transmitter/Receiver Block Diagram

such that either pilot can operate number one or number two system by selecting the required radio transmitter/receiver on his audio selector panel.

The avionic radio equipment installed nowadays is designed and manufactured employing a combination of integrated circuits, microprocessors, silicon chips and other new electronic components. The name used for this type of equipment is solid state. This method of designing avionic equipment has restricted the use of mechanical devices and circuits, resulting in fewer maintenance problems. The new equipment has brought big benefits to aviation including smaller size, less weight and greater reliability. The saving in fuel and space is also very welcome to airline operators.

To aid avionic maintenance personnel microphone and headphone socket jack-plugs are fitted on the front panel of the transmitter/receiver. This facility is often used by avionic maintenance personnel when testing radio transmitter/receivers from the electronic equipment bay. A test button mounted on the same panel is pressed to test the receiver signal input. When the test button is pressed it causes a circuit known as the 'squelch' to operate, which results in signal hiss or noise being heard in the headphones that are plugged into the radio jack-socket. The button permits a quick check of the very high frequency radio receiver to be carried out in the main electronic equipment bay. Fitted on the front panel is a transmit radio frequency power signal lamp. The lamp lights when the radio transmitted power output is above 12 watts. When testing the radio *in situ* it is a good indication that the transmitter section is working normally.

A coaxial cable from the antenna which is connected to the back of the transmitter/receiver feeds the incoming very high frequency signals into the radio unit. During the period when the transmitter is in operation the outgoing signals are passed through the same coaxial cable to the antennae for transmission. Relay circuits are used to switch the transmitter/receiver function from transmit to receive. The type of antennae used are shark-fin-blade-shaped devices and they measure about twelve inches long. They are easily picked up on an aircraft as they are normally situated on the top and bottom of the fuselage. The next time you are at an airport try to locate the very high frequency antennae.

CONTROL PANEL

A typical very high frequency radio control panel is divided into two sections, as shown in fig. 1–7. Each section has its own display window and frequency control knobs, so arranged that an outer knob selects the first, second and third frequency digits and an inner knob selects the fourth and fifth. If the pilot selected the frequency

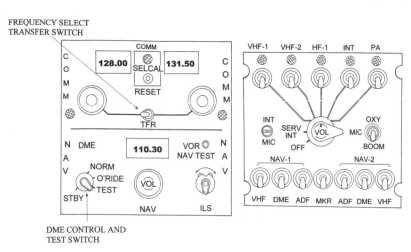

Figure 1–7   VHF Comm/NAV/DME Control Panel

131.00 megahertz, the control panel display window would show the following: reading from left to right, one three one, the first second and third digits plus zero zero.

The control panel also allows the pilot to dial in two different radio frequencies and have both displayed at the same time in separate display windows located on the controller. This feature of the controller is useful in that a pilot on approaching an airport can have the air traffic control frequency selected and operational and at the same time have his company's ground operation control frequency selected on the other display window ready for use. A transfer switch is fitted on the front panel of the controller for that function. The transfer switch allows the pilot to transfer quickly from one selected frequency to another. The very high frequency transmitter/receiver radio automatically tunes to whatever frequency is selected by the flight crew.

Each member of the flight crew has an audio selector panel (see fig. 1–7). This selector panel permits the crew member to choose the radio system needed at any particular time. Mounted on the front panel are toggle or push-button switches. Each switch is marked to indicate the specific radio communication or navigation system of which it is part. All systems are represented on this selector panel. A crew member can select any of the following systems: number one or two very high frequency or high frequency radio systems, number one or two automatic direction finding, omni-range navigation and distance measuring equipment systems. Flight or service interphone can also be selected with this panel. Oxygen or boom microphone can be selected by a switch mounted on the front of the panel. All oxygen masks in the cockpit have a microphone fitted. The advantage to a pilot of using the boom microphone fitted to headphones is that it leaves him with both hands free for other operations.

TRANSMITTER/RECEIVER OPERATION

The transmitter can be divided into separate circuits. Normally, a very high frequency radio transmitter is made up of a power amplifier, modulator, filter and a detector circuit. When the flight crew press the microphone push-to-talk button, control circuits within the radio unit disconnect the receiver and connect the transmitter circuits to the antenna. The transmitted signal is radiated from the antenna when the pilot speaks. When the pilot makes the transmission a small part of the audio, or sidetone, is passed back into his headphone. This sidetone permits the pilot to monitor the transmission and he would be aware of any weakness or distortion in the transmitted/signal. On completion of the transmission the transmitter/receiver switches back to a receive state of operation. The chain of events within the transmitter circuits when the pilot speaks is as follows:

(a) Audio is superimposed on to the radio frequency signal carrier wave.

(b) The stabilised master oscillator (SMO) is used to process the transmit frequency needed to carry the audio signal to its destination.

(c) Transmitter circuits used for transmission functions are the power output amplifiers. All power amplifier circuits are operated broadly tuned for best results.

(d) Modulator circuits consist of a pre-amplifier which is part of the microphone circuit and signal limiting devices. A modulator driver amplifier circuit is also used.

(e) The power output of a very high frequency transmitter/receiver is about 25–35 watts.

(f) The antenna is normally vertically polarised. It is omnidirectional, which means it can transmit and receive in any direction.

The receiver process starts when a signal is received by the antenna. From the antenna the signal is passed into the radio frequency amplifier circuit. From there the signal goes into an electronic radio frequency mixing circuit. It is then filtered and sent to a detector circuit. The output of the detector is an audio signal which is coupled into the aircraft interphone system. They can now receive the audio signal by plugging their headphones into the interphone sockets provided in the cockpit. If they wish the audio signal can be heard through the cockpit loudspeakers.

The heart of most transmitter/receivers is an electronic circuit called a frequency synthesiser, which is also known as a stabilised master oscillator (SMO). This generates the frequencies necessary for the processing of the receive and transmit signals. A simple explanation of this circuit is as follows. An electronic circuit called a voltage-controlled oscillator (VCO) produces a reference frequency, which is put to work by the synthesiser during the operation of the receiver circuits. The oscillator-produced frequency is then tuned by a device called a Varactor. The Varactor device allows the oscillator frequency to be used over a band of frequencies. A crystal-controlled oscillator keeps all radio frequencies from 118.00 to 135.975 megahertz in the very high frequency band in a stable condition. No frequency drift is allowed by the crystal-controlled oscillator when operating. The signal output of the reference oscillator is then passed to a frequency comparison circuit. If the frequency comparison circuit finds that the frequency of the oscillator is not correct it will automatically send a signal to the Varactor tuning device to remedy the error.

In a typical aviation radio transmitter/receiver frequency channels are spaced 25 kilohertz apart in the frequency band of 118.00 to 135.975 megahertz. Transmitted radio frequency power output would normally be about 25 watts; electric power to the radio is 28 volts DC. A very high frequency radio transmitter can operate from sea level to altitudes above 30,000 feet (fig. 1–8 shows two airborne aircraft and a ground station communicating). Line-of-sight radio transmissions are limited in the distance they can travel, which is the negative aspect; on the other hand they are less prone to distortion or bad reception by static and other types of interference.

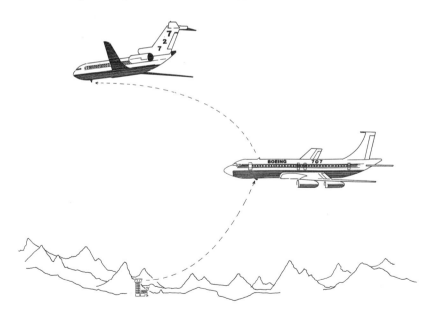

Figure 1–8   VHF Communications Between Two Aircraft

High frequency radio system

Due to the high radio wave energy being transmitted by the transmitter, safety precautions are necessary when operating this communication system on the ground. Before a transmission takes place all personnel working in the vicinity of the high frequency antenna are instructed to vacate the area. If fuelling or de-fuelling is taking place no transmission is allowed.

A high frequency radio system provides long-range communications. The frequency range is 2 to 30 megahertz. By using sky wave propagation long-distance transmissions are possible. When the transmitted radio signal waves are bounced back by the ionosphere they skip long distances and are then picked up by receivers located thousands of miles away. The skip distance phenomenon (see fig. 1–9) is very useful in high frequency communications as it extends the transmission and reception range. The drawback is that the conditions at that level in the sky never remain constant, and the signals fade in and out. Normally two high frequency radio systems are installed, each a self-contained system.

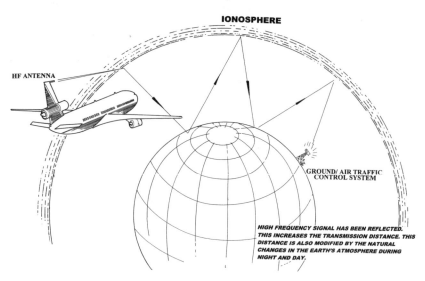

Figure 1–9   HF Radio Transmission

In many parts of the world facilities for very high frequency radio communications do not exist so aircraft flying into airports without

VHF ground control equipment depend on high frequency radio communications. This situation would affect long-haul transport aircraft flying over a large land mass or sea area. To make communication contact a high frequency radio system is essential.

CONTROL PANEL

The control panel is similar to the one already discussed in the section on very high frequency operation. Selector knobs are used for frequency selection in the 2 to 30 megahertz band. A function switch mounted on the front panel gives the pilot a means of selecting amplitude modulation (AM), or upper side band (USB). The control panel has an on/off switch fitted on the front. A squelch adjust knob permits the pilot to set receiver gain. The frequency display window is located in the centre of the front panel. Upper side band is the band used in aviation when operating the high frequency radio system. Each pilot has a controller and normally it is located on the forward instrument panel or the overhead panel in the cockpit. Fig. 1–10 shows the control panel, transceiver and high frequency coupler.

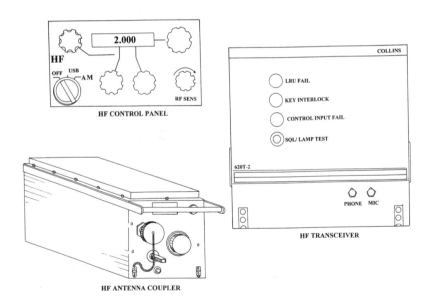

Figure 1–10

27

TRANSMITTER/RECEIVER OPERATION

The transmitter/receiver radio unit in a typical installation is mounted on an electronic equipment rack and secured with holding latches. The racks are located in the electronic equipment bay. In some installations the avionic radio equipment is located on racks in a special compartment in the cockpit. This radio transmitter/receiver transmits at a maximum of 400 watts in upper side band operation; in amplitude modulation operation the power output is 125 watts. The system tunes to a selected frequency in approximately eight seconds. Electrical power needed to operate the system is 115 volts AC 3 phase at 400 hertz plus 28 volts DC. The transmitter/receiver has a small cooling fan mounted on the front of the radio set which is operational during transmission, when the radio frequency power amplifiers get very hot. The cooling fan increases the air going into the transmitter/receiver during that time. Also mounted on the front of the radio set is a test meter whose function is to indicate the different voltages and current used in the transmitter/receiver. By checking the voltage and current values displayed on the test meter maintenance personnel have a good idea where a problem might be in the radio system. The front panel of the transmitter/receiver also has a headphone and microphone jack to allow monitoring of the audio sidetone signals being transmitted and received. To facilitate connection between the radio unit and the antenna circuits a coaxial connector is fitted at the front panel. In recent years avionic equipment has become smaller and lighter. The use of solid-state electronic components like microprocessors and integrated circuits has resulted in great savings in space and weight. Maintenance on the equipment has also been reduced.

The cycle of events in the transmission of a signal begins when the pilot switches power to the system. He then selects the mode of operation amplitude modulation (AM), upper side band (USB) or lower side band (LSB). Normally in aviation communications upper side band is used. The same frequency is used for transmitting and receiving. A frequency is inserted using the frequency knobs on the control panel. This selected frequency is displayed in the control panel display window.

The next step would be to set the level of the squelch control and audio volume controls for headphone and cockpit loudspeaker for sidetone gain. By pressing his press-to-talk microphone button the pilot tunes the transmitter to the frequency required. To indicate to the pilot the system is tuning to the selected frequency a one-kilohertz note is heard in the headphones. When the tuning cycle is completed correctly the note stops. He now listens awaiting his chance to speak without interrupting other transmissions which are taking place. When an opportunity to speak occurs he speaks into the microphone stating the name of the station called, followed by his own aircraft call-sign and location. Once the pilot begins to speak the transmission sequence of events starts to take place. A sidetone signal is coupled back into the interphone system and from that into the pilot's headphones. He will then know if the transmission is correct. In the transmitter the audio signal from the pilot is amplified and used to drive a modulator. From the modulator the signal is filtered and is prepared for upper side band operation. A radio frequency translator circuit then processes the signal and the output of the translator circuit is the operating frequency required. When the translator has completed its function the signal is then coupled to the radio frequency driver and power amplifier circuits. The output from the radio frequency power amplifiers is passed on to the antenna circuits for transmission to its final destination.

In receive the radio frequency from the antenna is amplified by radio frequency amplifiers, then mixed with an oscillator frequency to produce an intermediate frequency. That operation takes place in the translator (the radio frequency translator circuits are common to transmit and receive modes of operation in most transmitter/receivers). Having gone through the translator and been processed the signal is now sent to a detector circuit. The output of the detector circuit is an audio signal which is coupled to the audio amplifier before being processed through the interphone system and passed to the pilot's headphones. Fig. 1–11 shows a typical high frequency transmitter-receiver block diagram.

High and very high frequency radio communication systems use the flight interphone system (see Chapter Two). As already stated the advantage of the high frequency radio system is the long distance over which it can transmit and receive signals. The disadvantages of the system are that atmospherics caused by lightning storms interfere with transmission and reception of signals, the result of which is incomplete, garbled and unclear radio messages.

HIGH FREQUENCY ANTENNAE

Different types of antennae can be installed in a high frequency radio system. The most common types used are the probe, notch and wire antennae. Each of them has its advantages and disadvantages. A probe antenna is shaped like a round pole and it can be mounted on

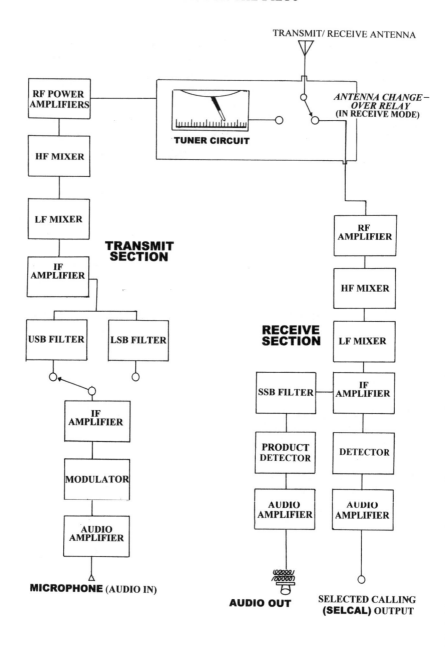

Figure 1–11   Aeroplane HF Transmitter/Receiver ("Transceiver")

the wing tips or at the tail, depending on the type of aircraft. Probe antennae are approximately 147 inches long and are covered with fibreglass material. Not all of the antenna would extend beyond the tail or wing; as the probe-type antenna sticks out lightning is liable to strike it, hence the need for lightning arrestors (see fig. 1–12).

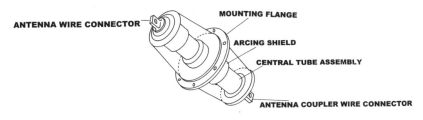

ANTENNA WIRE CONNECTOR

MOUNTING FLANGE

ARCING SHIELD

CENTRAL TUBE ASSEMBLY

ANTENNA COUPLER WIRE CONNECTOR

Figure 1–12   HF Antenna Lightning Arrestor

The lightning arrestor directs the lightning from the radio system antennae to the larger areas of the fuselage and wings. As the aircraft is composed of metal and other material structures properly inter- connected and earthed, the lightning is dispensed harmlessly. All radio system antennae are designed to be able to operate in an elec- trically isolated manner from the aircraft structure. A lightning arrestor is positioned between the antenna and the radio equipment. This is enclosed in a tightly sealed glass and metal case. When a light- ning discharge arc goes into the lightning arrestor case it is stopped from entering the radio equipment by a protective gap, which is designed in such a way that radio frequency signals are permitted to pass without causing arcing. The electronic circuit in the arrestor acts as a capacitor-type path, coupling radio frequency signals to and from the antenna but stopping any lightning electric energy from doing damage to the radio equipment. If a heavy lightning strike takes place a film of black or orange dust forms inside the glass surface of the arrestor. For that reason regular inspections are made. If a lightning strike takes place the pilot enters details of the event in the technical log book.

Another type of antenna used on short-haul aircraft is the notch antenna. The notch antenna is a slot cut into the vertical stabiliser. In some radio systems' installations a wire antenna is used. The wire antenna is fitted from the vertical fin at the rear end and extended forward to terminate at the lightning arrestor and antenna coupler. As this antenna is installed on the top of the fuselage special instal- lation procedures are carried out when fitting it. A fail-safe weak link is put in place at a predetermined point, preventing the wire from doing any damage or getting tangled in any moving surface controls. Safety is always paramount in all avionic installations.

When two radio systems are installed it is important that only one of the transmitters transmits at any one time. If the two systems transmit together induced voltages from the power amplifier output could damage either radio system's electronic circuits. The devices that prevent this happening are called interlock relays. When the transmission begins an interlock circuit relay will disconnect one transmitter and leave it set in the receive position. In some antennae installations the number one system and number two system avail themselves of the same probe antenna for transmitting. The same antenna might also be used for receiving signals for the number two system. In situations like that interlock and changeover relay circuits are used to ensure proper operation of the systems.

ANTENNA TUNER-COUPLER

This unit in the radio system is used to command a tuning impedance match between the radio frequency power output of the transmitter to the aircraft antenna at the frequency selected by the pilot. During the tuning cycle sequence servo amplifiers and control modules combine with discriminator circuits to carry out the operation. When the pilot presses the microphone switch the antenna tuner automatically tunes to a position which gives maximum transfer of radio frequency power to the antenna. On completion of a transmission a pilot can select a different frequency and the control module in the tuner control unit will automatically command a new tuning sequence to begin. If the system had no means of matching the radio frequency power in the connecting coaxial cable between the antenna and transmitter, the signal power would be reduced and a weak signal would result. The antenna control unit controls a unit called a tuner which is used as an impedance-matching device between the transmitter/receiver and the antenna. In the tuner a variable capacitor and inductor circuit functions as a matching network to couple the radio frequency signals to the antenna. In a typical installation the tuner is in a special compartment near the antenna. A tuner-coupler can be located at the wing tip or in the tail area. The tuner is pressurised with dry nitrogen to keep an inert atmosphere within the tuner at different altitudes. A tuner control unit is normally fitted on a radio rack in the electronic equipment bay.

STATIC DISCHARGERS

The elimination of noise in aircraft radio communication systems caused by an accumulation of electrically charged air and moisture as the aircraft moves through the atmosphere is carried out by fitting static dischargers at effective points on the aircraft. Normally they are fitted to wing tips, stabiliser, tail tip and aircraft rudder. The type of static that causes most problems is called perception static. Static dischargers act as discharge points for perception static. A discharger is made from resistive conducting material and can be a long type or short type, depending where it is to be fitted. The discharger is shaped like a rod and normally has fine metal needles or carbon tips on the end of the rod. On large, long-haul, high-speed, all-weather aircraft, static dischargers are easy to spot, protruding from the aircraft at the positions already stated. The base of a discharger is made of metal. When it is fitted the base is bonded to the aircraft structure.

SELECTIVE CALLING

Another communication unit involved with the radio systems in aviation is selective calling (Selcal). It sometimes happens that a ground control station would like to contact a particular aircraft to speak with the flight crew. The avionic unit designed for this purpose is called a Selcal decoder, an electronic monitor unit which continuously monitors the aircraft radio receivers. Every decoder has a four-letter code which is unique to the aircraft on which it is installed. Normally a four-letter code such as ABCD or any combination of letters in sets of four is inserted on the selective calling unit. The codes are inserted by using push buttons mounted on the front of the unit. When the decoder detects that code in the receiver it will operate a chime and flash an alert light on the Selcal control alert panel in the cockpit. This alerts the pilot and co-pilot that their aircraft is being called from a ground control station. Mounted on the control panel in the cockpit is a reset button which when pressed stops the flashing light and the chimes. The ground station uses a Selcal tone-transmitting unit to call an individual aircraft using a combination of tones which will key the airborne Selcal decoder. A ground station uses a radio frequency signal to transmit the four-tone code needed to alert the aircraft it wishes to contact. Every aircraft tuned to the frequency transmitted by the ground transmitter will receive the coded signal, but the only unit which can decode and produce the alert chimes and flashing lights for the cockpit crew is the Selcal decoder which is set up for the four-tone signal combination being received. A typical Selcal decoder unit uses vibrasponder reeds, manufactured in a special way which ensures they respond to audio frequencies. The resulting voltages caused by this response set off the chimes and lights in the cockpit. Solid state transistor switches are used in place of relays to operate circuits. A selective calling unit works in combination with the very high frequency and high frequency radio systems.

A Selection of HF Radio Systems Made by Rockwell/Collins

CHAPTER TWO
AUDIO INTEGRATING

System functions

The function of an audio integrating system is to provide a communication link between cabin crew, flight crew and ground service personnel. The system allows the flight crew and maintenance personnel to select the service required when they wish to contact each other. The system can be sub-divided into different functions:

(a) Service interphone. The service interphone system allows communications to be provided between ground service crews with either each other or the flight crew (fig. 2–1 shows typical service interphone locations). During a push-back from a terminal building apron you will often see a service crew

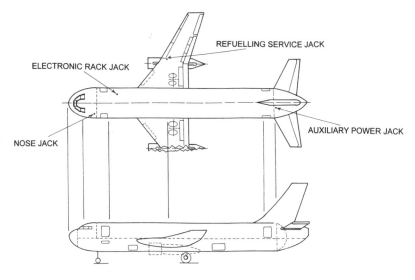

Figure 2–1   Typical Service Interphone Jacks Location

member talking to the pilot via a microphone headset plugged into an interphone jack, which is located in the nose area. Communication is essential during the push-back operation at an airport terminal building. When maintenance crews are communicating using this system at different points of the aircraft the service interphone switch located in the cockpit must be in the on position.

(b) Flight interphone. The flight interphone allows cockpit crew to communicate with each other or with ground service crews. A flight interphone system is the most important part of the audio integrating sub-systems. This system handles all radio commu-

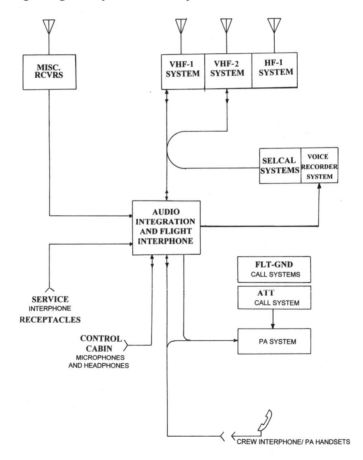

Figure 2–2   Communication Block Diagram

nication which uses microphones and headphones for transmitting and receiving audio signals. All other audio input and output signals from other systems are also processed through the flight interphone system. Fig. 2–2 shows a typical audio and flight interphone integrating system.

(c) Ground call. A push-button situated on the overhead panel can be utilised by the flight crew to sound an alert horn when they need to contact the ground service crew. Also located at the nose area is a similar facility for the ground service crew when it is necessary for them to contact the flight crew.

(d) Cabin Interphone. This system is a multi-channel phone communication system for interconnecting attendants' station positions during onboard cabin and cockpit telephone communications. Normally the stations are positioned at the doors and galley locations. The electronic equipment which is the heart of this communication system is known as the central switching unit, which operates as a compact mini automatic telephone switchboard. The electronic circuits in a central switching unit are housed in a black rectangular metal case and consist of interphone amplifiers, switching, decoder logic, filter and control circuits. Operations carried out by the central switching unit vary but its main function is connecting dialling circuits and providing a dial tone to handsets. It can automatically decode tone signals sent from attendants' and pilots' handsets. It amplifies voice audio and controls gain of voice signal. The central switching unit permits the pilot to override an attendant's call when needed. If a cabin interphone station makes a call and does not complete the dialling in eight seconds the central switching unit disconnects that station. Another function of this unit is to allow chime and light sensor units to be operated when a specific attendant's station is called.

Another unit employed in the cabin interphone system is the pilot's control module. It is located in the cockpit on an overhead panel. A typical control module has five dialling push-buttons. Each dialling button allows the pilot to dial a required number; for example, the PA button when pressed permits the flight crew to make announcements. The flight crew can also dial any specific cabin attendant's door position from the control module.

The chime-sensor devices are located at the attendants'

station positions. A sensor is put to work to sense the signal from the central switching unit and operate the attendants' call light and chime tone.

The handsets employed by the cabin attendants have a special type of microphone built in. It has the ability to reduce engine or cabin noise when the handset is in use. Push-buttons for dialling and a push-to-talk switch are fitted on the handset.

System units

The system units are as follows: audio accessory unit, audio selector panels, microphones, headphones, oxygen mask microphones, loudspeakers, attendants' cabin handset and microphones. Audio integrating also makes it possible during refuelling and maintenance checks for service crews to use the interphone and service jacks positioned around the aircraft. Components inside the audio accessory box consist of printed circuit cards containing microprocessors and integrated circuits. Each card is used for different functions. The interphone control card in the audio accessory box contains circuits covering the aircraft interphone operations. An interphone switching card provides switching for the interphone and service amplifiers. The service interphone amplifier circuit is used to increase audio input signal gain to give better reception at the interphone points on the aircraft.

Audio selector panel

An audio selector panel is a multi-function module permitting selection of transmit and receive functions on navigation and communication systems. It provides the flight crew with the means of selecting any of the navigation or communication system services they wish to listen or speak to. It has a toggle control switch mounted on the front of the panel for each system employed in the radio and navigation systems, and a microphone switch for transmit operations. A function switch permits the flight crew to select whatever system is needed. If, for example, the pilot selects the passenger address service or flight interphone system, the function switch is rotated until it is aligned with the service required. A small indicator light would illuminate to indicate the specific system selected. Also fitted on the front panel is a switch marked 'oxygen-boom'; setting the switch to oxygen permits the flight crew when wearing oxygen masks to transmit messages. When set to boom, normal transmissions from the boom microphone can be carried out. The advantage of using a boom microphone is that it leaves both hands free for other operation functions. This panel is also used to select and listen to navigation, very high frequency and high frequency radio signals.

Passenger address operation

All announcements to the passengers in the cabin pass through this system. A passenger address system normally consists of three public address amplifiers, announcement and boarding music tape deck, annunciator panel, attendants' control panels, plus loudspeakers which are located in the ceiling of the main cabin area, galleys and lavatory. A priority calling system is used in the passenger address circuit.

Within the PA system the pilot has priority over all other announcements. If an attendant is using a cabin microphone or handset to make a flight announcement, a pilot can break into the conversation. To put it another way, the pilot has override capability. PA messages also have priority over other audio such as entertainment music. PA announcements from cockpit crew and cabin attendants automatically interrupt the music channels being transmitted to cabin seats. The same procedure is followed when prerecorded messages interrupt the music or movie audio channels in the passenger entertainment system. The PA messages to passengers are operated in a precedence system: first priority goes to pilot's information announcements, second is attendants' messages, third is prerecorded announcements and fourth is boarding music. A no smoking or fasten seat belt sign is indicated by a chime signal to alert crew and passengers.

Each amplifier has a meter on the front panel for testing the service state of a PA system. The PA systems are numbered one to three and the amplifiers can be interchanged. If, for example, a problem has been reported in number one system it can be confirmed by interchanging number two PA amplifier into number one position. It is a quick way of eliminating PA amplifier snags. A circuit in the amplifier in co-operation with a switch on one of the engines increases the gain of passenger announcements when the engines are running and reduces the gain of the amplifier when the aircraft is on the ground.

Passenger entertainment

A passenger entertainment system produces a wide choice of services. Passengers can watch movies, listen to stereo or mono music channels and receive public address messages and pre-recorded announcements through the system. Telecommunications are now being installed utilising satellites to allow passengers to make telephone calls to anywhere in the world from the comfort of their cabin seat. Fax machines and access points for laptop computers are also being fitted to expand the communication link from air to ground. The new sophisticated passenger entertainment systems being installed will provide more options during long-haul flights (see Chapter 26).

A typical passenger entertainment system is composed of:

(a) videotape recorders, video projectors and a music tape reproducer

(b) a main multiplexer unit (multiplexing is a method of using one wire to carry many signals)

(c) zone sub-multiplexer units, one for each zone in the aircraft (in large aircraft the normal layout is A zone, B zone, C zone, D zone and E zone)

(d) seat electronic boxes, fitted to each group of seats (normally a seat electronic box is fitted in two-seat, three-seat and four-seat configurations)

(e) a passenger control unit fitted to each seat (also called a seat control unit). This unit has a channel selector allowing the passenger to select whatever music or video service is desired. A reading light and attendant's call switch is also fitted. When an inflight video system is installed an individual video monitor is fitted on the back of the seat directly in front of where the passenger is seated. In first or executive class the video monitor is part of a fold-away metal arm which is stored in the seat arm rest.

Control panels for switching on the system are located on the cabin sidewall near the door positions. The control panels have a test facility switch which permits maintenance to check the system.

The tape reproducers in the entertainment system contain magazines which serve to hold individual tape cassettes of pre-recorded music, announcements and boarding music. Music programmes can be arranged in a variety of ways. Many airlines have one set of music tapes for outbound flights and another set for inbound flights. Most reproducers can produce over sixteen channels of mono music. Stereo music channels are also available. Some reproducers being manufactured at present will be able to give passengers a choice of many more channels. The unit is normally located on an electronic rack in the electronic equipment bay. To produce a good standard of music in passengers' headsets, reproducers need maintenance, and the tape heads in the unit are cleaned on a regular basis.

A unit called the main multiplexer box is used to process the audio signals from the tape reproducer. The signals are received in an analogue form and are then converted to digital-type signals. When the signals are in a digital format a multiplexing process takes place. A thin, single coaxial cable running the length of the aircraft is used to feed the multiplex signal to the different zones. Units known as sub-multiplex boxes pass the signals to seat electronic boxes which are fitted on the bottom of the cabin seats. A seat cable harness brings the signal from the seat electronic box to the passenger's control unit on the arm-rest. Signals used in multiplexing are separated in time and frequency. In a multiplex circuit a sequence of continuous spaced square wave pulses maintain timing control when the system is processing the audio signals. Signals are transmitted in frames: when sixteen audio channels are used in the system, a sample signal of each of the audio channels is transmitted in sequence and in a set time period. The frames are held apart by a synchronising pulse. Conversion of the digital signal frames takes place at high speed and as frames arrive one after another an analogue signal is produced which is equivalent to the audio sent from the tape reproducer music cassettes. Normally, after the above process the audio signals are filtered before being coupled to the passengers' headsets. Many entertainment systems are able to give passengers audio in different languages. It is also possible to use the system to listen into the high frequency radio system; a passenger then has the facility of being able to hear worldwide broadcast stations.

CHAPTER THREE

AIR TRAFFIC CONTROL (ATC)

Modern aircraft air traffic control transponder systems are born out of the Second World War interrogation 'Friend or Foe' (IFF) airfield protection system. To protect airfields, Allied air forces installed a unit called a transponder on the aircraft. At the airfield another unit called an 'interrogator' was fitted. When an aircraft approached to land, a burst of radio frequency pulse waves were transmitted from the ground. If the approaching aircraft had a transponder installed, it answered the ground interrogator. This confirmation of identity gave the aircraft safe passage to land.

In the early days of flying, pilots had a wide margin of freedom. Air traffic control was not a big issue, and aircraft could fly on different tracks and height without permission. Due to the small numbers of aircraft involved, collisions hardly occurred. All that freedom ended as civil air transport expanded. Airspace around airports has become very busy. Aircraft fly faster and are much bigger. Tighter air traffic control was initiated and an area known as controlled airspace was introduced. In controlled airspace pilots must obey air traffic controllers' instructions to fly at a certain height, track and speed, and each aircraft must retain a predetermined distance from other aircraft.

All this control over aircraft movement has advantages. It has helped to make flying much safer than it would be otherwise and it also prevents long delays at airports. A pilot, before taking an aircraft to its destination, must first have a flight plan to follow. In the flight plan a pilot is told which path, or airway, in the sky to fly on. Air traffic control on the ground uses modern powerful computers combined with radar to control airspace. The result of all this can be seen by looking at the Civil Aviation Public Transport

Safety Record; in recent years, on completion of a million flights, only two aircraft have had accidents, and you can be sure the aviation industry will keep striving towards a risk-free, zero-accident airspace.

ATC radar

Primary

This ground-based radar is a system which sends out radio frequency waves in a narrow directed beam. This beam strikes the aircraft. Part of the beam signal is reflected off the outer skin of the aircraft. In a weak state this reflected signal is picked up by a ground radar antenna and coupled to a ground radar transmitter/receiver. The signal is made stronger by amplifiers, detected and filtered. It is then amplified and displayed on an air traffic controller's radar display screen. This display is known as planned position indicator (PPI). On the indicator the location and direction of travel is shown. Primary radar is important but the information given to a ground controller is not enough; for example, the controller has no way of knowing what aircraft he is watching and how high it is flying. A second radar system is installed on the ground to give him that information.

Secondary surveillance

The secondary radar is different from the primary in that it utilises another system installed on the aircraft to produce the information needed. On the ground a transmitter/receiver called the 'interrogator' transmits coded radio frequency pulses to an aircraft. The interrogator signals trigger an aircraft's transponder to reply. This reply from the aircraft is picked up at the ground station. The reply is actioned by equipment at the ground station and coupled to a display monitor screen. An air traffic controller will now have displayed on his screen the identity and altitude of the aircraft (fig. 3–1 illustrates the air traffic control operation). When primary radar and secondary radar information are combined, they give the controller all the information necessary: altitude, bearing, range and location of the aircraft are displayed. Another piece of information given is the speed of the aircraft. Air traffic control, by using the planned position indicator, can now position aircraft in an orderly manner.

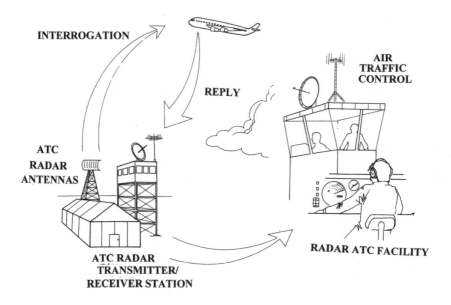

Figure 3–1

On the roof of the ground station radar building there is a rotating platform which has mounted on it two directional scan-radar antennae. The antennae are put to work in the primary and secondary air traffic control radar systems. As the platform rotates, both antennae are rotated together, both always pointing in the same direction at the same time. This means all received signals are from the same source and are in unison. The next time you are at an airport look out for the ground radar station building. A rotating platform with large antennae indicates it is functioning as an air traffic control radar scanning installation.

Air traffic controllers observing a display monitor see bright lines which represent aircraft. The lines can be moving or stationary. For example, when primary radar strikes an aircraft the reflected signal will show up on a display screen as one bright line. When secondary radar interrogates an aircraft and the aircraft transponder replies, two bright lines close together show up on the display screen. If the air controller tells a pilot to identify his aircraft, a brighter line appears behind the two lines already being shown on his display screen. The brighter line only exists for a short time period, then it fades away. Other information is displayed on the screen by means of symbols. In the equipment room great use is made of computers and telecommunications. Today, as in the past, contact by voice through very high frequency and high frequency radio continues to be an important part in controlling air traffic.

Aircraft transponder system

On a typical large civil aviation transport aircraft two air traffic control transponder systems are installed. Each system is self-contained. A dual control box enables the pilot to select either number one or number two transponder system. An air traffic control transponder system on an aircraft consists of:

(a) a transponder transmitter/receiver (radio frequency output about 500 watts)

(b) an antenna

(c) a control box.

The transponder is secured on an electronic rack located in the aircraft electronic equipment bay. Access for maintenance is via a flush-type hatch located on the belly of the aircraft. The antenna is a L-Band Blade type located aft of the nose wheel on the bottom of the aircraft. The dual control box is located in the cockpit. Electronic power for the system is supplied from circuit breakers located in the cockpit. The power needed to operate the system is 115 volts AC and 28 volts DC. An airborne transponder receives signals on a frequency of 1,030 megahertz and transmits on 1,090 megahertz. At the air traffic control ground station the 'interrogator' transmitter/receiver receives on 1,090 megahertz and transmits on 1,030 megahertz. Fig. 3–2 shows transponder and antenna locations.

Transponder

A transponder is a transmitter/receiver installed on an aircraft as part of an air traffic control secondary surveillance radar system. When an air traffic control ground station transmitter/receiver called an 'interrogator' transmits, it triggers a reply from the aircraft transponder. This reply contains coded signals giving

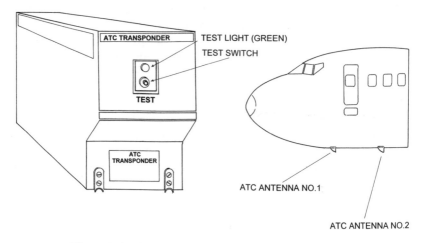

Figure 3–2   ATC Transponder and Antenna Locations

aircraft altitude and identification information. The information is decoded and displayed on the screen of an air traffic controller's display monitor scope.

TRANSPONDER SIGNALS

All transponder signals between ground station and aircraft are pulse-shaped coded signals. The same applies between aircraft and ground station. The coded interrogation signals are called 'modes'. Each mode has a different code name. To differentiate between modes the air traffic control ground 'interrogator' transmits coded signals with known spacing from the mode required. For example, Mode A pulses are spaced eight microseconds apart. Mode A signal information when decoded is 'What is your identity?' Mode B signal pulses are seventeen microseconds apart. This mode is also used for identification purposes. Mode C signal pulses are twenty-one microseconds apart. This mode is used for altitude information. Normally aircraft operate in Modes A and C. In Mode C the aircraft is replying to an interrogation with identification and altitude. When a pilot selects Mode C on the aircraft transponder control box, the system automatically sends Mode A information.

A transponder system on an aircraft operating in Mode C has to have altitude information supplied to it from another source. This source is a unit called a central air data computer (CADC). This computer is used to produce signals which are sent to different

46

indicators located on the pilot' and co-pilot's instrument panels. It also feeds altitude information to the aircraft air traffic control transponder system. A module in the computer containing an evacuated and sealed capsule is used to produce a signal which is amplified and processed for use by the transponder system. The capsule operates by expanding as the aircraft gains altitude, due to the decrease in atmospheric pressure as the aircraft flies higher. When the aircraft descends the capsule contracts. The expansion and contraction produce the necessary signal in the central air data computer.

Many aircraft are now being equipped with transponders able to operate in Mode S. When operating in Mode S the transponder is utilised by air traffic control and traffic alert and collision avoidance systems, and extra data are transmitted. An aircraft with a Mode S transponder are able to reply to an interrogation from an air traffic control ground station or traffic alert and collision avoidance system with identification, altitude, range and bearing. An important Mode S aspect is its coded address which is a unique binary number assigned to each individual aircraft. This allows traffic alert collision avoidance systems to communicate with specific aircraft.

Transponder receiver

On receiving an air traffic control signal from the ground station the aircraft transponder system antenna routes it via coaxial cable to the transponder receiver section. Inside the transponder is a duplexer, a circuit device that connects and disconnects an antenna during transmit and receive operations. A duplexer protects the receiver from strong transmit signals. From the duplexer the signal is routed to a pre-selector circuit; from there the signal goes to a frequency mixer. The output of the mixer process is a 60 megahertz intermediate frequency. This signal of 60 megahertz, known as a IF frequency, is amplified, then detected in a detector circuit. From the detector it goes to a code processor which determines air traffic control interrogator pulse shape and pulse amplitude. It also checks pulse spacing. When the code processor is satisfied the signal is a valid one and that it meets specifications, it is sent to a mode control circuit. If all is well the reply signal operation takes place.

TRANSPONDER TRANSMITTER
The first circuit to handle the signal in a transponder transmitter is code-processing. This circuit passes the signal to a modulator

circuit. The modulator converts the signal frequency pulses to high voltage pulses to drive the transmitter output tube. From the output tube the signal is sent via a duplexer device to the transponder system antenna. As you have no doubt noticed, certain electronic circuits and devices are common to receive and transmit in a transponder. Having been actioned, the signal is coupled via the coaxial cable to the aircraft transponder antenna. From the antenna, it is radiated back to air traffic control ground station. When a signal from an aircraft is received, air traffic control equipment decodes and processes it and the signal information is displayed on a controller's display screen.

It is possible for a pilot to select certain codes and employ the transponder system to inform an air traffic control ground station that an emergency has occurred on his aircraft. There are transponder codes for different events. A serious event would be a hijacking, radio system failure or any other emergency.

Antenna

An air traffic control transponder system antenna is omnidirectional. This means the antenna can transmit and receive from any direction. Each transponder system on a large civil transport aircraft has its own antenna. The same antenna serves for transmitting and receiving signals. Coaxial cable links the signal from the antenna to a transponder

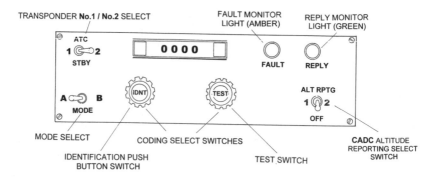

Figure 3–3   Typical ATC Control Panel

Control box

The control box is located on the pedestal. It has selection knobs for air traffic code inputs. A mode-selector switch allows the pilot to select A, B, C or D. A standby and off switch permits the system to have a warm-up period, which aids the system to be ready for operation quickly. On the front panel of the box an 'Ident' push-button permits the pilot to identify his aircraft when requested by air traffic control. An altitude switch allows the pilot to select altitude reporting. Also on the front panel is a test push-button and test monitoring light. On pushing the test button a quick check of the transponder system is performed; if all is well the monitoring light illuminates. Code selecting switches are mounted on the box beside code display windows (see fig. 3–3).

Chapter Four
Weather Radar

In 1935 radio signals were used in Britain to detect aircraft. The start of the Second World War increased the search for an advanced radar system which would give clear return signal displays from long range. During 1939, when the magnetron tube was invented in England, the key to developing a radar system which could meet the demands of the military was found. After the Second World War air traffic increased and radar was quickly utilised by air traffic control at airports to control air traffic. At the same time aircraft manufacturers of avionic equipment developed a weather radar for use on passenger and freight aircraft.

A small word of caution about weather radar systems. The radar system should at all times be treated with respect. Only fully trained professional flight crews and maintenance personnel operate the radar on commercial transport aircraft. All airline operators have strict safety rules to follow before switching on and operating a radar system. Firstly the radar should not be transmitting directly at terminal buildings, hangars, other aircraft and personnel. It should not be operated during refuelling or defuelling of an aircraft. A radar system must be switched off when containers holding fuel or flammable explosive liquids are present. Normal procedure when a radar system is being tested outside a hangar is to point the aircraft nose so that the forward area at approximately 180 degrees of arc is free of large trucks, hangars, and other aircraft. It is also safe practice to tilt the radar antenna upwards at about 10 degrees, otherwise strong reflected radar signals could damage the radar receiver circuits. All external service personnel must be cleared to a safe distance before transmitting. In general safety is the first and last rule when working with a radar system.

Radar system

The radar system is a reliable method of detecting moisture or rain in clouds; it can also detect thunder and turbulence ahead of an

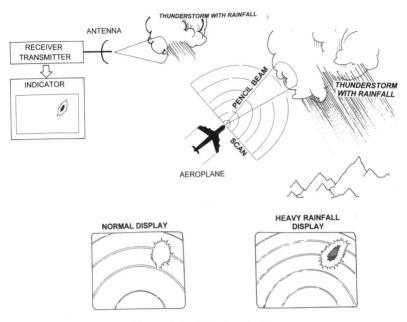

Figure 4–1 Weather Radar

aircraft (fig. 4–1 shows rainfall and storm display). Severe turbulence can damage an aircraft and it makes a flight unpleasant for crew and passengers. If a severe storm is on an aircraft flight path, it will be detected by the weather radar system and displayed on the cockpit radar indicator. The operating range of a weather radar system is between 30 and 300 nautical miles. The operating frequency of a C band radar is 5,400 megahertz, an X band radar 9,375 megahertz. X band radar is most often used in aviation and normally has a tolerance of plus or minus 40 megahertz. Peak output radio frequency power is 50 kilowatts of energy.

A typical weather system on a commercial transport aircraft would consist of the following equipment (fig. 4–2 shows radar controller, indicator and system component locations):

(a) Radar transmitter/receiver unit. Normally located in a compartment on an electronic rack on the bottom of the aircraft close to the nose area.

(b) Radar antenna. The antenna is located at the nose under the

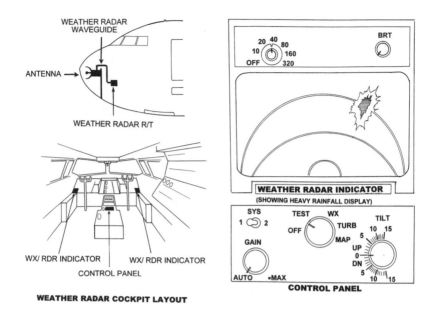

Figure 4–2 Weather Radar Unit Location

aircraft radome. (A radome is a protective dome made of a special honeycombed material which is utilised to house the radar and other antennae situated at the nose of the aircraft. It is detachable.)

(c) Radar indicator (depending on the aircraft the pilot and co-pilot would each have an indicator fitted on their instrument panels). The radar indicator permits a pilot to select different range distances. If, for example, a pilot selected 100 miles, five range marks would be displayed on the indicator, spaced at twenty miles apart; a selected distance of 300 miles would have five range marks spaced at sixty miles apart; a ten-mile range would be displayed as five two-mile range marks.

(d) Radar control panel; location, cockpit.

The function of the transmitter/receiver is to transmit and receive radar-pulsed energy signals. A transmitter section sends out high energy radio frequency pulses via a waveguide tubing which is joined to the antenna. (Waveguide sections are made of metal covered with an insulating material. The sections are detachable for maintenance purposes.) The antenna then radiates the pulse signal towards the target in front of the aircraft. A target can be rain clouds or ground features like mountains and large groups of buildings. The receiver section receives in return a much weaker reflected signal from the target, be it rain clouds or a mountain, and has it amplified. When processed the signal is sent to a radar indicator to be displayed for viewing.

Radar control panel

A typical radar control panel has the following different operations or modes.

(a) A master mode select switch.

(b) Off mode – this position or mode on the panel switches off AC and DC voltages to the radar system.

(c) Standby mode –in this position a radar system is warming up for operation. From initial switch-on, a time delay of about three minutes occurs before the correct operating temperature is reached.

(d) Normal mode – a position which switches-in the complete radar system. When the system is in normal mode of operation the transmitter/receiver is on.

(e) The radar indicator in the cockpit is displaying target returns.

(f) The radar antenna is scanning.

(g) The target range already selected by the pilot will display on the indicator.

(h) Contour mode – when operating like this a radar system looks ahead long range and indicates if severe storm clouds or turbulence are present. It gives the crew time to avoid severe weather.

(i) Map mode – in the map mode of operation a ground mapping effect is shown on the radar indicator. When map mode is selected the radar antenna is deflected. The display seen on the indicator will depend where the tilt control on the control panel is set. A tilt control moves the antenna up or down a maximum of 15 degrees from a zero reference point. This mode of operation can display a city or coastline.

(j) Gain control – this control operation permits the pilot to adjust the radar receiver's sensitivity. It would, for example, help to improve the picture on the indicator and highlight large high ground such as mountains.

(k) Test mode – this mode of operation is employed by the flight crew and maintenance to test the radar system. By switching to test mode the radar system transmits and receives, except that in this case the transmitted radio frequency pulses are sent into a device called a dummy load. This permits the transmission to take place without danger to personnel or objects external to the aircraft. A test pattern of different range marks in miles is displayed, and other system information is indicated; for example, it would show the radar system video bands. The contour operation can be checked in test mode. The serviceable state of the radar system can be confirmed by studying the test pattern on a radar indicator.

(l) Antenna tilt control – as already stated in map mode, it allows a pilot to tilt an antenna up or down 15 degrees.

Transmitter circuits

The magnetron, the biggest factor in the development of radar transmitter/receivers, is the means of generating powerful radio frequency pulses of energy. The radio pulses can be radiated from an antenna at a target with enough power for the weaker reflected signal to reach the radar receiver circuits via the same antenna (fig. 4–3 illustrates a basic aircraft radar system). The magnetron – the heart of the transmitter – normally operates in the frequency range 9,375 megahertz and a tolerance of 40 megahertz is allowed. A magnetron tube in a transmitter acts as an oscillator. It can develop radio frequency pulse power of 50 kilowatts in this manner.

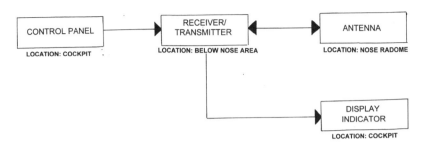

Figure 4–3   Simple Weather Radar System

MODULATOR CIRCUIT

A modulator circuit is a pulse-making network. A transformer is part of the output stages of the network. From the transformer, output pulses push the magnetron into oscillation for specific time periods. The output pulses are then passed to a duplexer circuit.

DUPLEXER CIRCUIT

A duplexer has the job of coupling the output radio frequency pulses of 50 kilowatts to the antenna. It also has to stop any output pulses from entering the receiver circuits. When the duplexer is satisfied the transmitter transmission cycle is finished it permits the received radar frequency return signals to pass into the receiver circuits.

Radar receiver operation

When a signal is reflected back from a target it is picked up by the antenna and passed on to the receiver circuits for processing. The circuit common to the transmitter and receiver is the duplexer and it is through this circuit a received signal must pass before going into the radar receiver.

A superheterodyne-type receiver, containing a balanced mixer, local oscillator and filter circuits, plus video amplifiers and automatic gain control circuits, provides most of the signal processing needed by the receive section. A circuit called a sensitivity time control (STC) provides a fixed signal-to-noise ratio. This means that the receiver signal gain is controlled so that the signal output is constant for weather radar targets of like density over approximately the first sixty miles . In practice it keeps the signal amplitude for targets close to the aircraft at the same level as targets further away.

When strong signals are received from a heavy rain and thunder cloud mass, a circuit known as 'contour' checks if the signal is above a certain minimum level. If so, the contour circuit inverts the received video signals so that they go above the contour level. This causes the display to change on the radar indicator and this change in the display alerts the pilot. Having got this advanced warning from the radar a pilot is able to take preventive action to avoid the bad weather ahead.

In a typical radar system the antenna receives pitch and roll signals from the aircraft's vertical gyro. This maintains radar antenna stabilisation and helps it to remain level during flight movements. If no vertical gyroscope signals were coupled to the antenna it would not be able to scan targets in a steady mode of operation.

Colour radar system

Colour radar transmitter/receivers produce lower power output than non-colour radar systems, about 125 watts compared to 50 kilowatts. In a colour radar system more efficient use is made of the transmitted radio frequency pulses. The transmitted pulse radio beam is produced in a narrow, sharp, concentrated form. New antenna technology has also been a factor in the development of better results from radar systems. Due to solid state technology which is employing microprocessors and integrated circuits, colour radar transmitter/receivers are much lighter and more compact than the older units.

SYSTEM INDICATOR

In weather radar operation, medium rainfall is shown in yellow; light rainfall conditions are displayed in green; heavy rain or thunderstorms are displayed in red. Some systems give an alert warning when heavy rain conditions are within 60 to 130 miles of the aircraft. The alert is displayed by means of a flashing sign appearing on the indicator. In map radar operation the display colours used are cyan, yellow and magenta. The range markers used in a colour indicator are cyan for weather radar operation. When in map mode the range markers are coloured green.

TEST SIGNALS

A test operation in a radar system of this type can be completed when a button is pressed on the radar control in the cockpit. When pressed the test pattern is displayed on the indicator, normally displaying four bands of colours. The bottom band on the indicator is green; a band in the middle is coloured yellow; this is followed by a red band; and the final colour band on the indicator is magenta.

Most of these new microprocessor-integrated weather radar systems have built-in test equipment. If any fault develops it will display a fault message on an indicator in the cockpit and also record the message so that a printout can be produced. In a typical radar system of this type, the fault message also appears on the indicator.

Another advantage the new weather radar system has is a built-in automatic monitoring circuit which checks transmitting and receiving circuits when the system is operating. If any defects are found a fault message is displayed on the indicator to alert the pilot. In the modern aircraft radar information can also be displayed on the new flat panel indicators such as an electronic horizontal situation indicator. It gives the airline operator the option of omitting the radar indicator and using the multifunction electronic horizontal situation indicator for radar displays.

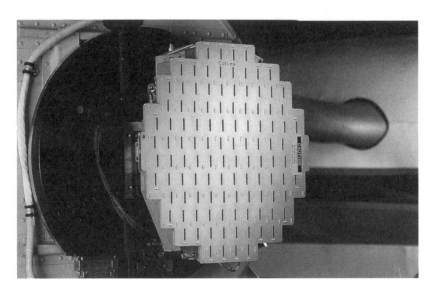

A Weather Radar Installation in the nose of an Aircraft. (*Rockwell/Collins*)

CHAPTER FIVE

INSTRUMENT LANDING SYSTEM (ILS)

The two world wars created a demand for a more efficient and safer method of landing aeroplanes, and funds for research and development in ground and airborne radio technology were released. From the first efforts in the 1920s, intermittent progress was made until the 1930s. During the 1930s a German company called Lorenz developed a runway radio beam approach, an audio system employing dots and dashes to guide the pilot to the runway. The system operated by transmitting a Morse code signal of the letter A on one side of the radio beam and a letter N on the other; in the centre of the beam the signals combined to give a long continuous tone. The pilot, by noting which signal was predominant, was able to direct his aircraft towards the airfield landing area. The Lorenz system served many countries for a long period.

During the time when the Lorenz system was being developed the air forces of Great Britain and the United States were also developing and experimenting with new runway approach technology. In fact both United States and British aircraft carried out a series of blind landings using new radio equipment. During September of 1929 Lieutenant James Doolittle made with the aid of instruments one of the first blind landings. The flight was made from Mitchell Field, New York. Using new avionic equipment, which included a barometric altimeter able to measure height to within a few feet, plus a Sperry artificial horizon and directional gyroscope, the blind landing was a success. The aircraft was also fitted with a radio receiver tuned to pick up the navigation ground beacons located at Mitchell Field. A system called a blind approach beacon system (BABS) was also produced by the British.

During the Second World War the United States increased the effort to develop a reliable runway approach system. By utilising the new radio equipment produced during the experiments, a new instrument landing system was created which is still being utilised worldwide. The equipment was the ancestor of today's ultra-modern radio technology now in operation at airports around the world. In 1949 the American system of instrument landing was made an international standard by the International Civil Aviation Organisation (ICAO). The new instrument landing system worked very well but it had serious disadvantages. Attempting to land an aeroplane in bad weather was one of them, and aircraft in a holding pattern over an airport waiting for weather to improve used up fuel and time. The big problem was visibility of the runway. In 1958 or thereabouts British Overseas Airways Corporation (BOAC), now British Airways, developed the idea of aircraft being able to land in all types of weather conditions. This idea got support from other airlines, and improvements to ground landing equipment took place. In line with the ground equipment improvement, airborne technology also advanced. Due to the new technology, delays in landing aircraft were lessened and cancellations due to weather problems also declined. The weather problem has not been defeated completely, as anybody waiting around an airport for a heavy fall of snow and freezing rain to clear knows. Mother Nature is hard to beat.

Before discussing the airborne avionic equipment which operates during approach and landing, an explanation of the ground radio equipment and air traffic control methods will help the reader to understand the instrument landing system better.

Airport landing facilities

ICO regulations have divided approach and landings into three category types.

Category 1 (Cat 1). This category permits a pilot to operate down to a landing decision height of 300 feet with a runway visual range (RVR) of over 800 metres. The pilot must also be confident the landing is possible.

Category 2 (Cat 2). When flying into an airport under Category 2 rules, a pilot can operate down to 100 feet decision height and 400 metres runway visual range. The pilot must be confident the landing is possible.

Category 3 (Cat 3). In this category a pilot can operate down to a decision height of below 100 feet. He must also have external runway visual range of 200 metres, and must be confident the landing is possible.

Category 3 has been extended to include a Category 3b and Category 3c. The 3b and 3c are used for aeroplane taxiing and tower guidance control of an aeroplane to a hangar or parking area.

Airport instrument landing equipment

A ground instrument landing system normally has the following equipment.

(a) Glideslope radio transmitter complete with antenna system. This transmitter transmits a radio beam that gives the pilot guidance in the vertical (up or down) direction when approaching a runway.

(b) Localiser radio transmitter complete with antenna system. The localiser transmitter transmits a radio beam that gives the pilot guidance in the lateral (left and right) direction when approaching the runway.

(c) Marker beacon transmitters. The marker beacons transmit a radio frequency signal modulated with three audio signals of different frequencies to indicate to the pilot that the aeroplane is passing over certain points along an instrument landing path.

The glideslope and localiser radio beams when transmitted are directed towards the approaching aircraft. The instrument landing system is a method of giving a pilot visual instructions allowing him to fly the aircraft along a set flight path to the threshold of a runway that has an ILS operating. In a real approach a pilot normally descends to his decision, or critical, height and at that stage, using a visual reference of the runway, makes the final decision to land or overshoot. When an aircraft is coming in to land it is common practice for a pilot to set the aircraft on the localiser radio beam first; that gives him horizontal, or lateral, landing guidance. The glideslope radio beam at the same time is giving vertical guidance. When the aircraft is lined up in the middle and on the centreline of the radio beams, and all visual signals on the navigation instruments in the cockpit are correct, the pilot is ready to land the aircraft.

Localiser ground signal

This signal is transmitted on the frequency range of 108.1 to 111.9 megahertz. The ground transmitter, which is located close to the runway, radiates the signal towards the incoming aircraft. Two directional lopes are sent out, one to the left of the runway and the other to the right of the runway. The left directional lope is modulated with a 90 hertz audio signal; the right lope is modulated with a 150 hertz audio signal. The centreline of the runway is where both signals are equal. When an aircraft is on approach and is left of the runway the 90 hertz predominates; right of the runway the 150 hertz signal beam is stronger. On board the aircraft a radio navigation radio receiver is able to process the ground-transmitted instrument landing signals and separate the different signals to produce visual instructions to the pilot so that he is able to position himself on the centreline of the localiser radio beam (see fig. 5–1).

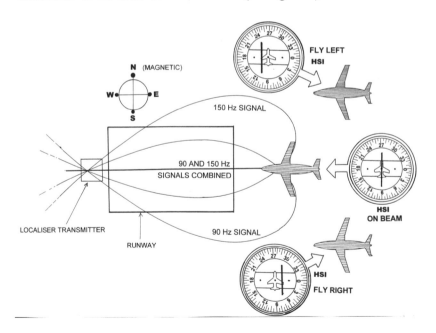

Figure 5–1   VHF Navigation – Localiser Theory

Glideslope ground signal

Normally a glideslope transmitter is situated near the side of the runway close to the aeroplane runway touchdown point. The glideslope transmitter operates in the ultra-high frequency (UHF) range, from 329.3 to 335.4 megahertz. Like the localiser a glideslope transmitter transmits two directional lopes, an upper and lower. The upper lope is modulated by a 90 hertz audio signal and the lower lope by a 150 hertz signal. A glideslope is positioned with the localiser signal so that they form a path on a line 2.5 to 3 degrees above the runway at a point where the two signals are the same. When the aircraft is approaching a runway and above the glidepath the 90 hertz signal beam predominates; below the glidepath the 150 hertz signal is stronger. When the aircraft is dead centre of both radio beams and in line with the runway centreline all navigation instrument pointers should be showing no deflections (see fig. 5–2).

Aircraft equipment

A typical ILS avionic suite consists of the following:

(a) A very high frequency omnidirectional navigation radio

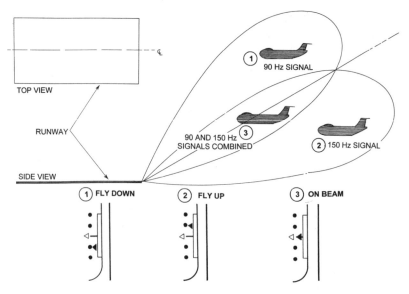

Figure 5–2   VHF Glideslope Theory

receiver (VOR/NAV RX). This navigation radio receiver has three functions: besides receiving radio signals for glideslope and localiser transmissions it also serves as a navigation receiver for omni-range ground station transmissions. As very high frequency omnidirectional range (VOR) will be explained in Chapter 8, we will only discuss the instrument landing system sections of the navigation receiver at this point. The frequency range the localiser section operates on is 108 to 112 megahertz (on odd decimal channel spacing); for example, 108.1, 108.3 and 109.3 megahertz are localiser frequencies.

(b) The glideslope receiver section of the receiver operates on the ultra-high frequency (UHF) range, from 329.3 to 335.00 megahertz. To make the instrument landing system more efficient a method called 'frequency pairing' was developed. This means that when a pilot selects a localiser frequency on the cockpit navigation control box, a glideslope frequency is automatically selected to match it. Each localiser frequency is allocated a glideslope radio frequency. One advantage of this is that only one frequency has to be selected on the control box. The localiser and glideslope navigation signals from the navigation radio receiver provide the pilot with visual deviation signals needed to carry out an instrument landing.

Navigation-communications control panel

The control panel used in ILS comes in many different shapes, sizes and designs. Some display frequency information in digital form, others use electromechanical digits. For this explanation a typical control panel as used in a large civil transport aircraft will be discussed. All electronic circuits are contained in a square metal case. Function switches, display windows and frequency select knobs are mounted on the front of the panel. The control panel is divided into two sections: one serves the radio communication system, the other half is utilised for navigation systems. In most cases the bottom half of the control panel will have the word NAV (navigation) marked on it. Also on the front panel are either two test buttons or switches. Marked on the test switches is UP/L (up, left) and DN/R (down, right) which are operated when testing the instrument landing system. Each switch operates test circuits inside the navigation receiver. Also on the controller are the distance measuring equipment and very high frequency omnidirectional range systems test switches.

Aircraft antennae

The localiser antenna is a fin cap type and is normally found on large aeroplanes located on top of the vertical stabiliser. The vertical stabiliser is situated at the rear or aft of the aeroplane. The antenna is made up of two balanced half loops and has a hybrid coupler to improve received signals. The antenna is also used by the VOR system, as can be seen from the name above (fig. 5–3 shows a typical localiser antenna). The glideslope antenna is a horizontally polarised type (see fig. 5–4). It is fitted just above the weather radar antenna in the aircraft nose radome.

Due to the fact that three navigation radio receivers are fitted on large transport aeroplanes, a system of relay switching is used to transfer the glideslope and VOR/localiser antennae from one system to the other as required. The antennae are connected to the radio navigation receivers by coaxial cable. A VOR/localiser antenna has the longer coaxial cable run of the two. It has to be directed and secured from the vertical fin to the main electronic equipment bay where it is connected to the navigation radio receiver. The glideslope coaxial cable has only a short distance to run as the antenna is located not far from the main electronic equipment bay.

Navigation receiver signals

The navigation radio receiver is divided into three sections. One electronic module is used for glideslope, another for localiser and a third for the VOR signals. Common circuits in the receiver are the power supply and warning flag circuits. The glideslope receiver only receives radio signals in the ultra-high frequency (UHF) range. For an aircraft glideslope receiver the frequency range is from 329.3 to 335.00 megahertz. Glideslope and localiser frequencies are paired. This means that when the pilot selects a localiser frequency the navigation electronic equipment automatically selects a matching glideslope frequency. In the navigation receiver as the processing circuits are tuning and amplifying the localiser frequency, the same is being done with the glideslope signal. When the glideslope signal enters the receiver from the antenna it is sent to a 90 hertz and 150 hertz filter and detector circuits. After being processed, the signal outputs are glideslope deviation signals. Two types of signal are created. One is a negative direct current voltage which is used for the 90 hertz part of the glideslope runway radio beam. This negative voltage signal when used with the 90 hertz is the up signal, indicating

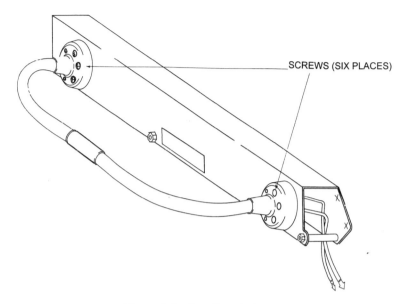

Figure 5–3   Localiser Antenna

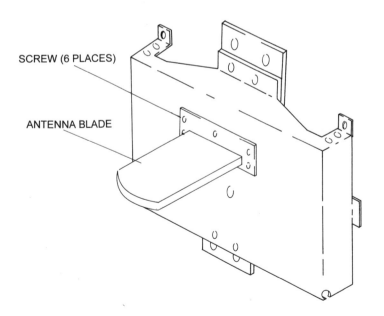

Figure 5–4   Glideslope Antenna

65

to the pilot that he is above the runway centreline. The other signal is a positive one, indicating the aircraft is below the runway centreline. When the localiser and glideslope voltage signals are zero output, no deviation on the indicator is displayed, and this indicates the aircraft is on the runway centreline. At that stage of the instrument landing approach the aeroplane triangle symbol is lined up centrally between the command bars on the attitude director indicator (ADI), with all instrument positions level and no warning flags showing.

A circuit called a comparator is used in the glideslope receiver section of the navigation radio receiver to monitor and compare all received ground radio landing signals. It also monitors voltage levels. If any defect in the signals or voltage level occurs, a warning flag appears on the navigation instrument to alert the pilot to the fact.

When the ground localiser radio beam signal is received by the aircraft localiser antenna, it is coupled via the coaxial cable from the vertical fin to the VOR/ILS navigation receiver. The navigation radio receiver is located on the radio rack in the electronic equipment bay. When the pilot selects a localiser frequency on the navigation control panel, automatically the VOR section of the navigation receiver is switched out of the circuit. All VOR AC and DC voltages are removed from that section of the receiver. Also, the radio magnetic indicator (RMI) heading pointer is parked at a set position on the compass card. In an instrument landing system approach the VOR circuits in the navigation radio receiver are not needed. As in the glideslope receiver, the signal received from the ground transmitter is first processed through filters and monitor electronic circuits. Signal outputs from the filter detector circuits are amplified and used to give left or right deviation movements on the horizontal situation indicator and attitude director indicator. The deviations are governed by the stronger signal; if the two audio modulating signals 90 hertz and 150 hertz are equal no deviation takes place: in other words a zero voltage situation exists. Voltages and signals are monitored constantly to prevent errors appearing in the system. When the localiser ground signals are good, a level sensor logic circuit will pass the signal for use by the localiser receiver. If the signals do not meet the tolerance required a warning flag circuit is switched on. The warning flag will then appear in the navigation instruments and alert the flight crew to a system fault.

HORIZONTAL SITUATION INDICATOR (HSI)

This instrument is sometimes called a course deviation indicator (CDI); for the purpose of this explanation we will call it a HSI. Normally on civil transport aircraft two instruments are fitted, one on each of the instrument panels. The primary function of these instruments is to provide the flight crew with a pictorial outline view of the aircraft's position in the horizontal plane. It outlines, in the form of glideslope and localiser, signal deviations with the use of moving pointers, and a moveable deviation bar with marked spaced reference dots, an aircraft's position on a runway radio beam. The deviation pointers move up or down for glideslope signals and left and right for localiser radio beam signals. The HSI also shows when operating in VOR radio mode heading to the omni-range ground navigation station.

In the centre of the HSI a small triangle aeroplane symbol is fixed in a steady rigid position. This symbol is used to indicate position with reference to vertical and horizontal planes. A course arrow pointer is used to show the selected course in degrees. Display windows located at the top of the instrument indicate the distance in nautical miles to a ground navigation station. This instrument also shows ground speed. Another small inset box indicates which navigation radio receiver the pilot selected. Warning flags which are retracted behind shutters until needed are built into the instrument. If a fault develops the relevant warning flag appears to alert the pilot. A course knob is fitted to permit a selected navigation course to be inserted. Glideslope and localiser deviations are measured with dots. The instrument has five dots, divided into two and half dots for the left side and the same for the right side. When the deviation pointer or bar is located hard right or left on the instrument it means full deflection has been reached. When the deviation pointer or bar is lined up dead centre on the instrument this means the aircraft is flying level and on course. This instrument is a very important one and must be accurate and reliable. It is tested frequently both on the aircraft and in avionic workshops. Fig. 5–5 shows a typical horizontal situation indicator.

ATTITUDE DIRECTOR INDICATOR

This instrument is also known as a flight director indicator (FDI). The function of this instrument is to display the aircraft attitude in flight. The instrument indicates the pitch and roll attitude of the aircraft to the flight crew. This is normally shown in pitch by a fixed aeroplane symbol set against a pitch tape marked in lines. A

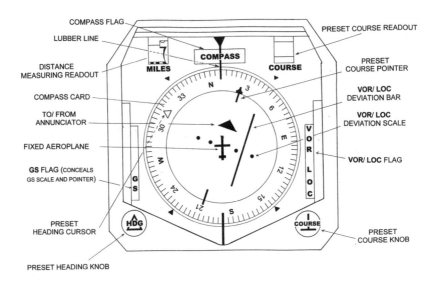

Figure 5–5   Horizontal Situation Indicator

pitch tape can rotate up or down to indicate degrees of aeroplane pitch; it can also rotate left or right to display degrees of aeroplane roll.

The dial of the ADI is marked out in blue for the sky and black for ground. A fixed triangle symbol coloured orange represents the aircraft. When the pilot moves the control column to position the aircraft in a nose-up or pitch-up attitude, the pitch tape moves and the symbol will then be located further up the pitch tape markings. The tape does not move the symbol.

The instrument is also used in the flight director and autopilot systems. When the flight director system is being used by the pilot, flight command V-bars appear on the ADI. These command bars are V-shaped and move up or down and can also roll left or right depending on the attitude of the aircraft. Command bars inform the flight crew of the attitude in which the aircraft is flying. When a pilot aligns the fixed aircraft symbol located in the centre of the command bars and they are level with each other, this means it is correctly positioned for flight. In flight director system operation the command bars in the ADI are used to direct the pilot when positioning the aircraft. Fig. 5–6 illustrates a typical indicator.

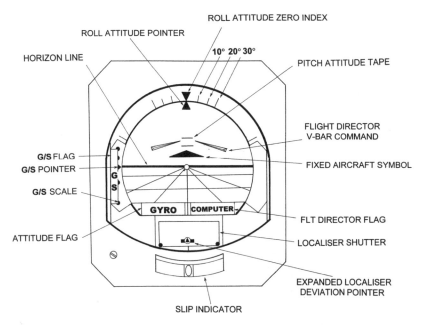

Figure 5–6   Attitude Director Indicator (ADI)

Navigation receiver self-test

A typical ILS navigation system has self-test functions built into the radio receiver and navigation instruments. First let us look at the test facilities on the navigation receiver. Located on the front panel of the unit are two test buttons; one button is marked UP/L (up, left), the other is marked DN/R (down, right). When the up/left or down/right button is operated the following actions take place:

(a) Warning flags appear in the navigation instruments for VOR, localiser and glideslope receiver radio sections. The warning flags are only visible for about two seconds, after which they are retracted from view.

(b) Glideslope deviation pointers on the horizontal situation indi-cator and attitude director indicator move up one dot. When the down/right button is pressed the glideslope deviation pointers move down one dot.

(c) Localiser deviation pointers on the horizontal situation indicator and attitude director indicator will deflect left or right depending on the test button pressed.

The course deviation bar on the horizontal situation indicator will deflect left or right one dot depending on which button is pressed. When the test is being carried out the glideslope and localiser deviations are displayed at the same time. This test of the instrument landing system is a good overview of all units in the system. It is a check often employed by flight crew and maintenance when testing the system.

This Flight Control Indicator is Part of the Instrument Landing System

CHAPTER SIX
MARKER BEACON SYSTEM

The marker beacon system installed on civil transport aircraft serves with the instrument landing system (ILS) as a landing aid. The ground air traffic control has located a series of marker radio beacon transmitters to assist pilots when a landing approach is being made. Ground marker radio beacons help the pilot in two ways:

(a) Ground marker radio beacon signals are transmitted at different locations along an instrument landing system approach path.

(b) When an aircraft is en route to an airport runway the ground marker beacon will provide the pilot with the exact point where that specific beacon is located.

In this chapter the ground marker beacon transmitters and the aircraft airborne marker receiver are discussed. Also explained is how an aircraft flight crew uses the information provided by them.

Ground marker beacons

The ground marker beacons involved when an aircraft is using its instrument landing system on a runway approach are as follows:

(a) An outer marker beacon which is located about four or five miles from the runway end. This beacon transmits a cone-shaped radio frequency signal of 75 megahertz modulated by a 400 hertz audio tone. Normally this beacon is directly under the position where an aircraft on an ILS approach would start descending. In the cockpit an outer marker beacon radio signal is indicated to the pilot and co-pilot by a blue flashing light combined with a 400 hertz audio tone heard in their headphones or on the overhead cockpit loudspeakers.

71

(b) A middle marker beacon which is located about half a mile from the runway end. It transmits a radio signal exactly like the outer marker except that the signal of 75 megahertz is modulated by a 1,300 hertz audio tone. The flight crew will be alerted by an amber flashing light and a 1,300 hertz audio tone from the loud-speakers or headphones.

(c) An inner marker beacon. The inner marker beacon is located about one-tenth of a mile from the runway end. This marker beacon transmits a radio signal of 75 megahertz modulated by a 3,000 hertz audio tone. The visual signal in the cockpit to the flight crew is a clear white flashing light plus a 3,000 hertz audio tone which is heard from the loudspeakers and headphones. Fig. 6–1 shows a marker beacon system.

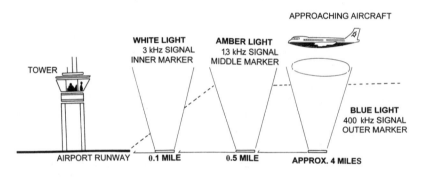

Figure 6–1   Marker Beacon System

Marker beacon ground signals are very useful to pilots because of the information they give when an ILS approach is being made. The marker beacon lights and audio tones work in a specific sequence when the approach is being attempted. First the pilot receives a visual and aural signal at the outer marker, followed by the same at the middle marker, and finally the inner flashing light and aural tone takes place. The inner marker beacon is also known as the airways beacon. This beacon is often used to indicate to pilots that the aircraft is positioned over a runway intersection.

The cockpit navigation chart books have a record of the marker beacon locations at all airports. The books can be referred to by a flight crew when needed. All ground marker beacons are transmitted on the same frequency of 75 megahertz. The 75 megahertz ground signal is shaped like an ice-cream cone. A typical radio wave of that type would be about 2,300 feet wide by 4,000 feet long at an altitude of 1,000 feet from runway level. If an aircraft is approaching a runway at 110 mph it will take it approximately sixteen seconds to pass through the ground radio wave. During that time the airborne marker beacon radio is also receiving the signal. To aid the identification of the marker beacons at different locations Morse code signals are sent with the ground radio wave.

Marker beacon receiver system

The airborne marker receiver system comprises a marker radio receiver, light assembly module, antenna and a sensitivity switch. The units are located on the aircraft as follows:

(a) The marker radio receiver is located in the main electronic equipment bay. It is secured with metal holding latches. Normally this avionic unit is situated on a radio rack. Marker radio receivers are very small and narrow in shape (see fig. 6–2).

(b) The light assembly module consists of three different coloured lights, blue, amber and white. It is located on the pilot's and co-pilot's instrument panel. The module is a three-light assembly. It can be positioned vertically or horizontally on the instrument panels (see fig. 6–2).

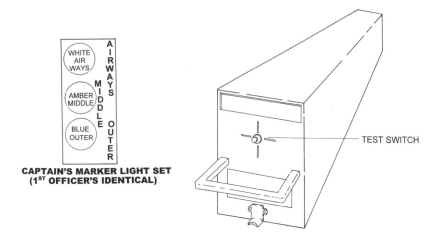

CAPTAIN'S MARKER LIGHT SET
(1ST OFFICER'S IDENTICAL)

TEST SWITCH

Figure 6–2 Marker Beacon Receiver

(c) The sensitivity switch is located on an instrument panel in the cockpit. The function of the sensitivity switch is to increase or decrease a marker radio receiver's sensitivity to ground beacon signals. Depending on the altitude of the aircraft a pilot can select a high or low sensitivity setting. If the pilot sets a high position the marker beacon signal should be heard for a longer period than on a low switch setting.

(d) The marker beacon antenna is designed to receive a frequency of 75 megahertz. It is used as the means of receiving the ground marker beacon signal. The marker beacon radio receiver antenna is located on the bottom of the fuselage. This antenna is only used for receiving, it does not transmit signals. The antenna can be boat- or rectangular-shaped depending on the installation.

The marker radio receiver is much more basic than other radio transmitter/receivers used in communications and navigation operations. Most of the airborne radio equipment operates on various different frequencies, which means more complicated electronic circuits to handle the incoming and outgoing signals. As the receiver is using only one frequency the tuning circuits can be of simpler design; for example, the marker receiver needs only a single-crystal-controlled circuit to produce selectivity, but in other radio receivers many crystals are used. Another difference between a marker receiver and other radio receivers is its sensitivity to incoming signals. A typical marker receiver's sensitivity to incoming signals is between 800 and 1,000 microvolts (1 microvolt = one millionth of a volt) compared to a sensitivity of 3 microvolts for a very high frequency (VHF) or high frequency (HF) radio receiver. The marker sensitivity governs how long the pilot will receive the ground marker signal as the aircraft passes through it. If the ground signal received is weak the marker lights on the instrument panels in the cockpit will glow very dim, and when the signal is strong the lights glow brighter. The rejection of unwanted signals is important and the ability of the receiver electronic circuits to stay on frequency at 75 megahertz to receive ground marker beacon signals is important. No pilot wants a marker beacon receiver on board which is weak or fading when an ILS approach is being made. Instability in a marker radio receiver is not tolerated and any sign of it would mean the removal of the radio receiver.

The receiver is a small, low, black, rectangular unit and weighs about 3.5lb. All electronic circuits are enclosed in a black metal case. Electrical power required to operate the receiver is 28 volts DC. Normally the onboard marker receiver has a self-test button mounted on the front panel. This is used by avionic engineers when testing the marker beacon system on the aircraft. When the self-test button is pressed an in-built generator circuit sends a signal through the receiver which results in the light assembly module on the instrument panels in the cockpit operating as if the aircraft was passing through the ground marker beacon signals. When the lights flash through blue, amber and white, audio signals are heard in the cockpit loudspeakers and headphones. The self-test operation lasts about six seconds. A self-test does not check the marker beacon aircraft system antenna.

Aircraft marker radio receivers are only as good as the signal received from the antenna. The antenna is an important part of the aircraft marker system. When the ground signal is received by the antenna it is passed to the receiver through coaxial cable. In the receiver the signal is increased in strength by radio frequency amplifiers. It is then sent to a filter circuit. From the filter circuit it passes into a mixer or converter network. In the converter circuit the signal is mixed with a 70.4 megahertz oscillator frequency. The output signal of the converter is an intermediate frequency of 4.6 megahertz. From the converter the 4.6 megahertz is filtered to shape the signal for the next stage in the receiver. When finished in the filter circuit the signal is amplified once more. It then enters a detector circuit. In the detector the original audio signals sent with the 75 megahertz radio frequency are detected and sent to an electronic switching circuit to operate the blue, amber and white marker light module assembly in the cockpit.

Chapter Seven

Low-Range Radio Altimeter System (LRRA)

This system is used to measure the height of the aircraft from the ground when on a low-level approach and landing approach (see fig. 7–1). It measures from zero to 2,500 feet. The frequency of operation is 4,300 megahertz. When in operation the radio altimeter transmitter/receiver transmits on number one antenna and the reflected signal from the ground is received on number two antenna. In the transmitter/receiver the received reflected signal is compared with the transmitted original signal. The output from the comparison of the two signals is called a difference signal. This difference signal is

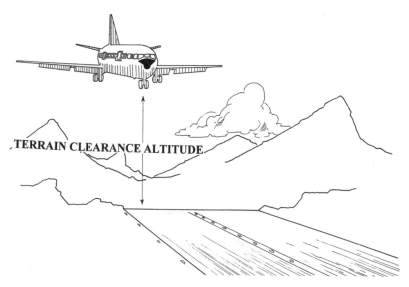

Figure 7–1   Low-Range Radio Altimeter

proportional to the time it took the transmitted signal to strike the ground and return to the aircraft radio altimeter system's transmitter/receiver. The difference signal is changed to a voltage which is used to drive the radio altimeter indicator pointer located in the cockpit. The automatic pilot and flight director systems also receive signals from the radio altimeter transmitter/receiver. Radio altimeter signals are needed during an approach and landing operation to indicate height from the ground. An aircraft cannot make an automatic pilot landing if the low-range altimeter system is defective.

Aircraft equipment

It is normal procedure for civil transport aircraft to have on board two or sometimes three low-range radio altimeter systems. Both pilots have a system and the third is used for back-up. A typical system comprises:

(a) a low-range transmitter/receiver

(b) a radio altimeter indicator

(c) transmit and receive antennae.

Transmitter/receiver

The transmitter section generates a frequency-modulated continuous wave (FMCW) signal output centred at 4,300 megahertz. When the transmitted signal strikes the ground it is reflected. The radio altimeter system's receive antenna picks up the reflected signal and couples it via a coaxial cable into the receiver section of the unit. Inside the transmitter/receiver, mixing circuits process the transmitted and reflected signals. An output signal from the transmitter/receiver – a difference signal – is used to drive the pointer on the radio altimeter indicator to the height in feet the aircraft is from the ground.

A monitor circuit is built into the transmit and receive sections of the unit. The monitor electronic circuits check all signals for proper operation. If a signal is defective a warning flag is displayed on the radio altimeter indicator to alert the pilot. To aid maintenance personnel in the checking of the radio altimeter system a group of monitor lights is mounted on the front panel of the transmitter/receiver. A system self-test button fitted on the same panel permits a system test to be carried out. When the button is pressed it starts the electronic monitor test circuit operation. Normally six monitor lights are fitted to the panel of the transmitter/receiver, each used for a different purpose. In the monitor circuit when a weak signal is received, the sensitivity (SENS) light located on the transmitter/receiver front panel will come on as well as a warning flag on the dial of the radio altimeter indicator to alert the pilot. If the system developed an antenna fault the monitor circuit would light the monitor light marked 'antenna'.

The transmitter/receiver is located on a radio rack in the electronic equipment bay. On some large civil transport aircraft the equipment bay containing the radio altimeter transmitter/receiver is located away from the main electronic equipment bay. In the bay one radio rack hold the radio altimeter's transmitter/receivers and the two automatic direction finder receivers.

Radio altimeter indicator

A low-range radio altimeter indicator indicates from zero to 2,500 feet. The dial of the indicator goes from zero to 500 feet on an expanded scale to give a more accurate readout to a pilot at that height. From 500 feet up to 2,500 feet the scale changes to a logarithmic scale. Mounted in the middle of the dial is a pointer. Also fitted on the outer rim of the dial is a small triangle arrowhead indicator, utilised when setting the required decision height reading on the radio altimeter. Should the pilot fly below the decision height, a light is illuminated, and in some systems an audio tone is sounded in the pilot's headphones or through the cockpit loudspeakers. The pilot sets the decision height with a knob mounted on the front of the indicator. Decision height is a visual reference check, the height at which the runway should be in view when on an approach. It is measured in feet of radio altitude above the runway. When the aircraft is flying above 2,300 feet the indicator pointer is retracted behind a shutter or mask. Most indicators have a test button fitted which when pressed drives the pointer to a pre-set altitude. This altitude changes for different radio altimeter systems. In some cases the pointer might be pre-set to stop at 40 feet, on others it could be 100 feet. The test pre-set altitude is always confirmed by checking the aircraft maintenance manual or manufacturer's instructions.

System antennae

Each system has its own individual transmit and receive antennae. Normally the radio altimeter system antennae are round and flat, with the connector for the coaxial cable located on their base. Also fitted on the bottom of the antenna is a positioning key, important when fitting the antenna to the aircraft. If the antenna is fitted in an incorrect manner errors may be introduced into the system. The top of the antenna is smooth and fits flush into the bottom of the aircraft fuselage. Due to the time-and-distance signal comparison process used in a low-range radio altimeter system to measure aircraft height from the ground, the length of the run of coaxial cable from the transmitter receiver to the antenna is also critical. The coaxial cable must be fitted within a certain tolerance; if it does not meet the specifications height errors would appear in the system. Best results from a radio altimeter system are obtained when transmitting the signal downwards at a water surface, as water reflects the signal better than other materials (on saying that, it must be remembered water runways are not the best to land on). Snow is a good surface but not as good as hard-packed earth. A badly reflected signal will result if the signal strikes dry, fine, disturbed soil.

New system equipment

In modern systems, microprocessors and integrated circuits have reduced the weight and space a system takes up in the aircraft. The output signals are processed by the microprocessor and produced in analogue and digital format. Another advantage the new systems have is that no separate radio altimeter indicator is needed. The aircraft altitude can be displayed to the pilot on his electronic attitude director indicator. This instrument is also used to display other flight information. Most altitude readouts of this kind of system are in digital form. The low-range radio altimeter system is an important avionic aid to pilots when in the approach and landing operation mode. The system gives the pilot the aircraft's actual height above the ground. It is an essential system on an approach and landing operation.

CHAPTER EIGHT

NAVIGATION

Modern navigation has its roots in ancient Greece, where the celestial location of the different groups of stars were noted and catalogued. A key navigation and mathematical tool, trigonometry, was invented. At that time sea voyages only went as far as Britain and Ireland in the west, beyond which it was believed an empty space existed; in the east, navigation was confined to known sea routes.

At a later period in history a new type of navigator appeared. The new navigators were also explorers wanting to find out what was over the horizon. In the west St Brendan with a crew of monks sailed from Ireland into the then unknown Atlantic ocean. It is believed he reached as far away as Greenland, Iceland and North America. As a result of these epic sea journeys St Brendan became the patron saint of navigators. In the years between 867 and 986 another group of seamen also managed to navigate across the Atlantic – the Norsemen (Vikings). The long sea voyages carried out by the Norsemen and St Brendan indicate that they had a good knowledge of navigating by the stars.

The next big expansion in navigation methods and technology took place in Portugal. In the year 1485 King John of Portugal, who was interested in navigation and subjects related to it, decided to gather all scientists and navigators in Lisbon for a conference, called Junta dos Mathematicos. This conference was to have a lasting effect on the world. During their time in Lisbon inventors, scientists, mathematicians, soldiers, diplomats and navigators discussed methods of discovering new lands. King John, who was keen to expand Portuguese power, took over the chairmanship of the meeting. Navigators who attended were later to sail vast distances at sea in their quest to discover new lands, and in the process opened up new sea routes for mankind. Great Portuguese navigators like Ferdinand Magellan gained support for his voyages because of King John's broad interest in navigation. In 1521 Magellan sailed through the straits separating the Atlantic and Pacific oceans – now known as the Magellan Straits –, reached the Philippines, and subsequently became the first man to circumnavigate the globe. Portugal at that time had the world's best navigators, held in high esteem due to their ability to navigate by the stars and also because of their knowledge of mathematics. All navigators were skilled in the use of trigonometry, and in a world where most men could not read, write or calculate, being able to use trigonometry was a considerable advantage. Two of the great Portuguese navigators at that time were Bartolomeu Diaz, the first European to reach the Cape of Good Hope and to open a route round South Africa, and Vasco da Gama, who opened up the route to India. In 1502 he founded the Portuguese colony of Mozambique.

During this period of great navigation sea journeys, Brazil was discovered. At that time another means of navigating was found: the magnetic compass was invented. The magnetic compass was used by the Italian navigator Christopher Columbus when he discovered the Bahamas in 1492. The first island sighted was Watling Island, now called San Salvador Island. From the Bahamas he went on to discover Cuba and Haiti. On his second voyage he discovered America, Guadeloupe, Montserrat, Antigua, Puerto Rico and Jamaica. He also explored along the South American coast and discovered Trinidad. It is said Columbus never told any of his ship's officers or crew he had a magnetic compass. It was a useful piece of knowledge when navigating unknown parts of the world's oceans. Maybe it was a means of keeping himself safe from harm from a fearful crew wishing to return home, for if they harmed Columbus, who would be able to navigate back to Europe? A Spanish navigator named Vasco Nuñez de Balboa, who was also a *conquistador*, crossed the Isthmus of Panama. Shortly after this crossing Hernando Cortes landed in Mexico. The Spanish navigators also sailed round the California coast. By the year 1650 many oceans of the world had been navigated.

The next big expansion in navigation methods and technology took place in England. In the year 1700 Greenwich Observatory was founded. In Greenwich a gathering of scientists and navigators discussed methods of determining longitude with certainty at sea, and set a universal time standard for ships at sea no matter where they were positioned in the world. The time standard was called Greenwich Mean Time (GMT). It was also agreed that Greenwich would become the zero line of longitude (Greenwich Meridian) for navigation purposes. In the year 1730 an Englishman called John Hadley invented the sextant. This fine new navigation tool made possible more voyages of discovery. The sextant is used to determine latitude by measuring the angle between some heavenly body and the horizon. It has one disadvantage in that it can be used only when the sky is clear; a cloudy sky limits its use. Navigators by sea and air are still taught how to use a sextant. At the time of the Greenwich gathering of navigators England had men like Captain James Cook, a native of Yorkshire, who was a great explorer and seaman. Cook navigated his way around the Pacific and sailed round New Zealand and Australia, in the process discovering new lands. One sea voyage took three years to complete, during which his ship sailed 60,000 sea miles. Before we leave this period of navigation another man deserves a mention, Captain William Bligh of *Bounty* fame. After being set adrift in a ship's longboat loaded to the brink with sixteen seamen Bligh managed with the aid of a sextant and his skill of navigating by the stars to bring the longboat to Timor Island in the Dutch East Indies. The distance he had navigated was 3,618 nautical miles (5,822 km), a remarkable feat considering it was across unknown seas.

From the conference of 1485 in Portugal to 1998 is only 513 years. In that time navigation has developed from using the stars, magnetic compasses and sextants to the satellite; however, part of the technology invented in the ancient world, such as the compass, is still in use today. When Magellan sailed around the world in 1521 the navigation equipment on board the ship consisted of sea charts and maybe a compass; a modern jet leaving for a long-haul flight has twenty radio navigation system antennae fitted. On board the aircraft, navigation systems able to receive satellite signals give the captain of an aircraft navigation information that the sea captains of old could only dream about. (Fig. 8–1 shows the new and old methods of crossing the Atlantic ocean.) The new artificial stars – the satellites – are now being used to transmit navigation information and probably in the future will be used to send to air traffic control ground stations information on an aircraft's speed, height and course position.

Radio signal navigation is a common method of guiding aircraft from place to place. The invisible nature of radio signals makes it very different from using a compass or sextant to navigate. Navigation systems which are fitted to modern civil air transport are divided into two types, one for short-range operations and the other for long-range operations. The short-range navigation systems are automatic direction finding (ADF), very high frequency omnidirectional range (VOR) and distance measuring equipment (DME).

Figure 8–1   Navigation – Old and New

Aircraft long-range navigation systems are Omega, Decca, Loran C, inertial navigation system (INS) and global positioning system (GPS).

New avionic navigation systems are still being developed; 1996 saw the development in the United States of a global positioning system. With the help of Navstar satellites it is reported that the navigation accuracy is such that the system can give an operator a position anywhere in the world to within forty-five feet. The next section will give a brief summary of most avionic radio signal navigation systems. In later chapters each major system will be looked at in detail.

Very high frequency omnidirectional range (VOR)

This is a short-range navigation aid. A VOR system determines the position of the aircraft with respect to a ground navigation station. The ground station can be compared to a lighthouse. It transmits navigation signals from zero to 360 degrees. The signals radiate outwards like spokes of a wheel and are known as radials. The signals received by the VOR system are processed by a navigation receiver and passed to an instrument called a radio magnetic indicator (RMI). This instrument displays the bearing on a compass card in degrees. Also during VOR operation a horizontal situation indicator is used to indicate course deviation. Deviation is displayed by means of a course deviation bar which consists of a moveable centrepiece, a course arrow pointer and a tail. When the aircraft is flying along an omni-range radial and is on track the display on the instrument will show the deviation bar centred and aligned with the arrow and tail of the bar. A VOR system operates in the 108 to 117.95 megahertz range. This is the most widely used navigation system. VOR ground navigation stations are located along aircraft airways permitting the pilot when he selects the correct VOR bearing radial to fly from station to station. The selected radial bearings can serve other navigation systems such as the flight director and automatic pilot. On short-haul overland flights the VOR system is very useful. See Chapter Ten.

Automatic direction finding (ADF)

This was the first radio navigation system; 'automatic' was not in the name when it first appeared. This system is a short-range navigation aid. An automatic direction finding system provides the flight crew with the bearing to a ground navigation beacon or ground station. It can receive normal broadcast stations. The development of radio direction finding navigation aids started in the 1920s. Many readers have at one time or another used the direction finding ability of a normal home radio to pick up a broadcast station by moving the radio to a better position. The principle is the same for aircraft direction finding (DF) except that it is done automatically and with different equipment. An automatic direction finding system operates within the frequency range 200 to 1,700 kilohertz. The information received by the airborne radio receiver is coupled into a radio magnetic indicator (RMI) instrument. On the RMI the radio bearing to the ADF beacon or station is displayed in degrees on a compass card. The RMI is located on an instrument panel in the cockpit. See Chapter Nine.

Distance measuring equipment (DME)

This system is another short-range navigation aid. Distance measuring equipment (DME) is utilised to measure distance in nautical miles to a DME ground station. On the ground distance measuring equipment is normally located with or close to VOR navigation transmitters. The DME system operates in the frequency range 960 to 1,215 megahertz. A DME transmitter/receiver is fitted on the aircraft and this is called an interrogator. The airborne interrogator is used to interrogate a system on the ground called a transponder. A system of distance and time measurement by the interrogator results in a readout on an indicator in the cockpit of the number of nautical miles to the DME ground station. The normal operating range for this system is fifty miles; a 390-mile override operating range position is available when needed. The range to the ground station is called the slant range. A distance measuring indicator is used in the cockpit to display the distance in nautical miles. See Chapter Eleven.

Inertial navigation system (INS)

An inertial navigation system is used for long-range navigation. This system is self-contained, which means it does not need external ground station signals to navigate. It has internal gyroscope devices and electronic circuits which automatically calculate the aircraft position to keep it on course. Another feature of the INS is its ability to use attitude information from other systems when navigating. When it is operational an INS uses additional signal inputs from the distance measuring equipment and a central air data computer to make the navigation calculations more accurate. The signal output containing the navigation information is passed to the attitude director indicator (ADI) and horizontal situation indicator. Both of these instruments are located on the pilot's and co-pilot's instrument panels in the cockpit. If a pilot chooses he can use this system to feed the flight director or autopilot systems, and it would aid an automatic flight to be carried out. To operate correctly, the system needs the navigation information punched into it before leaving the aircraft's departure point. It is normal practice for the longitude and latitude of the departure airport to be inserted before beginning the flight, and the navigation details of all way-points to be met en route to its destination to be entered into the system. See Chapter Thirteen.

Omega

Omega is a long-range all-weather global navigation aid. It operates in the very low frequency (VLF) range. An Omega navigation system can operate worldwide. It receives navigation from eight Omega transmitters operating at 10.2, 11.33 and 13.6 kilohertz. Omega ground transmitting stations are located in the United

States, Liberia, Norway, Japan, Argentina and Australia. The average distance or separation between stations is about 5,000 miles. The Omega receiver in the aircraft receives the signals from the ground stations and by timing the transmissions is able to identify the signals' source. It can then process and compare the signals and convert the results into longitude and latitude. From this information the system informs the pilot via indicators in the cockpit where exactly the aircraft is positioned. The Omega navigation system was developed by the United States Navy. Because it operates in a very low frequency band it needs to transmit with big antennae. The system is served by different types of antennae, two of which are tower antennae about 450 metres high. Another type used is a valley horizontal antenna which can cover an area 3,500 metres in length. Radio systems using frequencies in the high range need only small antennae. See Chapter Twelve.

Decca

Decca is an area coverage navigation system. Unlike very high frequency omnidirectional radio range (VOR), which is a direct line navigation aid, Decca permits flexibility en route. On the ground a Decca navigation chain consists of a master station and three slave transmitters. Each station is located at a specific geographical location. Decca operates in a low frequency range of 14 to 14.33 kHz assigned to each transmitting ground station chain. When operating each station transmits a harmonic of the fundamental frequency. The master station transmits a 6f harmonic which is equal to 84 kHz. Each slave ground transmitter sends out an individual harmonic signal, which are 5f, 8f and 9f. The three slave transmitters are also given a colour code of purple, red and green. The 5f purple slave transmitter operates on a frequency of 70 kHz, red on 8f at 112 kHz, and 9f at 126 kHz. The Decca navigation system has the ability to operate at long range or short range. This system, invented by W.J.O. Brian in the United States, is very accurate and reliable. The first use of the Decca navigation system near the end of the Second World War was by the British; it was a success and ships and aircraft started to use it on a regular basis. To widen the use of Decca the system is located in different areas, creating a web of navigation position lines which with the aid of charts permit the operator to plot his position. Automatic means of calculating the input signals are normally done by onboard computers.

Loran

The word Loran is derived from the term 'long-range navigation'. Loran, like Decca, is an area coverage long-range navigation system operating in the low frequency band. The system known as Loran C is used on aircraft. Loran, like Decca, consists of a radio transmitter chain of ground stations comprising a master transmitter and three slave transmitters. All transmit on a frequency of 100 kHz. Loran C is very accurate due to the use of atomic clocks which are so reliable they lose only one second per year. The clocks are used to synchronise the transmission times of the master and slave ground stations. To ensure accuracy is held within laid-down tolerances a monitoring station checks all transmitting stations on a continuous basis. Loran's principle is the use of the known fact that radio waves travel at 300,000,000 metres per second. By using that speed as a reference and inserting the elapsed fixed time delay of slave station transmissions and the master station signal transmission, the Loran receiver calculates the distance an aircraft has travelled. Loran computer receivers are very useful and many models supply range and bearing which includes distance in nautical miles plus bearing in degrees. Up to nine way-points can also be stored along with estimated time en route and ground speed in knots. On the ground the slave transmitters and the master station are separated by large distances. By synchronising slave transmissions with the master radio waves they are interwoven in a net pattern across the area of sky used by the transmitters. The result of this is a map drawn in a hyperbola line effect. The aircraft Loran receiver uses these radio wave patterns to determine its position and bearing.

Magnetic heading reference compass

An aircraft uses a magnetic heading reference system (MHRS). This system is a descendant of the magnetic compass used by so many of the world's great navigators. On modern aircraft a magnetic heading reference system is used to sense the earth's magnetic flux lines. The system utilises a device called a flux valve which contains a flux line detector. The flux valves are normally located near the tip of each wing and fitted as far away as possible from large areas of metal or electric wire looms. When the flux valve picks up the earth's magnetic lines of force it converts them into an alternating cycle signal. The signal is then amplified and passed to the aircraft instruments. If the aircraft is flying at high latitudes in the North and

South Pole areas of the earth the signal becomes unreliable. To over-come that problem the pilot would then switch to a more stabilised navigation system, for example inertial navigation system (INS), which unlike MHRS uses true north and not magnetic north as its reference. An ordinary magnetic compass is located in the cockpit as a stand-by in the event of all other navigation systems becoming defective. See Chapter Fourteen.

A Pictorial Navigation Indicator Showing a Heading of 115 degrees

CHAPTER NINE

AUTOMATIC DIRECTION FINDING (ADF) SYSTEM

Direction finding (DF) is an old timer among aviation navigation systems. In the 1930s it was a primary navigation system; later, due to progress in other navigational methods, DF was reduced to a secondary navigation aid. In the first direction finding systems a pilot or navigator had to manually plot and calculate direction and bearing to a transmitting radio station or navigation beacon. This operation can often be seen in old films and photographs. Trying to work on a plotting chart and do calculations must have been a stressful business during wartime or in bad weather conditions. A mistake by the pilot or navigator would have had serious results for the flight crew and aircraft. The new technology has made it unnecessary to have a navigator on board modern aircraft. A pilot no longer has the worry of working out his direction or bearing as it is done automatically by the automatic direction finding (ADF) system.

Even though ADF has been reduced to the role of a secondary navigation system in many parts of the world, it is still very important due to the absence of other navigational aids at some airports. When a pilot meets a situation like that, the ADF system can be used to tune in a local amplitude modulation (AM) radio station. He can then use the signal for direction and relative bearing to that specific station. This is not encouraged as precise bearings can be difficult to determine from commercial broadcasting stations.

System function

Automatic direction finding is a short-range navigation aid which would normally use radio frequency signals in the range 190 to 1,750 kilohertz. The ground navigation station radio signals are used by the system radio receiver to process the bearing information and display it on a radio magnetic indicator. The signals are prefaced with a three-lettered Morse code identification signal, which is transmitted with the normal signal. For example, when an aircraft is on the approach path into Dublin, Ireland, the flight crew will, when tuned to the local frequency, hear in the headphones dah-dit-dah (= K), dit-dah-dit-dit (= L), and dah-dit-dah-dah (= Y) which when decoded is the three-lettered Morse code signal for Killaney (KLY), an ADF ground station situated on the east coast approach path to Dublin airport. The radio frequency range the ADF system operates in contains the common broadcast band. It also receives air traffic control navigation ground stations and non-directional beacon (NDB) signals.

The ADF system on a transport aircraft uses 115 volts AC and 28 volts DC. Each system has its own circuit breakers, marked ADF system number one and two. Within the system 26 volts of alternating current are used in the servo circuits.

System components

A system on a large passenger transport aircraft would have the following avionic equipment fitted (fig. 9–1 shows component locations). Most aircraft of that type have two self-contained ADF systems on board. The system would consist of:

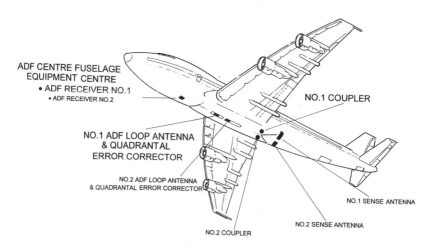

Figure 9–1   ADF System Component Location

90

(a) an ADF radio receiver

(b) a control panel

(c) a loop antenna

(d) a sense antenna

(e) a radio magnetic indicator

(f) a quadrantal error corrector

(g) an ADF sense antenna coupler.

ADF control panel

A typical control panel has several switches, knobs and controls fitted. A variable switch permits the flight crew to select any of the following functions:

(a) Off position.

(b) ADF position – when in this position the system is using the sense and loop antennae combined to produce a bearing to the ground navigation station being received. The bearing is displayed on a radio magnetic indicator which is located in the cockpit.

(c) Ant – this position only allows the receiver to process sense antenna signals. When this is selected normal broadcast radio stations and non-directional beacons can be received for station identification. The bearing pointer on the radio magnetic indicator is left at 90 degrees relative bearing and it does not move when signals are received.

(d) Beat frequency oscillator (BFO) – when receiving continuous wave radio signals a beat frequency oscillator signal of 1,020 hertz is inserted into the receiver circuits and by beating with the incoming signal an audio tone is heard in the pilot's headphones. This tone helps to tune in a received radio station accurately for best reception. The beat frequency oscillator signal also serves to detect the Morse code identification signal.

(e) Audio gain control – a control which allows a pilot to increase or decrease the signal volume.

(f) Receiver tuning meter – displays the tuning state of the receiver. When the station is tuned in for maximum signal strength a pointer in the meter will deflect to the right, and if the signal is weak or fading the pointer will stay at a minimum position.

Radio receiver

The most common type of radio employed in ADF navigation systems is the common superheterodyne radio. It operates in three bands and is tuned by a variable capacitor which is controlled by a servo motor. The receiver must be very sensitive to signal reception due to the antenna installation layout on aircraft. It also has to have good radio station selectivity due to a large number of stations operating on the crowded radio bands utilised by ADF receivers. A superheterodyne type of radio design meets the requirements as it has good sensitivity and selectivity. The superheterodyne radio is probably what you have in your house and car. Aviation radios have extra electronic circuits for other specific functions needed in the system, but in all other respects they are working on the same basic principle. Today most receivers are solid state and the electronic circuit components are microprocessors and integrated chips. In recent years the receivers have become smaller and lighter.

The front panel of the receiver has two connectors fitted. One connector serves the sense antenna triaxial cable and the other is for the loop antenna cable. Also mounted on the panel is a test display window and a test button. When the test button is pressed this pointer is driven to a calibration line, and if it lines up correctly this indicates the receiver is tuning in a proper manner. When in the test operation a signal from the receiver to the radio magnetic indicator will cause the indicator pointer to take up a certain bearing position.

The output of the receiver is a synchro signal which is coupled to the radio magnetic indicator. This signal drives the pointer in the indicator to the relative compass bearing of the navigational radio station that is transmitting on the frequency selected by the pilot.

The receiver receives signals from both the sense and loop antennae. Electronic circuits in the receiver process and calculate the bearing to the ground radio station; the bearing information is changed into a synchro signal and coupled to the radio magnetic indicator for display in the cockpit. When the flight crew select the

ADF position on the controller the system automatically determines the bearing to the ground station. The electronic circuits used in the receiver are solid state and consist of intermediate frequency amplifiers, radio frequency amplifiers, audio amplifiers, automatic gain control, beat frequency oscillator, balance modulator and servo circuits. On modern aircraft the receiver is secured on a radio equipment rack. The rack is located in the electronic equipment bay, situated at the bottom of the fuselage. Fig 9–2 illustrates an ADF receiver and control panel.

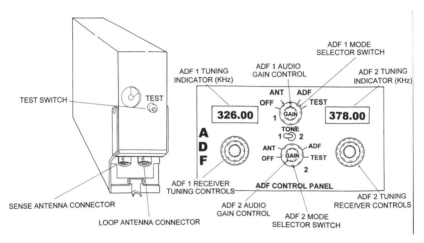

Figure 9–2   Automatic Direction Finding (ADF) Receiver

Loop antenna

The special feature of a loop antenna is its directional quality which makes it very useful in this type of radio system. An example of what directional quality is can be shown by a little experiment in the reader's own home. If the reader rotates manually his domestic portable radio to receive a better signal from a station he will have noticed how strong the signal is in one direction and how weak in another. That is the basic direction finding quality of a loop antenna operation. The weak signal position in this small experiment is called the 'null'. A null position is used in ADF systems to locate the radio station that is transmitting. When a receiver receives a station signal from the loop antenna operating in the null position and combines it with the sense antenna signal, an accurate, stable, ADF signal output occurs. The result is a good indication of the ground station location on the radio magnetic indicator in the cockpit. The loop antenna can be used for manually determining the bearing of a ground station signal being received. If the loop antenna is used on its own without the sense, signals from ground radio stations will be unreliable.

Sense antenna and coupler

This antenna is used in combination with the loop antenna to develop a signal which when processed in the receiver circuits drives the radio magnetic indicator to a relative compass bearing in the direction the received radio signal is coming from. This antenna is also used to receive normal broadcast radio stations. When the antenna position is selected on the control panel the bearing pointer is parked at a fixed setting on the radio magnetic indicator. The coupler is used to match the sense antenna to the radio receiver. If on receiving radio signals the capacitance of the antenna was not matched to the receiver's input capacitance a weak signal would result.

Quadrantal error corrector

This device is used in the loop antenna circuit and is positioned between the loop antenna output and the radio receiver. It is used to correct the error introduced into the ADF system by signals re-radiating from the aircraft fuselage. Normally the signal waves are reflected by the aircraft fuselage and wings. These reflected signal waves then mix with other incoming signals and are received by the loop antenna; the result of this mixing of signals is an error in direction bearing. The name 'quadrantal' comes from the fact that these signals when they strike the aircraft fuselage at cardinal points have little effect, but when they strike the quadrantal area of the fuselage and then mix with the loop signals maximum effect is noticed. The cardinal and quadrantal points are the same as on a compass.

Radio magnetic indicator

A radio magnetic indicator, besides being used in an ADF mode of operation, can be operated as part of the omni-range navigation system or ADF system. A switch permits the pilot to select either ADF or VOR mode of operation.

In an ADF system this instrument is used to display a visual indication to a pilot of the bearing in direction and degrees of a received ground radio station. The radio magnetic indicator displays the bearing of the station being received on a compass card in degrees. The outer front of the compass card is marked in degrees from zero to 360. An inner card, which is variable in movement, is also marked in degrees from zero to 360. Normally the indicating lines are marked two degrees apart.

The magnetic bearing signals are indicated by a pointer on the radio magnetic indicator which can be driven by the received signal in the required direction. On a modern transport aircraft when two systems are being used the instrument has two pointers. A single narrow bar pointer serves the pilot and a double bar pointer is employed by the co-pilot. Both pointers are controlled by the signals being received from the receiver, and when a ground station is situated at a bearing of 180 degrees, the pointers take up a position pointing to 180 degrees on the compass card. The bearing pointers indicate navigational station bearing with respect to aircraft heading (see fig. 9–3).

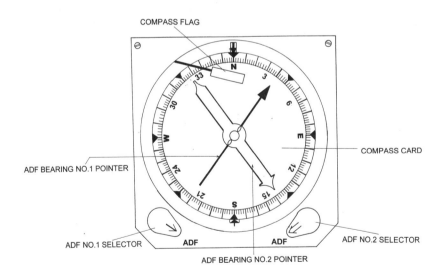

Figure 9–3   Radio Magnetic Indicator

CHAPTER TEN

VERY HIGH FREQUENCY OMNIDIRECTIONAL RANGE (VOR)

This navigation radio aid is the system most commonly used by aircraft en route from one destination to another. Omni-range navigation ground beacons are found on most airways and are nearly always located close to airports. The only other navigation aid that is as popular as this system is ADF. VOR operates in the frequency range 108 to 117.95 megahertz. Ground navigation stations are used to transmit radio signals which are picked up by the aircraft antenna and passed to a navigation receiver. The receiver processes the received signal from the ground station and converts it into bearing and position information. The frequency of the desired ground station is selected on the aircraft VOR control panel. This system of navigation was developed in the United States, and like many other aviation systems it was a product of the two world wars. In 1946 the United States made omni-range a standard navigation aid at all American airports. A chain of navigation beacon stations was installed across the United States for aircraft to use en route to their destinations. The rest of the world followed suit in 1949. Due to the size of the aviation industry in the United States any changes which took place in navigation systems, flying procedure and equipment were normally adopted by other countries.

For a very high frequency omni-range system between an aircraft and ground system to give best results, it must have good line-of-sight (LOS) transmission and reception paths for the radio signals. It means that the transmitting and receiving antennae should see each other unobstructed.

Ground navigation station

An omni-range navigation ground station or beacon (see fig. 10–1) can be compared to a lighthouse or a rotating wheel. Look at the centre of the lighthouse as being the rotating light beam and the centre of the wheel being the hub. Like the lighthouse or rotating wheel an omni-range ground station transmits its navigation signals in all directions, radiating out like the spokes of a wheel. The signals which are radiated out like this are called radial lines. Radial lines are the signals along the transmission lines in a magnetic direction from the ground station. For example, if an aircraft is north of the station it is on a radial of zero degrees; when it is east of the station a 90 degree radial is being used. The reference point used in the system to aid the pilot is magnetic north. In the aircraft a radio magnetic indicator, which has a compass dial or card marked out in degrees from zero to 360, is used by the pilot to confirm the aircraft is in its right position and on the correct navigation track. When the ground station transmits, two signals are sent out. One signal is radiated in an omnidirectional manner, and a second signal is called a rotating directional signal. The reference signal from the station is the omnidirectional signal and is radiated at certain intervals. This signal is followed by a variable rotating directional signal. When the two signals are received by the aircraft

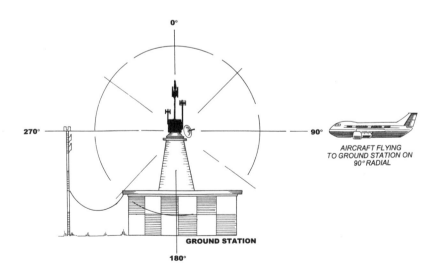

Figure 10–1   VOR Ground Station

navigation radio receiver it does a phase-comparison check in time between receiving the reference signal and the later arrival of the variable signal. If the signals are received in phase the aircraft is flying on a radial radio signal track indicating it is north of the station. On the radio magnetic indicator compass card the indicator needle will be pointing at zero degrees. An omni-range ground station can give a pilot a navigation track to steer by, but it cannot tell a pilot how far he is from that station. A distance measuring equipment system gives the pilot slant distance as measured in nautical miles from the station. Also transmitted from the station is a Morse code identification signal to inform the pilot which ground station signal he is receiving. The Morse signal consists of three letters which are the first letters of the transmitting ground station name. All very high frequency omni-range ground station locations and Morse code identifications are marked on the pilot's navigation charts.

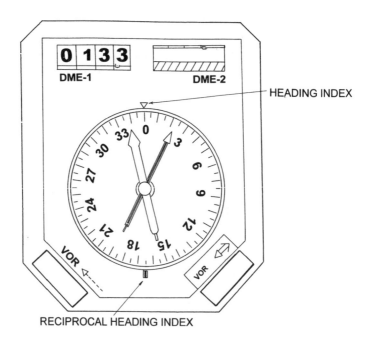

Figure 10–2   Radio Magnetic Indicator (RMI)

Aircraft system equipment

A typical aircraft system would comprise:

(a) a navigation radio receiver

(b) a radio magnetic indicator (see fig. 10–2)

(c) a horizontal situation indicator, also called a course deviation indicator (CDI)

(d) a navigation control panel

(e) an antenna.

On a large aircraft it is normal practice to have on board two complete self-contained, and in some cases three, navigation systems.

A navigation transfer relay switching system permits the pilot and co-pilot to select any of the systems when needed (fig. 10–3 shows a VOR block diagram). The navigation radio receiver used on the aircraft is a dual-purpose type. It means the radio receiver is also used to receive localiser and glideslope radio beam signals when the instrument landing system is being utilised on runway approach. In this discussion a basic explanation of the elements of the receiver will be given. The instrument landing system (ILS) section of the receiver is covered at a later stage.

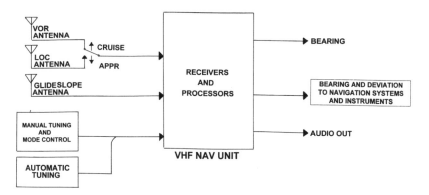

Figure 10–3   VOR Block Diagram

Radio receiver

This navigation receiver is designed to be able to do three major operations: to receive and process navigation signals from navigation ground stations or beacons; and to receive and process instrument landing system localiser and glideslope radio beam signals on a runway approach path. When the pilot selects an omni-range frequency in the operating range of 108.00 to 117.95 megahertz the navigation receiver automatically switches off the localiser and glideslope sections of the receiver. All frequencies are used in the range except any frequency on odd tenths up to 111.90 megahertz. The odd tenths of the frequency range are used for localiser frequencies. An example of an odd tenth frequency used for localiser is 108.1 or 108.3 megahertz. The navigation receiver provides signal outputs to operate the radio magnetic indicator, and couples the ground station Morse code identification signal into the aircraft audio interphone system. Signals from the navigation receiver are also coupled into the flight director and autopilot systems.

All electronic circuits are contained in a square metal case (see fig. 10–4). Inside, the receiver is divided into electronic board modules which are detachable for testing and servicing purposes when the receiver is in avionic workshops. Each module is complete with solid state electronic components and synchro devices. In a typical navigation radio receiver three board modules are used, one for VOR/localiser, another for glideslope, and the third for power supply, system self-test and the radio magnetic indicator synchro driver. The average weight of this avionic radio receiver is about 12.5lb (5.7kg). Later models of navigation radio receivers weigh much less due to the use of miniature solid state technology.

RECEIVER OPERATION
The incoming ground station signal is picked up by the aircraft omni-range antenna and sent to the receiver through coaxial cable. A filtering circuit is used to pass the signal on to the variable and reference signal sections in the receiver. The signal is also fed to a tuning detector and audio amplifier circuit. From the audio amplifier the amplified audio signal which contains the Morse code ground station identification is passed to the interphone system to be received on the pilot's headphones or the cockpit loudspeaker. In the tuning circuit a very high frequency synthesiser is used to tune in the selected frequency. The tuning detector circuit is used to detect

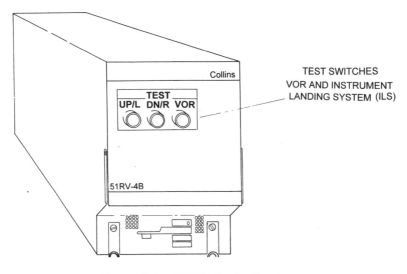

Figure 10–4 VHF Navigation Receiver

the frequency. The tuning process has to be accurate or the circuit will reject it. Processing of the variable and reference ground station phase-difference signals creates output signals that are used to position heading pointers in the navigation instruments in the cockpit.

Control panel

On wide- and narrow-body civil aircraft this control panel is often used for other navigation systems. It can, for instance, be used for localiser and glideslope and distance measuring equipment (DME) frequency selection. The system self-test press buttons or switches are also fitted on this controller. It is a square-shaped panel and all electronic circuits plus switch rotating wafers are enclosed in a metal case. Mounted on the front are frequency select knobs and a frequency display window. A function switch which permits the pilot to select DME is fitted on the front panel. Also mounted on the front panel is a self-test switch which is used for testing, and when the pilot selects an instrument landing system frequency the same switch is used for up–right and down–left operations for localiser and glideslope.

A self-test system allows the pilot, co-pilot and avionic mainte-nance personnel a means to test the system in the cockpit or from the electronic equipment bay. The navigation radio receiver is located on a radio rack in the electronic equipment bay under the aircraft fuselage. Mounted on the front panel of the receiver is a self-test button. The control panel in the cockpit has a similar self-test button. For a pilot or avionic personnel to carry out a self-test the following procedure is used. Firstly, a local omni-range ground station frequency is selected. Secondly, a course of zero degrees is aligned on the radio magnetic indicator in the cockpit. Thirdly, the test button is pressed. A good test would give the fol-lowing results:

(a) A red warning flag shows for about three to seven seconds.
(b) Red warning flag is retracted.
(c) Radio magnetic indicator needle pointer moves round to read 180 degrees on the compass card.
(d) The horizontal situation indicator deviation bar moves to the centre and aligns itself with the pre-set course pointer.
(e) The to–from triangle flag indicates 'from'. The to–from arrow-head-shaped flag is used on the instrument to inform the flight crew when the aircraft has left an omni-range ground station behind and is moving towards the next station en route.

Antenna

On civil transport aircraft the antenna is normally located on the top of the vertical fin. It is connected to the navigation receivers in the electronic equipment bay by a long run of coaxial cable. Access to the antenna and connectors is allowed by removing a section of the vertical fin top. Other panels allow access at intervals on the coaxial run to the equipment bay. To help the antenna cover the navigation frequency range a device called a 'Balun' (a matching transformer device) is used to give an impedance match between the aircraft antenna and navigation receiver coaxial cables. The antenna in the omni-range navigation system is normally tuned to the centre of the frequency range in use. To prevent the antenna being damaged during thunder and lightning storms, static lightning strips are inserted on the external cover of the antenna. A system of switching relays is used to allow the pilot and co-pilot to change the antenna from number one navigation receiver to number two, or if need be to the number three receiver. This is a very necessary feature as it gives the flight crew the ability to change systems if a fault develops when the aircraft is en route to its destination.

Horizontal situation indicator

This instrument is also known as a course deviation indicator and is used in other navigation functions besides the omnidirectional range system. When it is displaying information it indicates to the flight crew the selected course by means of a course deviation bar. Course is the direction the aircraft is travelling with respect to the ground. A horizontal situation indicator, just like the radio magnetic indicator, has a compass card inserted on the face of the instrument. When a pilot has selected a ground station radio radial and is flying along it with no deviation, the course deviation bar will be centred. The course deviation bar is split into a course arrowhead pointer, a middle portion which can deviate left or right, and a tail. When the portion which can deviate is aligned with the arrow pointer and tail to make a complete deviation bar the aircraft is on the selected course (see fig. 5–5).

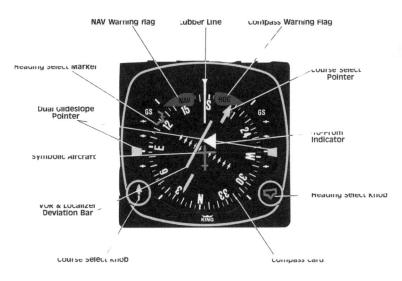

A VHF-Directional Instrument Showing VOR – to and from – and Deviation Bar

CHAPTER ELEVEN

DISTANCE MEASURING EQUIPMENT (DME) SYSTEM

A distance measuring equipment (DME) system serves to give flight crews correct and constant visual line-of-sight or slant range distance to a ground navigation station. The distance from the aircraft to the ground station is measured in nautical miles. A DME indicator located in the cockpit displays the miles to the destination. Indicators can be digital or electromechanical type. Normally in today's modern aircraft DME systems provide a digital readout. Flight crews normally operate the system in the fifty-mile range, which is the system's limit. The exception to that is a mode called override which permits the DME to operate up to 390 nautical miles.

A typical DME system comprises:

(a) an interrogator, which is a combination transmitter/receiver (see fig. 11–1)

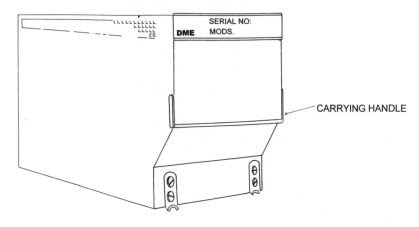

Figure 11–1   DME Interrogator

(b) an indicator

(c) a control panel

(d) an antenna (omnidirectional type).

All large civil transport aircraft are fitted with two DME systems. Each system is self-contained and has individual components. Fig. 11–2 shows a typical system layout.

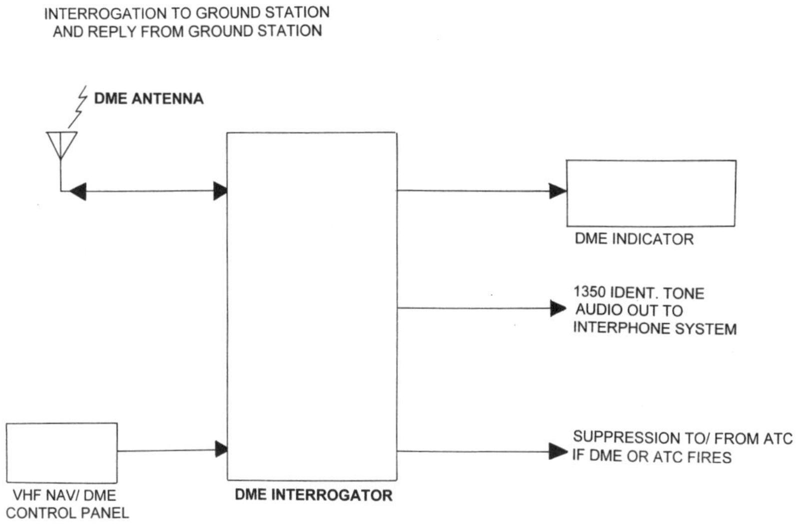

INTERROGATION TO GROUND STATION
AND REPLY FROM GROUND STATION

DME ANTENNA

DME INDICATOR

1350 IDENT. TONE
AUDIO OUT TO
INTERPHONE SYSTEM

SUPPRESSION TO/ FROM ATC
IF DME OR ATC FIRES

VHF NAV/ DME
CONTROL PANEL

DME INTERROGATOR

Figure 11–2   DME System Block Diagram

DME operation

Located at the air traffic control navigation ground station is a transponder transmitter/receiver. This ground transponder is interrogated by the airborne DME interrogator. The aircraft interrogator transmits a constant series of coded, shaped signal pulse pairs. A method called random transmission is used to vary the time distance between pulse pair signals. The normal time interval between pulses is twelve microseconds. In the aircraft interrogator random transmission takes place by making the pulse repetition frequency erratic within certain time tolerances. At the identical time that the pulse pair signal is being transmitted from the aircraft interrogator, the receiver's circuits begin a timing operation and start hunting among the ground transponder signal replies for the specific pulse pairs it transmitted to the ground station. The transponder at the ground station is answering many aircraft at the same time. It transmits by sending out bursts of signal pulse pairs in a method called 'squitter'. In the aircraft the onboard interrogator senses the ground squitter pulse signals coming from the ground station and it then starts transmitting. The ground station is transmitting to many aircraft but the onboard interrogator only accepts returned signal pulse pairs from the station which matches its own transmitted pulse repetition frequency (PRF). The received signal is then processed and converted into distance in nautical miles and displayed on the indicator in the cockpit. Distance is calculated from the understanding of the speed of the radio wave signals and the period of time taken by the interrogator pulse pairs to travel out to the ground station and back to the aircraft.

The DME interrogator transmitting or receiving pulse signals operates on the same frequency range as the air traffic control transponder system. Both are secondary-radar-type systems. To prevent either system interfering with the other a suppression pulse is transmitted from the DME interrogator during its transmission cycle which cuts off the transponder. The transponder in the air traffic control system on board the aircraft does the same thing to prevent the interrogator operating when it is transmitting.

DME ground stations

For this avionic system a ground station would be located at or near an omni-range navigation station. A dual frequency pairing in the cockpit controller means that when a pilot selects an omni-range navigation station he is at the same time selecting a distance measuring equipment frequency. Ground station transponders transmit pulses in a squitter fashion. A typical transmission would be 2,700 pulses per second at random. When aircraft distance measuring equipment senses the squitter pulses it interrogates the ground transponder. If interrogated by more aircraft than it can handle, the ground transponder will give priority to the nearest aircraft. It then accepts aircraft located further away from the ground station.

System description

DME systems operate in the frequency range 962 to 1,213 mega-hertz. Normally the frequency operation is sub-divided into 252 transmitting channels between 1,025 and 1,150 megahertz; these channels are known as X and Y and they vary in frequency. They use different spacing between pulse transmissions: X uses a twelve-microsecond interval and the Y spacing is thirty-six microseconds. The receive frequency range of the aircraft inter-rogator is between 962 and 1,213 megahertz. The power needed to operate the system is 115 volts AC and 28 volts DC. Each system has a separate power supply. The circuit breakers on the power panel reflect this and are marked number one system and number two system.

The interrogator is installed on a radio rack in the electronic equipment bay. The control panel is normally located on the pedestal in the cockpit. A DME indicator is situated on the flight crew's instrument panels. DME L band antennae are located on the bottom of the fuselage.

When in operating mode an aircraft interrogator will always start a search for a navigation ground station in an outbound manner. Normally this means the interrogator searches out up to 390 nautical miles. On finding a ground station which is replying to its interrogations, and if the reply signal from the ground is strong enough, the interrogator locks on to this signal. The received strong signal is then converted into distance in miles in the interrogator receiver circuits. The receiver also checks the timing, space and shape of the received signal pulse pairs to confirm they originated from the aircraft interrogator. When flying outbound away from a station, miles displayed increase, and when going towards its destination the miles shown decrease. If an interrogator is receiving a weak ground station signal or when a pilot selects a different frequency the reading will disappear from the indicator and a new search will begin.

An operation known as a signal controlled search is utilised to stop an unnecessary search for a ground station if the aircraft is out of range. During this time a warning flag or shutter displayed on the indicator will alert the pilot to the situation. When back in range of a ground station the distance measuring equipment will automati-cally go into normal operation.

An aircraft system is tested by pressing a test-button which is located on the control panel. When the button is pressed a display of '0' miles appears on the indicator in the cockpit. The test result informs the pilot that the system is accurate in the measuring circuits of the interrogator.

CHAPTER TWELVE
OMEGA NAVIGATION

Omega is a long-range, all-weather global navigation aid operating in the very low frequency (VLF) range. Coverage is worldwide. Omega employs eight transmitters located in different parts of the world to provide this navigation service. In the aftermath of World War Two the US Navy Electronic Research Section worked on developing VLF for navigation. In 1958 the US Navy started the practical use of a VLF Omega system using the 10–14 kilohertz frequency band. Continuous development and experiments showed the Omega system to be suitable for navigation. The research and practical tests done by the American Navy showed the Omega system was accurate to one nautical mile within the area covered by the VLF transmitters. During the period of developing Omega, the US Navy also had the co-operation of many other groups of scientists from around the world. In Europe, Great Britain, France and Norway made contributions to developing Omega; Canada also helped the Omega research trials. The final outcome of all this was the birth of a new navigation aid.

Omega operation

The eight Omega transmitters transmit three continuous wave (CW) radio signals of 10.2, 11.33 and 13.6 kilohertz. The time interval between each signal is 0.9 seconds and 1.2 seconds. Every ten seconds the transmissions are repeated in the same order. To ensure the transmitting pattern is precisely timed, it is synchronised to worldwide time by the use of atomic clocks. Atomic clocks are very accurate and are a part of the US Navy worldwide communication system. Each signal is transmitted omnidirectionally from the transmitters. The ground station transmitter signal output is 10 kilowatts. The Omega computer receiver processes all input from the ground stations plus other external sensor signal inputs from the aircraft navigation systems. The receiver then processes and calculates the aircraft position.

Omega transmitting antennae

Because very low frequency is being utilised the physical size of the antennae is above average. Operating with very low frequencies has disadvantages. Omega ground station antennae are tall, vertical towers up to 450 metres high or a valley horizontal span antenna (sometimes called an umbrella antenna) covering an area 3,500 metres in length. Each Omega ground station transmits a 10 kilowatt signal. The antennae normally have transmitting devices on

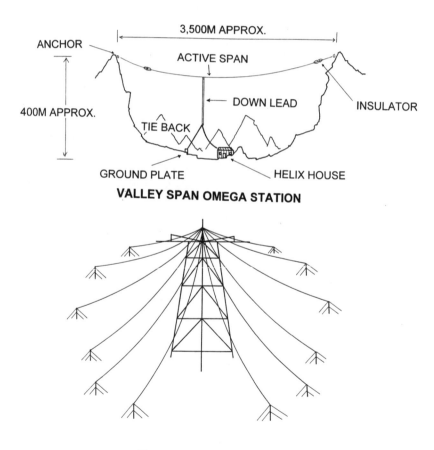

Figure 12–1   Omega Stations

their infrastructure. Due to the fact that eight ground stations were needed, worldwide agreements between the USA and other countries had to be organised. Fig. 12–1 shows typical Omega antennae.

Ground stations

The eight ground stations are located in the following countries:

(a) USA (two stations: North Dakota and Hawaii)
(b) Liberia
(c) Norway
(d) Japan
(e) Argentina
(f) Australia
(g) La Reunion.

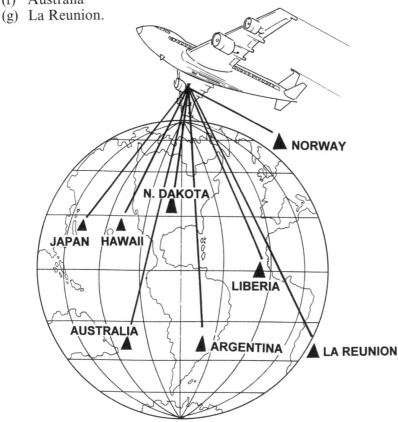

Figure 12–2   Omega Navigation Stations

111

The average distance separating the transmitting stations is about 5,000 miles (see fig .12–2).

Very low frequency signals

These radio signals have certain characteristics which make them the best signal to use with Omega navigation. The first advantage is that very low frequencies can travel long distances with high phase stability. The second advantage is that they have a low attenuation rate. Combining these results in a signal with good stability and low losses over long distances. In higher frequencies radio signals travel shorter distances and are frequently unstable.

The location where an Omega signal can be received was a major factor in deciding if it could be used for world navigation. Most of the research and development was carried out at sea. In later experiments, airborne equipment was tested. An aircraft could be anywhere in the world en route to its destination. Travelling to and from airports worldwide takes aircraft over vast tracts of deserts and water. In the situation mentioned, for Omega to be useful as a navigation aid signals have to reach everywhere. By using navigation stations sited at specific worldwide geographical locations, it was discovered that eight stations could cover the earth.

A feature of this navigation system is that a receiver must be able to receive three of the transmitted ground signals from anywhere in the world. To get a navigation fix on an aircraft position, a minimum of three or four good Omega signals must be picked up by the receiver. Because propagation problems arise due to the ionosphere varying from day to night, Omega-transmitted signals are changed in phase. The largest change occurs at sunrise and sunset when the ionosphere layer moves closer and further away from the earth. This problem is called a diurnal effect. As the varying changes are known and are predictable, corrections are inserted using computer software. The radio signals are also interfered with by the different types of terrain they cross. Around or near large stretches of ice an Omega-transmitted signal can be retained or attenuated. The earth's magnetic field also affects radio signals, producing navigation errors. An occurrence called a sun spot cycle disturbance causes solar system flares. The Omega radio signals are changed during solar flares to minimise errors. Navigation errors of up to six nautical miles and more are produced during solar system flares. Because most of the disturbances in the sky are predictable, alert notices can be issued to airlines and other interested bodies to warn of impending sun spot cycle action.

Aircraft system

An airborne Omega system normally comprises:

(a) an antenna coupler unit (ACU)
(b) a receiver/processor unit (RPU)
(c) a control display unit (CDU)
(e) an antenna.

Control display unit

This unit is used to key in reference information to the Omega navigation system. The control display unit has a function switch permitting the pilot to select different operating modes. On the keyboard the punch buttons numbered 2, 8, 4 and 6 are inscribed with the four compass cardinal points: number 2 is inscribed North, number 8 South, number 4 West and number 6 is East. When the flight crew are inserting a navigation instruction to the Omega system the initial procedure is normally to punch in the present position in longitude and latitude plus time and date. Up to nine navigation way-points to be used en route can be inserted. When en route the system will display updated way-point positions and status.

Omega receiver

The airborne receiver unit is the main part of the system. All Omega ground station and other external sensor signals are processed in this unit. Microprocessor computing circuits calculate the data supplied by the incoming signals, then generate output data which give the aircraft position and other information needed by the flight crew. Memory circuits operated with random access memory serve to store data. Random only memory circuits store programs which are utilised in the correction functions of the receiver. Other circuits in the receiver are power supply, built-in test equipment, analogue and digital interface hardware, and finally antenna switching devices.

Aircraft antenna

Normally a loop-type antenna is used in the Omega system. A radio frequency amplifier is built into the antenna unit. Omega antennae come in different shapes, a common type used frequently being the brick type, shaped, as its name indicates, like a square brick. In the system installation on a large civil transport aircraft the brick antenna would be fitted at the tip of the horizontal stabiliser. Loop antennae are fitted because of their ability not to be affected by precipitation static. Precipitation static caused by thunder and lightning rainstorms can cause problems to radio signal reception. On the other hand Omega loop antennae are vulnerable to electrical generating equipment interference. When a system is installed on an aircraft great care is taken to minimise any trouble which can come from electrical sources of interference.

CHAPTER THIRTEEN

INERTIAL NAVIGATION SYSTEM (INS)

An inertial navigation system is a self-contained long-range navigation aid independent of external signal inputs (fig. 13–1 illustrates system layout). It does, however, employ other aircraft navigation systems to update and check its accuracy. Navigation information is provided by utilising inertial sensing units, gyroscopes and a digital computer. Inertial navigation can sense the aircraft attitude in pitch and roll. The signals created within the system are put to work to direct the aircraft over a pre-selected global circle course. When a selected course is being followed an inertial navigation system will maintain the aircraft at a level attitude, stabilise

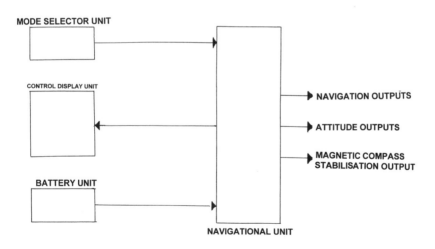

Figure 13–1   Inertial Navigation System

magnetic compass systems, and display navigation information on the instruments in the cockpit. When installed this navigation system only needs electric power for it to be fully operational.

For the inertial navigation system to navigate the aircraft correctly it is necessary to insert the starting point and destination of the flight. Normally this is done by giving the INS the latitude and longitude of the starting and finishing points of the flight. Alignment of the INS will not take place until the present position of the aircraft in terms of longitude and latitude is entered into the INS computer. The intermediate destinations (way-points) are also entered into the system before the flight begins. All this information is processed by the digital computer unit (DCU), which then determines the desired navigation track the aircraft will fly. Unlike the short-range navigation system VOR, the inertial navigation system uses true north and not magnetic north as its reference point.

INS units

(a) Mode selector
(b) Control display panel
(c) Battery module
(d) Navigation unit.

Navigation unit

Normally on civil transport aircraft three INS self-contained systems are fitted. The first unit in this system to be discussed is the navigation computer unit, the heart of the system. It contains the devices and electronic circuits needed to make the system operate. The system is served by accelerometers, gyroscopes and a stable platform. Another module in the navigation unit is the digital computer, which keeps a record of all changes of time, speed and direction sensed by the accelerometers. A battery unit and charger are part of the inertial navigation system. The battery unit is a 28 volt DC nickel-cadmium type. If during a flight the aircraft electric power is cut off or interrupted the inertial navigation system battery will supply power for approximately fifteen to thirty minutes. The navigation unit is located in the electronic equipment bay. The initial start of the system takes place with the help of its own battery, and when started 115 volts AC are supplied by aircraft power. The battery is then used as a back-up supply in case of a power failure. The navigation unit is cooled by an air circulation fan which is fitted on the electronic shelf where the inertial navigation unit is installed.

Mode selector unit

This unit controls the operating state of the system. A mode selector unit is a square-shaped panel with a selector switch and two indicating lights mounted on it. It has five positions which can be selected by a pilot:

(a) Off
(b) Standby (STBY). In this position the INS is warming up and the gyro devices are running up to speed. A typical speed for the gyros is 20,000 rpm. This mode of operation is only used when the aircraft is parked on the ground.
(c) Align. When this position is selected internal levelling of the sensing devices is completed. The INS also decides the sensing devices' direction in relation to true north. When in the align position the aircraft should not be moved. If the aircraft is moved an error in the navigation data being inserted into the system will occur.
(d) Navigation (NAV). In this operating position the internal modules and devices calculate the navigation instructions for the pilot. When it has finished computing, it presents the pilot with a continuous display of the aircraft heading, position, ground speed and distance to the next navigation way-point. Indicator lights on the mode selector are used to inform the pilot of the operation status the system is in. A ready light will glow green if the Align position is selected and the INS is aligned correctly.
(e) A battery (BAT) light glows red if the INS battery voltage drops below a certain level.

This unit permits the flight crew to insert navigation instructions and also to read navigation information which is indicated in the display windows fitted on the front panel of the control display unit. Normally the displayed information is shown in a digital format. The unit is a square-shaped metal box which has mounted on the front panel a keyboard numbered from one to nine. The zero key is separate. On the key numbered two the letter N representing North is inscribed; number eight has S inscribed representing South; number four has a W representing West; the E for East is inscribed on number six. Inscribed on other keys on the keyboard are operation positions like Insert, Alert, BAT (Battery) and Warn. The keyboard is used by the pilot to punch in the present longitude and latitude position of the aircraft. Also inserted at the same time is the longitude and latitude of all the different navigation way-points which will be used on the intended flight. The INS is very flexible and allows the pilot to check when in flight what distance it is to the next way-point and also how long it will take to arrive there. On the control display unit three lights are mounted on the front panel. One light is marked Alert, and is used to let the pilot know he has reached a certain way-point en route to the aircraft's destination. The second light is part of the battery alert circuit used to inform the pilot that the INS is being powered by the battery and not the aircraft power. Finally there is a warning light which glows red when the INS has a fault. This light will not extinguish until the defect is corrected.

Also on the front panel a thumbwheel permits the pilot to insert way-point numbers. For example, if he was on way-point three en route, by inserting number three all navigation information about way-point three would be displayed on the control display unit. A test switch is fitted which when pressed will check certain sections of the system. This facility is used by maintenance personnel when checking out the system.

System operation

When the system is installed on an aircraft it is not in isolation. Signals from the inertial navigation are used to supply attitude reference in pitch and roll to the flight director and autopilot systems. A signal is also sent to the yaw damper. The weather radar system receives a stabilisation signal which is used by the radar antenna. Navigation instruments such as the attitude director indicator (ADI) and horizontal situation indicator receive signals from the INS. Other systems such as the autothrottle computer, compass coupler and central instrument warning system (CIWS) also receive signals from the same source. Aircraft input signals to the INS are from the central air data computer (CADC), and the DME systems are used by the computer to update the position of the aircraft and distance to the way-point. A central air data computer is used to send altitude and true airspeed (TAS).

Before the system can operate correctly it has to have certain information to use as a reference base. A flight crew start the procedure by inserting the longitude and latitude of the place from where the aircraft is going to begin the flight. After the computer has been given the starting point, the destination of the flight is inserted. All way-points en route are punched into the computer. All the navigation information is inserted into the system in longitude and latitude format. When the system computer has the selected flight path or navigation instructions, while the aircraft is flying it will keep comparing this required flight path with the actual path being sensed by the accelerometers. The accelerometers measure the movements of the aircraft, no matter how small they are. Other major devices in this system are the gyroscopes, which are used to keep the platform that the accelerometers are resting on stable. The output signal of the accelerometers supplies acceleration to the computer. After the computer processes all signals from the accelerometers it converts them into time, speed and direction. The computer issues flight commands to the flight director or autopilot so that the aircraft is steered in the direction required.

Accelerometers

This sensing device operates on the principle of centring weight balanced by two springs in a signal feedback circuit. It is essentially a spring balance device which measures the G forces of the aircraft. The weight is marked from the centre: left of centre is a negative signal, right of centre a positive signal. When the aircraft accelerates the weight is displaced. The displacement from the centre whether left or right causes an electric pick-up signal to be created which is proportional to the amount the weight has moved. The pick-up signal is then amplified and sent back to the weight pointer to re-centre it. This feedback signal is directly representative of the amount of aircraft acceleration which created it to begin with. An accelerometer is very sensitive to aircraft movement, acceleration and sense change over a wide range. If the aircraft was flying in only one direction all the time, the system would need a single accelerometer to provide the navigation information. Due to the fact that aircraft fly in all directions two accelerometers are used. The output signals from the two accelerometers are added in a vector manner to produce the aircraft distance and direction.

When the aircraft is parked on the ground it is important that the INS stable platform is not moved or upset. Any tilting movement of the platform will make the accelerometer believe an aircraft acceleration has taken place. The displacement of the weight from the centre reference point will create a signal. This signal will become a distance flown when processed by the computer, even though the aircraft is still on the ground. On subsequent navigation calculations an error could be produced, causing problems for the aircraft flight crew. To prevent this error from taking place the gyros are used to sense platform disturbance and correct for it. The gyros can only correct for a certain amount of platform tilting. The earth's rotation also has an effect on the INS accelerometer horizontal platform. This results in the accelerometers sensing gravity and navigation errors being introduced into the system. To prevent this and to compensate for the earth's rotation, a compensation signal, derived from the rate and direction of the earth's normal movement pattern, is applied to the platform. As the earth rotates in a west to east direction, and as the rate of rotation depends on latitude (15 degrees an hour at the equator), the amount of compensation can be worked out reasonably easily. The compensation signal nudges the platform back on track when it becomes unstable due to the earth's rotation. The navigation unit and other units in this system are handled with great care by avionic personnel during aircraft overhauls.

Gyroscopes

Three gyroscopes are installed in the INS system. The system needs three gyroscopes to handle the three axes of pitch, roll and azimuth movement of the aircraft. When the pilot rolls or pitches the aircraft, the gyros sense the movement and immediately create a signal to drive the platform to a level position, otherwise the movement of the aircraft would tilt the platform, which would result in the accelerometers creating navigation errors. In the azimuth movement of 90 degrees the azimuth gyro senses the aircraft changing direction. It then develops a signal output to rotate the stable platform 90 degrees away from the aircraft movement. This results in the platform staying as it was relative to space. Inside the gyro case the gimbals rotating around the platform create a signal in the gimbals position transmitter. This signal is sent to the magnetic compass system to drive the heading indicators on the navigation instruments located on the pilot's and co-pilot's instrument panels.

System transfer switch circuits

On the aircraft up to three complete systems can be fitted. A transfer switch arrangement is used to allow the flight crew the means of switching from a radio navigation mode of operation to an inertial navigation system operation. If the pilot selects the radio navigation it means all the information being displayed on his navigation instruments is coming from the magnetic compass and the navigation receiver. The opposite is the case if he selects INS.

A switching transfer module which permits selection of other sources of navigation is normally located below the front instrument panels. The module consists of a flight director computer system switch. The module will also have an omni-range, INS, compass and attitude switch. The transfer switch also serves to select another source of attitude (pitch and roll) information if the normal supply develops a defect.

CHAPTER FOURTEEN

MAGNETIC HEADING REFERENCE SYSTEM (MHRS)

A magnetic heading reference system serves on an aircraft to sense the earth's magnetic north flux lines. A device called a flux valve is used to sense magnetic north. It receives the magnetic flux lines and from them generates a voltage which is then processed and coupled into a radio magnetic indicator (RMI), where it indicates magnetic heading. The flux valve device which senses magnetic fields is normally mounted on the wing tips of civil transport aircraft. A flux valve is always protected against other types of electromagnetic forces such as radiated electrical energy. Great care is taken when handling this device.

Aircraft system units

A system consists of the following units:

(a) Flux valves. Normal location wing tips. A flux valve must be kept away from electrical and magnetic fields. This device senses the direction of the earth's magnetic north. It is very sensitive to electromagnetic fields.

(b) Compass coupler unit. Location electronic equipment bay. A compass coupler has the function of coupling all synchro signal outputs to the navigation instruments.

(c) Magnetic compensator. This unit is located in the electronic equipment bay. These devices are utilised to adjust the flux valve signals for errors produced by other magnetic fields. The sources of errors are other electrical fields.

(d) Instrument amplifiers. The amplifiers are used to power the flight crew's compass system instruments' servo and warning flag circuits. They are located in the electronic equipment bay.

(e) Instrument transfer panel. Location overhead instrument panel in the cockpit. This switch is employed to transfer compass or directional heading information from number one to number two system. It can also transfer all heading information onto the auxiliary system in the event of problems developing in the other systems.

(f) Directional gyroscope. Location electronic equipment bay. The directional gyroscope produces the heading reference for the compass system.

(g) Compass switching relays. Location electronic equipment bay. The switching relays are part of the transfer system circuit.

(h) Horizontal situation indicator. Location forward instrument panels.

(i) Radio magnetic indicator. Location forward instrument panels.

(j) Transfer instrument switches. Location instrument panel in cockpit.

(k) Radio inertial navigation system (RAD/INS) transfer switch. Location forward instrument panel.

In a civil transport aircraft it is normal to have two magnetic heading reference compass systems fitted. Each system will have a complete set of units and instruments.

Flux valve operation

The flux valve device employs pick-up coils to sense the horizontal magnetic lines of force from the earth's magnetic field. The voltages created by the earth's magnetic lines are coupled to a stator of the slaving synchro in the radio magnet indicator. If the magnetic heading signal input from the flux valve and the heading displayed on the RMI compass card are in sync, a magnetic heading in degrees will be indicated by the pointer on the compass card. When the two heading signals are out of sync (the compass card and RMI slaving synchro are not aligned with the flux valve signal), a heading error is created in the system.

To hold the heading on course as the aircraft turns in the sky a stabilisation signal from a device called a directional gyro is used to create heading change signals. This function can also be carried out by an inertial navigation system (INS) instead of a directional gyro. The stabilisation signal is normally aligned with the flux valve signal. The compass coupler unit has the function of aligning both signals. A compass coupler unit is utilised to couple all the synchro signal outputs to the navigation instruments. The signals drive the instrument cards to the correct compass heading, which is displayed in degrees. Signals from this compass coupler unit are also passed to the aircraft flight director and autopilot systems.

The flux valve device is installed on an aircraft in a pre-indexed condition. This means the detector coils in the flux valve are aligned in a correct position to pick up the earth's magnetic north horizontal magnetic lines of force. Markings on the flux valve indicate to avionic personnel which way it must be fitted on the aircraft's wing tips. It is important that a flux valve is aligned correctly when fitted to an aircraft; if it is not fitted correctly wrong signals are generated, resulting in navigation heading errors. During major aircraft overhauls the flux valves have to be moved. When they are replaced on the aircraft a test or alignment procedure called a compass swing is carried out. The aircraft is taken out to a special area away from the hangars. The area the compass swing takes place in has to be free of underground electric cables and should not have large amounts of iron or metal nearby. In the area maintenance crews rotate the aircraft to different known compass headings and comparisons with the headings displayed on the aircraft instruments are made. The test includes the four cardinal points on a compass, and other compass readings are also checked and deviations noted. A certain tolerance is allowed during the compass swing. Normally the tolerance allowed is plus or minus two degrees on a navigation instrument such as the radio magnetic indicator. A standby magnetic compass is allowed a greater deviation tolerance: plus or minus five degrees would be considered acceptable.

System instruments

A radio magnetic indicator can display either automatic direction finding or omni-range navigation compass bearing information.

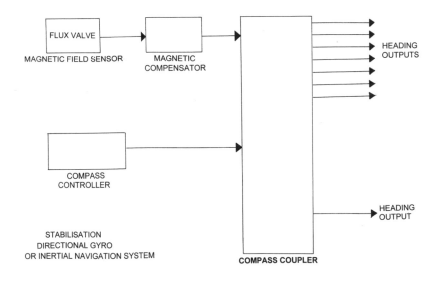

Figure 14–1   Magnetic Heading Reference System

What this instrument displays is determined by the system selected. A small push or slide switch allows the flight crew to choose the navigation they need. When they select automatic direction finding the letters ADF will be visible at the bottom of the instrument. Two pointers, one narrow and the other broad, are fitted on a swivel and depending on which systems are operating the pointers move around the compass card taking up bearings in degrees as required. On a typical indicator a single-bar pointer is used for number one navigation system and a double-bar pointer for the number two system indicator. In the instrument the pointers are driven to their positions on the compass card by synchro circuits. The synchro circuits receive their signals from devices in the ADF and very high frequency omnidirectional range navigation systems. A warning red flag will appear on the indicator dial face if a fault occurs in the compass navigation system. The other instrument utilised in the system indicates heading information from the radio or inertial navigation systems. The horizontal situation indicator can receive navigation signals from a radio source like a navigation radio receiver or it can receive signals from the inertial navigation system (INS). A switch mounted on the instrument panel allows the pilot to select which system he wants to use. If he chooses INS this will be displayed on the instrument in a small display box. When the pilot selects an inertial navigation system in which to navigate, the aircraft will then be taking information from the self-contained INS. No outside signals are being utilised. In the Radio position the horizontal situation indicator is part of radio navigation and the instrument indicates magnetic compass and VOR navigation bearing information. Fig. 14–1 shows a magnetic heading reference system block diagram.

Chapter Fifteen

Gyroscopes and Synchro Devices

In many navigation systems a device called a gyroscope is utilised (see fig. 15–1). A basic gyroscope, or gyro as it is commonly known, is constructed from metal. The main part is a spinning metal material mass called the rotor. The rotor is supported within two gimbal rings and the rotor and its gimbals are in turn mounted in a

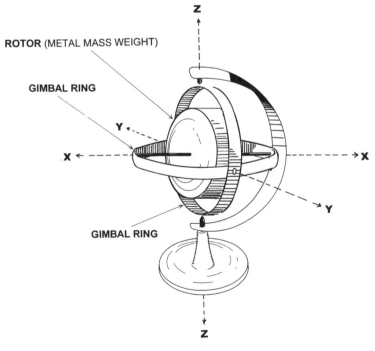

Figure 15–1   Gyroscope

metal instrument case. When they are mounted in this manner one gimbal is called the inner, and the other the outer, gimbal. This method of mounting the rotor gives the gyro movement in three mutually perpendicular directions without moving the spin axis, which means the gyro has freedom to move in three planes of direction.

A gyro has two characteristics: rigidity (speed of rotation of the rotor mass) and precession (torque – force of supply velocity). An example of rigidity is the fact that a spinning rotor can maintain its spin axis in a fixed direction unless an external force deflects it. The ability of the gyro to spin makes it very efficient as a stable reference from which an aircraft pitch, roll and turning operation can be measured. A practical experiment showing how a gyro keeps itself rigid can be carried out using an ordinary spinning top. When a child's toy spinning top is manually rotated to start it spinning it will continue spinning until a strong force knocks it over or the spinning slows down and it falls on its side. When spinning fast, the top (like the rotor mass spinning in the gyro) will resist bending and will stay rigid. If the gyro is spinning very fast it will have greater rigidity; a big rotor has greater rigidity than a small rotor. Precession is a force (torque) which when applied to a gyro will upset the spin axis and the gyro will act as if that force was applied 90 degrees around the rotor in the direction of rotation. In modern wide- and narrow-body aircraft an electric motor spins the gyro rotor.

Aircraft gyro types

Most navigation and altitude systems installed on an aircraft employ the following gyro types:

(a) vertical gyroscope (measures pitch and roll aircraft attitude)
(b) directional gyroscope (measures aircraft heading or turning)
(c) rate gyroscope (measures the rate of an aircraft turning about on an axis).

Gyroscopes, like most devices, have disadvantages. They are prone to what is known as gyro drift. Two types of drift from rigidity occur: real drift and apparent drift. Each can cause problems which interfere with navigation and attitude instrument indications. Real drift can be caused by having a defect in the rotor or gimbals; apparent drift is caused by the earth's rotation. If a directional gyroscope was situated at the equator with its spin axis horizontal and pointing east to west, then the earth's rotation once every twenty-four hours would create an apparent vertical gyro tilt at a rate of 15 degrees per hour. To make the gyroscope more efficient an erection system is utilised to keep its spin axis in a fixed position with respect to the earth's surface. The vertical gyro spins on a vertical plane, hence the name vertical gyro (VG). The other erection system does the same for a directional gyroscope, only in this case the spin axis is held in a horizontal direction with respect to the earth's surface.

An erection system consists of a mercury level switch or an electrolytic switch. The mercury level switch operates like a bubble spirit level. The idea is that when the gyroscope tilts, the mercury bubble will move to one side and will then apply power to a winding of a torque motor. The torque motor will then move the gyro back to its proper position. An electrolytic switch operates the same way except that the switch is filled with a conducting liquid and a bubble of inert gas. Electrodes are used to pass current outputs which drive the torque motors and keep the gyroscope in the position needed.

Gyroscopes are located in the electronic equipment bay. They are usually bolted down on a level surface, and on a large civil transport aircraft three vertical gyros are fitted. Number one and two gyroscopes are utilised in the number one and two systems. The third gyro, called the auxiliary gyro, is used as a back-up in case of problems in the other systems. In this type of gyroscope, synchro devices serve to pick up the pitch and roll movements of the gimbals and pass the output on to the navigation instruments in the aircraft cockpit. The vertical gyro is utilised in the flight director and autopilot systems to provide pitch and roll attitude indications on the attitude direction indicator (ADI). A vertical gyro signal also serves to stabilise the radar antenna.

Synchro devices

Many avionic navigation instruments and systems are served by a synchro to drive instrument pointers to certain positions. In the compass coupler unit, which is part of the magnetic heading reference system, a total of seven synchro signal outputs are put to work to drive navigation indicators on instruments that show magnetic heading. The ADF system also utilises outputs from these devices to drive a navigation instrument. This elementary explanation is included to help the reader become familiar with the terms and principles used in avionic synchro circuits. A basic synchro is in effect a transformer. The function of a transformer is to change an alternating voltage from one value to another, and it is composed of two coils known as the primary and secondary. The two coils are not connected electrically. Normally the coils are wound on top of each other or side by side on an iron frame; they can also be mounted on an air core or dust core material. A synchro is created by changing physically the orientation of the two windings in a transformer. If the primary winding is fixed and the secondary is made variable, changes can be made in input and output signals. A movement of an instrument pointer located far away from where a synchro is positioned is possible using less power and in a more efficient manner than if a manual method of moving the pointer was employed. A synchro is a small electric motor which can be utilised to cause a deviation in a device or instrument. The fixed winding is normally called the stator and a variable winding is known as the rotor. Synchros have certain names and abbreviations. A list of the most common:

(a) torque transmitter (TX)
(b) control transmitter (CX)
(c) torque differential (TDX)
(d) control differential (CDX)
(e) torque differential receiver (TDR)
(f) control transformer (CT).

Each of the devices listed has different characteristics with regard to signal input and output. A system consists of two or more devices interconnected plus capacitors and indicators. When a synchro system is driving a small indicator pointer or moving a very light load it is called a torque synchro system. Another use for interconnected synchros is to provide an electrical output in error detectors and automatic control systems. When used in that manner they are called control synchro systems. A torque unit can do a control synchro job. Control units are not employed for torque unit work.

Synchro operations

This is a basic summary of the more common functions these devices do.

(a) Torque transmitter (TX). This serves to electrically transmit angular displacement according to where the rotor is placed physically to its stator. It can work with torque differential receivers (TDR).

(b) Torque differential transmitter (TDX). A device which can electrically transmit angular displacement signals equal to the difference between the electrical input signal supplied to its stator from a torque transmitter, and the angular physical position of its rotor, with respect to its stator. When used in a system, output signals from a TDX can be coupled to a TX or a TDX.

(c) Control differential transmitter (CDX). Mostly utilised as part of control circuits in receiver circuits.

(d) Torque receiver synchro (TR). When this device receives input signals from a torque transmitter or a transmitter differential receiver it will take up an angular position determined by the input signal voltage amplitude.

(e) Control transformer (CT). This unit works when an electrical signal from a torque transmitter is applied to the stator. The rotor is positioned mechanically or it can be moved manually.

Chapter Sixteen

Pitot and Static Pressure System

To help the pilot and co-pilot to fly an aircraft in the civil transport class, external air pressure input information is needed. The air pressure outside the aircraft is converted to clear readable displays of vertical speed, altitude, airspeed and Mach number. Two types of air pressure are used during the external air conversion process – static air pressure and pitot air pressure. On an aircraft the vertical speed indicator instrument makes use of static pressure. The altimeter instrument which indicates aircraft altitude from the ground also makes use of static pressure. The Mach airspeed instrument needs static and pitot air pressures to indicate the Mach speed. The following are the air input definitions of pitot and static air pressure:

(a) Static air pressure: the static pressure of the motionless air surrounding the aircraft.
(b) Pitot air pressure: the air pressure measured when the active or dynamic pressure of the air is brought to a standstill in a pitot tube.
(c) Mach number: a Mach number is altitude plus airspeed.

Air input information instruments are designed to handle pneumatic (compressed air) and static air inputs.

Pneumatic indicators

On an aircraft with a pilot and co-pilot two instrument panels are installed. Instruments fitted into the number one side (captain's side) are repeated on the co-pilot's instrument panel. On a typical instrument panel the pneumatic (compressed air) indicators are:

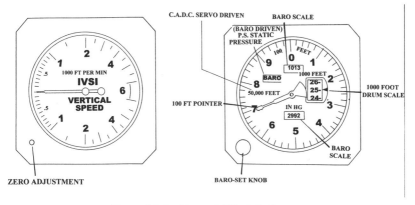

Figure 16–1   Rate-of-Climb Indicator

(a) pneumatic altimeter indicator
(b) Mach airspeed indicator
(c) instantaneous vertical speed indicator (IVSI).

IVSI

The instantaneous vertical speed indicator (IVSI) will be discussed first (fig. 16–1 shows altimeter and vertical speed indicator). When operating, this indicator produces a forecast of the aircraft's vertical speed during ascent or descent by joining together the effects of an accelerometer vertical pump, and an air leak through a bypass barrier moves a pressure-sensitive diaphragm. The movement amplifying element joined to the diaphragm (pressure-sensitive capsule) drives the indicator needle around the dial or face of the instrument. The dial of the indicator is calibrated in feet per minute. Static air pressure serves as the air input to the instrument. Accelerometer devices were discussed in Chapter Thirteen. To remind the reader of the basic operation, a brief explanation is repeated here.

Located inside the metal housing case of the indicator an accelerometer comprising two cylinders is fitted. In the cylinders a piston held steady by a spring and its own weight is moved up or down by the vertical speed of the aircraft. Depending on the direction of the aircraft's vertical acceleration, the piston movement develops and an instant increase or decrease in the indicator diaphragm causes it to move, producing the anticipated indication of vertical speed. This change on the accelerometer may only hold for a matter of seconds before it is lost. When the pressure that caused the change is lost a new pressure replaces it. The new pressure is in the diaphragm (pressure-sensitive capsule), which at that stage is equal to static air pressure and the pressure in the metal housing case. Both pressures serve to hold the indicating pointer on the indicator dial steady until another change in the aircraft's vertical speed causes a displacement of the pointer. Airspeed is displayed on the instantaneous vertical speed indicator in thousands of feet per minute.

Pneumatic (compressed air) altimeter indicator

This indicator displays static air pressure altitude in feet above a reference point at an airport or in the air (standard conditions of air temperature and pressure have to apply for the reference point to be valid). The standard is known as the Q code for altimeter setting. The International Civil Aviation Organisation (ICAO) has set out a universal code known as the International Standard Atmosphere (ISA). This is utilised by flight crews worldwide. In order to keep constant separation distances between aircraft the setting of altimeters to the barometric pressures prevailing at different flight levels and airports has been made part of flight operating procedure. To make sure all aircraft keep a safe separation distance between them during ground clearance, take-off and landing, certain altimeter settings are inserted which the pilot receives from ground meteorological stations. A three-letter code is employed in connection with these settings:

(a) QFE. Setting the pressure current at an airport to make the altimeter read zero on landing and take-off.

(b) QNE. Setting the standard sea-level pressure of 1013.25 millibars, which is 29.92 Hg, to make the altimeter read the airport elevation.

(c) QNH. Setting the pressure scale to make the altimeter read airport height above sea-level on landing and take-off.

The typical altimeter indicator is round shaped and is enclosed in a metal case. The dial of the indicator is marked out in graduations of hundreds of feet. Smaller graduations of twenty feet are also indicated on the dial. A cut-out display window shows altitude in hundreds, thousands and tens of thousands of feet. The barometric setting of the airfield or airport is displayed by dual-counter digit indicators. One counter displays inches of mercury (in Hg), the other counter indicator shows millibars (the millibar name is now being changed to hectopascal). A masking shutter covers either of the counter indications when necessary. The flight crew can adjust their altimeters with a barometric knob mounted on the indicator. Altimeters are calibrated on a regular basis to ensure no dial or scale error has developed within the instrument. If a defect occurs a warning flag will appear on the face of the indicator to alert the flight crew. Even with a defect the indicator is still able to measure altitude, but to a less accurate level.

Mach airspeed indicator

The Machmeter is used to measure the speed of an aircraft in relation to the local speed of sound in the prevailing atmospheric conditions in which it is operating. Different densities of air pressure and other factors make it necessary to use the local speed of sound as the reference point. This indicator combines two functions in one case. Airspeed is indicated by a linear scale from zero to 160 knots marked out in two-knot steps and from 160 knots to 420 knots by a logarithmic scale in 10-knot steps. Mach is displayed by the Mach sub-scale in 0.01 steps, from 0.50 to 1.0 Mach. Mach 1.0 equals the speed of sound. The Mach is read from the rotating indicator display window. Airspeed readings are taken from the outer dial scale. A wide-tip pointer is used to indicate airspeed. Another smaller pointer which normally has a coloured tip is used to indicate the maximum operating airspeeds at specific altitudes at which the aircraft is permitted to operate. This is also known as the velocity-maximum operating (VMO) indication. If the pilot exceeds the airspeed at certain altitudes an over-speed switching device fitted in the indicator will cause a Mach airspeed audio warning alert. A manual knob is fitted to the indicator to permit the flight crew to set in the required airspeed.

Pitot-static system

The system measures dynamic and still air pressure. Both pressures are used to define aircraft altitude and movement through the air mass. A system is composed of pitot-static probes and static ports

135

connected by tubing to instruments which measure or indicate dynamic or ambient air pressure. A typical installation consists of pitot-static probes which are normally fitted externally on the forward nose area. On large aircraft two probes are located on the left side of the fuselage and two on the right side (see fig. 16–2). The probes are made of metal and are a combined pitot and static device. Auxiliary static ports are also located on each side of the fuselage. When the probes are installed on the fuselage they are mounted one above the other. A probe heater control panel is part of the system and is located in the cockpit.

Pitot-static probes are physical devices designed in a specific way to allow pitot pressure air to flow into the system through a hole in the front of the probe. Static air is allowed access through ports located on the side of the probe.

Heater control panel

This control permits the flight crew to apply electric heat through a heater filament inside the probe. The heater is essential in cold weather. If no heat was applied to the probe access ports, ice would block off the mass of external air pressure from entering the system. Power needed to operate the heaters is 115 volts AC. Monitor lights indicate to the flight crew the operating status of the heaters. When the aircraft is in flight the heaters give out maximum heat. This heat

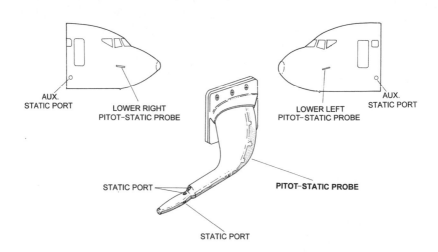

Figure 16–2   Pitot-Static System Component Location

is reduced when it is on the ground. Special care has to be taken when handling pitot-static probes when the heaters have been on. Severe burns can be received if they are handled incorrectly.

Pitot-static probe location

Pitot-static probes are easily recognised on most aircraft. They are fitted in the nose area and have a distinct appearance. When being fitted great care is taken not to scratch, dent or damage the surface or port access holes in any way. Before being fitted to the aircraft fuselage, pressure gaskets are inserted between the skin of the fuselage and the probe base. Metal bolts secure the probes in position. The use of any object to widen port holes or probe openings is not allowed. If the openings are widened the air data indicators in the cockpit will display incorrect readings. The pitot-static probes and the system are subject to regular checks. A system called flushing is carried out using a dry air pressure source set at zero to 15 lb per square inch. All interconnecting tubing in the system is flushed out on an individual basis to clean out any dirt lodged in the tubing. Before beginning this cleaning all indicators are removed from the system. During this maintenance procedure the pitot-static probes are also inspected and checked for serviceability. On the ground special tests are conducted by avionic maintenance engineers using test equipment which stimulates flight operating conditions. A pitot-static test operation includes making the aircraft descend at approximately 3,000 feet per minute for the static section and at an airspeed of 200 knots per minute for the pitot. Many other variations of these rates in ascend, descend and airspeed are conducted during the test. Great care is taken during ground tests and checks to stay within the recommended specifications, otherwise the cockpit air data indicators could be damaged. All indicators in this system are very sensitive devices.

CHAPTER SEVENTEEN

VOICE RECORDER AND EMERGENCY LOCATOR TRANSMITTER SYSTEMS

A voice recorder system on an aircraft serves to record the last half hour of communications that take place to and from the flight deck. It also records all communications between pilot and co-pilot. The voice recorder unit receives all sound in the cockpit and also receives audio from the audio integrating system. Radio transmit and receive signals between air traffic control or other ground control stations that take place are also recorded. When the aircraft is on the ground and the parking brake set, a tape erase circuit is used to bulk erase any conversations on the tape. This bulk erase circuit is not used if

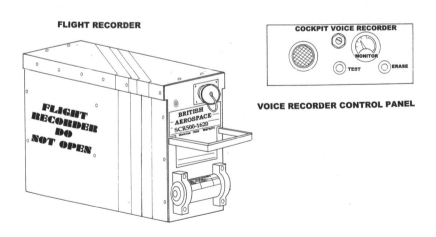

Figure 17–1 A Flight Recorder

138

a voice recorder tape is needed to investigate an incident that took place during the flight. Fig. 17–1 shows a combined flight and voice recorder and a cockpit control panel.

Voice recorder system

The system employs a:

(a) voice recorder

(b) control panel.

The voice recorder is an orange-coloured case and it weighs about 21 lb (9.4 kg). Inside the metal case are a recording tape and tape transport deck, both protected in a crash-proof module. Also in the case are electronic circuits, test circuits and monitor circuits. On the front panel of the voice recorder unit are mounted the following:

(a) Test switches to check the voice recorder audio channels individually. The test can be done one channel at a time. A switch which can test all channels in sequence is also on the front panel.

(b) A monitor meter to check the audio channels for good operation. The meter has a red and green area. When a test of the system is positive an indicating pointer stays in the green area. It stays in the red area when the result of the test is negative.

(c) Headphone input jack to check audio as it is being recorded on the four channels. This input jack is also used to check that the bulk erase circuit is operating correctly.

(d) An underwater locator beacon, fitted to the recorder. This underwater locator beacon is a battery-operated acoustic device which when submerged in water transmits a sonar signal and helps in locating the voice recorder unit.

The system starts operating when 115 volts AC is switched into the voice recorder. Internal electronic circuits produce 28 volts DC from the 115 volts AC. When the recorder begins operating it makes a 30-minute recording. Each channel is recorded by a four-channel recording head. Three of the audio recording tracks are recordings from the interphone system; the fourth recording track is the conversation picked up by the cockpit area microphone located in the control panel. Inside the unit a monitor circuit monitors all four recording tracks. Fitted on the front panel of the voice recorder is a monitor meter which allows the flight crew to check the four tracks. The flight crew or maintenance personnel can test the system by using the headphone input jack located on the front panel. When the test button on the voice recorder control panel is pressed a 600 kilohertz signal is sent to each channel. The signal is monitored by the tape monitor head and is then amplified; if everything is operating correctly a needle in the test meter which is divided into a red and green area will move on the control panel. If it moves into the green area the voice recorder has passed the system check, but if it has failed the needle stays in the red area. At the same time as the meter needle is indicating, a test signal should be heard in the headphones plugged into the input jack on the control panel. All the tests which are carried out at the cockpit control panel can also be done from the front panel of the voice recorder unit.

The voice recorder is normally fitted in the aft section of the aircraft. Depending on the type of aircraft it may be situated in an overhead electronic rack in the inside cabin ceiling area. Many narrow-body aircraft flying short-haul routes install the voice recorder in the aft freight hold. The unit is built to withstand great stress and physical pressure. A voice recorder can be in extreme heat, cold, and deep water for very long periods without the thirty-minute recorded tape suffering any defects. It can also be subject to heavy physical blows without any harm coming to the tape. When in a situation of high melting temperatures a chemical phenomenon sets up a protective thermal barrier of chemical steam. This chemical barrier prevents the recorded tape from being destroyed. The tape is also protected by the metal module it is encased in.

Control panel

The panel is located in the overhead electronic panel in the cockpit ceiling. Inside the control panel are monitoring and testing circuits. A microphone fitted into the panel is called the cockpit area microphone. It records all conversations in the cockpit. The channel used for this function is channel four. Also on the control panel is a bulk erase button which can be pressed to erase the last half-hour of recorded conversation. The erase operation can only take place on the ground and with the parking brake set.

Underwater locator beacon

The recorder has an underwater locator beacon fitted on the front panel of the unit if it goes into water. The locator beacon will begin operation when submerged in water. An acoustic signal of 37.5 kilohertz is transmitted into the water surrounding the beacon. Search teams with portable receivers that have directional hydrophones dive into the water and using a receiver follow the beacon's signal until it is found. If the flight or voice recorder to which the beacon is fitted has gone into shallow water the search can be conducted from small boats using long rods with directional hydrophones fitted on the end. The beacon can operate to a depth of up to 20,000 feet. A beacon battery will supply power to the electronic circuits for thirty days. The beacon has a built-in battery power supply. Most beacons use an oscillator circuit to transmit a pulse voltage output which is coupled onto a transducer. The output of the transducer is fed to the metal case of the underwater beacon. The effect of the transducer signal on the metal case is a mechanical movement which sends out into the surrounding water an acoustic signal which is then received by any search team in the vicinity. Pulse signals that are generated by the oscillator last for about ten milliseconds and happen once per second. A beacon signal can be heard through a receiver up to a range of approximately 2,000 to 4,000 yards. The underwater beacon is a very useful device and is a great aid in locating voice or flight recorders.

Emergency locator transmitter system

This system is installed to help search and rescue teams locate the main fuselage if a crash takes place (see fig. 17–2).
An emergency locator transmitter (ELT) system comprises:

(a) an emergency locator transmitter located at the rear of the aircraft, normally close to the tail
(b) a remote control switch situated in the cockpit
(c) a battery pack
(d) an antenna.

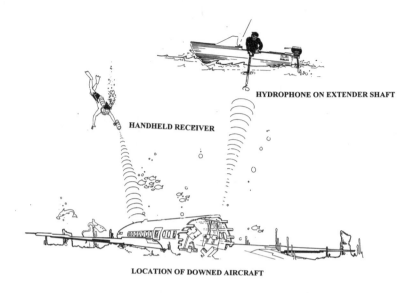

HYDROPHONE ON EXTENDER SHAFT

HANDHELD RECEIVER

LOCATION OF DOWNED AIRCRAFT

Figure 17–2   Locating Aircraft After Crash in Water

The transmitter has three switches fitted on the front panel:

(a) On-off-arm switch.

(b) Impact switch. This switch operates when a force of sufficient impact and duration strikes the emergency locator transmitter. For this switch to operate the on-off-arm switch must be set in the arm position.

(c) Reset switch. This switch just resets the transmitter after an operation.

The remote control switch is situated in the cockpit. The switch allows the flight crew to test or operate the locator transmitter manually from the cockpit. It has three positions: on-off-auto. In auto the emergency locator transmitter is prepared for transmission at all times. A metal shield is used to cover the switch when set in the auto position to prevent it being accidentally knocked out of the auto position.

The antenna used in this system is normally a short stub type or it can be a whip rod. In a typical installation it is mounted on top of the fuselage at the rear of the aircraft. The antenna is always fitted close to the emergency locator transmitter position. Coaxial cable is used to connect the transmitter to the antenna.

Before a test is carried out the air traffic control station is informed. No maintenance engineer would want to be responsible for an unnecessary search and rescue alert. The test procedure is to select the aviation emergency frequency, which is 121.5 megahertz using the very high frequency, radio system. Then using the headphones or cockpit loudspeakers they listen for the emergency locator transmitter output signal. Normally the test is kept as brief as possible. Besides the signal heard on the headphones a light mounted on the remote control panel in the cockpit illuminates to indicate the test operation is taking place. When the test is completed air traffic control is notified.

British Aerospace SCR500 Cockpit Voice/Flight Data Recorders are Available in Seven Variants Offering up to Two Hours Voice and 25 Hours Data Recording.
(British Aerospace Systems and Equipment)

Chapter Eighteen
Flight Data Recorder

The flight data recorder unit has been made famous by media reports of air crashes, which normally mention the search for the black box. Flight data recorders and voice recorders are not black. The boxes are coloured a bright orange to aid their recovery by search teams if the main fuselage is lost in rough terrain. During an investigation into a crash the flight recorder and voice recorder tapes are employed by the aviation authorities to assist in finding out the cause of the accident. The four methods of monitoring and reporting avionic, engine and flight control systems are the flight recorder, voice recorder, engine log book and technical log book.

In the aviation industry records are always held on file for long periods on anything which concerns the operation of the aircraft during its lifespan. The technical log book as used on a daily basis is a very necessary recording method of detailing any problems or incidents that happen on a flight. When the destination is reached the captain completes the technical log, reporting any defective system or equipment. A technical log, book is always consulted by maintenance to obtain information on the operating status of systems and components. Defects recorded in the log are repaired and work carried out must be entered in the technical log. When no action is taken, the reason for not correcting the defect must also be recorded in the technical log. The technical log book is an excellent medium for daily flight monitoring and defect reporting; on the other hand a technical log has its limitations and with the increase in number and complexity of aeroplane systems the log book has proved unable to handle the in-depth monitoring and reporting needed. Another great disadvantage of the technical log book is that it can be destroyed if the aircraft crashes.

To overcome this problem aviation equipment manufacturers developed the flight recorder and voice recorder to record the operation of an aeroplane system or systems using a means which could withstand the effects of severe shock and damage. About thirty-eight years ago, the United States made it mandatory by law that certain types of aircraft had to have on board a flight and voice recorder system. Shortly after, Great Britain also made it mandatory by law to install a flight and voice recorder system on certain categories of aircraft. Recently aerospace companies such as British Aerospace have developed a solid state combined flight data recorder which combines a voice recorder and a flight data recorder in the one orange-coloured box. The new solid state recorders use the latest digital memory and material technology. The new cockpit voice recorder and flight data recorder provide a full two hours' voice recording and twenty-five hours' digital data from the flight recorder. Due the use of solid state parts it needs no routine maintenance or overhaul.

Power consumption is 12 watts maximum. The weight of the combined recorder is 15.5 lb. An underwater beacon is fitted which can be inspected and tested without having to remove it. Also developed for use with the new combined recorder is ground support test equipment. The test equipment permits on location the high-speed retrieval of data from the recorder. Recorded data can be viewed or printed both on and off the aircraft. Advanced test equipment is also available to show a graphic display of in-depth data analysis needed to investigate an aircraft crash.

A flight data recorder is useful to the following groups of people:

(a) Civil and military aviation authorities investigating air crashes or incidents.

(b) Manufacturers of aircraft. The flight recorder records operation details of manoeuvres during flight. It also records the actions of the flight crew during flight.

(c) Airline operators, who are often interested in the record tapes of flight recorders for operational reasons.

The development of magnetic flexible tape which could be used to record flight events was a big breakthrough for the design engineers. The tape used in a flight recorder can be made from various materials; a commonly used type is made of stainless steel and nickel. Another type of tape is made of a material called vicalloy which is a combination of alloy and another metal. It is a process employed by manufacturers to create a very thin, pliable, strong tape. The recording tape is always being improved to give a better quality service and storage ability.

Flight recorder function

The flight recorder function is to record and store information and data on certain specific systems. The recording starts from the time of departure to the time of arrival. During that period it also records the movements of the flying controls and certain radio communication systems. In a typical flight recorder system (see fig. 18–1) the following operations are recorded:

(a) Altitude. The information about altitude is received from the pitot-static air data system. Data are also received from the central air data computer.

(b) Airspeed.

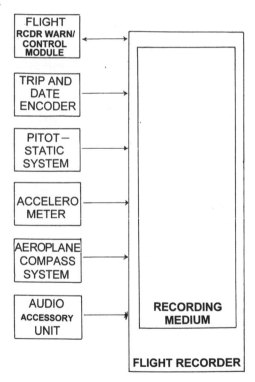

Figure 18–1   Flight Recorder System

146

(c) Vertical acceleration. A unit called an accelerometer supplies this information.

(d) A trip and date information code is inscribed on the tape for use as a reference point.

(e) Magnetic compass heading information.

(f) Communications. This information is received from the very high frequency and high frequency radio systems.

All of the operations listed have to be recorded in a flight recorder during a flight to conform with aviation authority regulations. It is mandatory by law that this is done. In the latest modern aircraft, flight digital data recorders are recording, in addition to mandatory operations, many other system operations and actions. The information from the tapes is being used by airline operators and builders of aircraft to increase their knowledge about material and component performance during take-off, cruising, descend and landing.

A typical flight recorder installation operation starts when electric power of 115 volts AC and 28 volts DC is switched into the system. To prevent the system from operating when an aeroplane is on the ground without engines running an electronic on-off relay circuit is used. A recorder has the ability to supply on tape, in the event of an incident or crash, the aeroplane's vertical acceleration, airspeeds up to about 430 knots and altitudes up to about 45,000 feet. In many recorders it is possible to include pitch and roll attitude, rudder pedal positions, marker beacon ground station passage, VHF and HF radio events, air traffic control events and engine pressure ratio plus thrust reverse positions. An important item also recorded is the aircraft radio altitude at the time the event occurred. Flight recorders are also available for supersonic aircraft such as Concorde.

All signals containing information from the aeroplane systems are indented onto the recording metal foil tape. This tape is five inches wide and is very thin, normally about one thousand of an inch thick. On the edges of the tape, sprocket holes allow the tape to be moved at a steady speed of six inches an hour. Each sprocket hole is spaced 0.2 inches apart. A sprocket hole is spaced from the next hole at two-minute intervals. As tape timing records can sometimes vary, they are inserted at regular thirty-minute periods to help analyse the recorded information. Stylus needle head scribers are simulated by the input signals from the aeroplane systems, and when the needles start moving they indent tracks on the metal foil tape. After a crash the magazine containing the tape is sent for decoding. The aviation authorities have special equipment, and in the case of metal foil tape, a transparent stencil designed to decipher the tape is utilised in the investigation. The decoding equipment is different and more complex when a digital flight recorder is involved.

Flight recorder system units

The flight recorder is divided into two sections: a mechanical assembly and the electronic circuits. A well-constructed metal magazine designed to withstand severe damage contains the recording tape. The recording tape is on a spool, the typical length of which is 200 feet; using both sides, this gives the flight recorder the ability to record 400 hours of flying operations. The tape moves at a steady controlled pace to give a correct time reference for the information recorded on the tape. Information is passed to the recorder from the navigation and communication systems; the stylus inscriber needles indent the metal foil recording tape with the signals received. This process is very like the method used in industrial graph chart recorders whereby a needle pen charts out information on a moving graded paper. The front panel of the flight recorder has a latch door which when opened allows the magazine containing the tape to be inserted or removed from the recorder.

Also connected to the recorder is a pitot and static pipe. Pitot-static probes are fitted externally on both sides of the aircraft nose. From the pitot-static probes dynamic and static pneumatic air pressures are received which are then converted into altitude and airspeed. Connecting pneumatic flow tubes feed the pitot-static air to the flight recorder. Inside the flight recorder the air data signals drive a cam that positions the stylus inscriber into the recording indication operation. Dynamic pneumatic air pressure is used to indicate airspeed on the recording tape and static air is used to record altitude. Fitted to the recorder is an underwater locator beacon. Normally a flight recorder is located in the rear of the airplane secured on a metal rack with holding latches. Many recorders have a meter on the front panel which displays the hours remaining on the recording tape. Fig. 18–2 illustrates recorder and location.

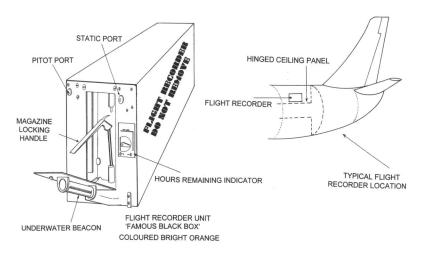

Figure 18–2   Flight Recorder Location

Recorder indicator panel

This unit displays evidence that the recorder is working correctly. If the recorder has an electric power defect or if the recording tape is defective in any way a warning light comes on. A test switch permits maintenance personnel to test the recorder when the aeroplane is on the ground and the engines are not operating. The indicator panel is normally situated on the overhead panel in the cockpit.

Trip and date encoder

The trip and date signals come from the selected flight and date numbers inserted by a crew member on the front panel of the encoder unit. Six numbered switches are fitted to the front of the encoder. Four switch digits are used for the trip section and the other two digits are used for date selection. The switches are round and easily moved and selection of trip and date information can be done swiftly. A button on the panel allows the crew to operate the encoder as required.

Digital flight data recorder

A digital flight data recorder, while doing the same work as the recorder explained above, has certain differences. It records a lot more data or information and it also works in combination with other digital units in the flight recorder system, such as a flight data acquisition unit and, on some aircraft, the master caution Mach airspeed module. Signal inputs in analogue and digital format from different systems are passed to the flight data acquisition unit. The signals process and convert all analogue signals to digital and pass the output to the flight recorder. A magnetic recording in digital format is made by the flight recorder. A typical digital recorder stores the last twenty-five hours of recording on tape. When needed the tape can be retrieved and the data on it sent for analysis.

Special equipment is utilised when tape analysis is being done. The tape has four tracks and is normally stored on two spools or reels. To prevent damage the tapes are held in a very strong module. To assist with recovery the flight recorder metal case is painted a bright orange. All electronic circuits and devices are housed in a metal case. Mounted on the front panel of the unit are an automatic test equipment connector and a 'bite' indicator. The unit has an underwater locator beacon fitted. A flight data entry panel permits the flight crew to enter trip, date, airline, flight number and weight before departure.

All of the following information is passed on to the digital flight recorder from the flight data acquisition unit in a digital binary format:

(a) The microphone transmitting key if pressed during radio transmissions is recorded. Thrust reverse lever positions and leading edge flap positions are also recorded.

(b) Synchro signals normally recorded include altitude, airspeed, heading and pitch and roll status of the aeroplane. Other signals recorded are control column operations, control wheel movements.

(c) Signals are also taken from the instrument landing system. This would include signals from the low-range radio altimeter system, localiser and glideslope deviation circuits.

(d) Pitch and roll attitude signals from the gyroscopes or inertial navigation system.

(e) Control wheel position taken from the control wheel column in the cockpit.

When all this information is decoded from the recording tape a very detailed examination can be made of the functions of the aircraft systems. Information on the crew's performance during flight is also available from the recorded tape. The information taken from the flight recorder tape is also utilised to find out which aircraft system has a developing defect, and with this knowledge preventive maintenance can be undertaken to correct the problem.

CHAPTER NINETEEN
PRESSURISATION

The primary function of a cabin pressurisation system is to allow passengers, flight crew and cabin crew a pleasant cabin and cockpit air pressure during the flight. The system stops extreme swings of air pressure during changes in the aircraft altitude. Regulations govern the temperature, humidity and fresh air quality in a aircraft cabin. To make flying more pleasant for passengers the rate of change in aircraft ascent and descent is also monitored. During a pressurisation operation the structure of the aircraft is put under great stress. Modern aircraft are built to withstand all of that stress. The aircraft is pressurised by bleed air from the engines supplied to and distributed by the air conditioning system. Within the air conditioning system, different sensors serve to protect from overheating problems. The system receives a supply of hot air from the main engine compressor before mixing it with cold air to produce a pre-selected air temperature ready for cabin use. It is then employed to send a continuous flow of conditioned air into the aircraft. The purpose of the pressurisation system is to manage the rate at which this air flow leaves the aircraft fuselage so that a comfortable air pressure is enjoyed in the cabin. Normally a system will hold cabin air pressure as close to sea level air pressure as possible. The system when set up correctly is able to keep cabin pressure at an altitude which makes it easy to relax in.

The advantages of having a pressure cabin are many:

(a) Oxygen equipment is only needed for emergency situations.

(b) Aircraft can operate at high altitudes without any ill effects to passengers. An aircraft which is not pressurised must keep down to a very low rate of climb and descend. A pressurised aircraft has the option of staying at high altitude for long periods of time.

(c) It gives an aircraft the option of flying over bad weather.

(d) Aircraft carrying horses and other animals can operate on routes which are not accessible to non-pressurised machines. No oxygen masks have to be worn for long periods of flight.

The disadvantage of pressurisation is the extra heavy equipment needed on board for this type of high-altitude flying.

System operation

As an aircraft flies to higher altitudes the more outside air pressure decreases. Aircraft structure materials reflect this and are designed for normal operation at what is called a differential pressure. What this means is that the difference between the air pressure inside the cabin and outside air pressure is held at 7.5 psi. As the aircraft climbs or descends the cabin pressure change will be proportional to the rate of upward or downward movement of the aircraft. If, for example, you were on an aircraft flying at an altitude of 30,000 feet and the outside air pressure is 4.6 psi, the inside cabin pressure would be about 4.6 plus 7.5 psi (which is 12.1 psi). That would give you a cabin altitude pressure of approximately 5,750 feet, which is just the right pressure to relax in. Outside the aircraft it would be a different situation. The aircraft fuselage structures are designed to take differential pressure of 1.5 times 7.5 psi. A self-contained back-up pressurisation system is available if the other system fails. In the systems use is made of different types of pressure relief valves. The function of the pressure relief valves is to prevent the differential air pressure from exceeding 8.5 psi. The normal differential is 7.5 psi and the tolerance allowed is very tight, only 1.0 psi. A valve known as a negative relief valve is available in the unlikely event of the pressure outside exceeding the pressure in the cabin. A main outflow and forward valve serve to maintain cabin pressure.

To allow the flight crew to operate and control the system a controller is located on the overhead instrument panel in the cockpit. The controller permits control and operation of the forward outflow valve, aft outflow valve, pressure sensing input devices for cabin and outside air pressure and monitoring cockpit indicators. In flight the rear outflow valve operates between an open and closed position, allowing cabin air to exit the aircraft and thus changing cabin pressure. The forward outflow valve is a slave of the rear valve and depends on signals from it to decide what way it should operate.

153

To control and give command voltages, a unit called a pressure controller is used. The unit is located on a radio rack in the equipment bay. The operating positions on the cockpit controller are:

(a) Manual AC – this position permits the flight crew to control cabin air pressure directly using alternating current. In this position the flight crew have to constantly monitor the pressurisation level as shown on the overhead indicators. A further check has to be made to make sure the cabin air pressure setting is correct with reference to the external altitude air pressure. A differential pressure gauge is provided for this purpose.

(b) Manual DC – this position allows the system to be controlled by direct current.

(c) Standby – this selected position is semi-automatic. It is used in the unlikely event of a defect in the automatic operation.

(d) Automatic (auto) position – this is the position which the system is normally operated in. When this position is selected the system automatically controls the cabin pressure for the complete length of the flight. The cabin pressure is held at a constant level from departure to arrival. To ensure this will take place the flight crew must set all altitudes at which the aircraft will be flying. The settings inserted include climb, cruise and descend altitudes. Inside the controller electronic circuits use this information to calculate an ascent, cruise and descent altitude pressure cabin program. The system also gives the airport elevation the aircraft should achieve. It needs this information to calculate a cabin air pressure when it starts to descend from the cruise altitude.

When the aircraft is taxiing towards the airport terminal sudden changes in cabin pressure can occur. To prevent this happening a flight-ground switch located on the cockpit control panel permits the flight crew to close the outflow valve to a certain degree. The result of this is that the cabin will be pressurised to about an altitude of 186 feet or approximately 0.1 psi below the runway elevation.

A landing gear safety switch supplies a signal to tell the pressure controller what position the aircraft is in. This signal will indicate whether the aircraft is on the ground or in the air. The signal's function is to establish landing and take-off operations for the controller. The actual cabin air pressure is monitored and sensed by a transducer device through an open port situated forward of the pressure controller. By using this signal as a reference, cabin pressure can be maintained at a pleasant level set by the controller.

Outside air pressure is sensed from a static air system. The pressure controller utilises this signal from the static air system to set cabin pressure during climb, cruise and descending operations. When the aircraft wheels touch down on the runway a signal is sent from the landing gear to the controller. That signal changes the controller's operating function from descend position to a ground pressure operation. As the aircraft moves towards the terminal building the flight crew move the flight-ground switch to ground; this drives the outflow valve full open at a controlled rate and depressurises the aircraft on the ground. The air pressure system on a civil transport aircraft has a complete warning and monitoring procedure built in, plus a standby system that keeps air cabin pressurisation problems to a minimum.

CHAPTER TWENTY

AIRCRAFT ELECTRICAL POWER

Alternating current (AC) serves as the main power supply. The engine generators supply a regulated 115 volts alternating current, 3 phase at a frequency of 400 hertz. Direct current is supplied from the alternating current system through devices called transformer rectifiers. The transformer rectifiers convert alternating current to direct current. Another source of direct current is the battery, which is normally a nickel-cadmium type. A unit called a static inverter is employed to convert the battery's direct current into alternating current. In the unlikely event of the generators being unable to supply electrical power the battery is utilised to supply both alternating and direct current.

Other systems need lighting, monitoring, control and indicating electrical circuits. This means various values of voltage are needed. To supply these voltages devices known as auto-transformers and transformer rectifiers change the 115 volts AC into different values. Depending on the type of aircraft, a primary power supply could consist of 2, 3 or 4 constant-speed engines driving alternating generators. During operation the generators are driven through a unit called a constant speed drive which holds them to a constant frequency output of 400 hertz, even with diverse engine speeds. A typical generator would produce 40 kilovolt-amperes.

Power supplies

The various power supplies employed are:

(a) AC power
(b) DC power
(c) auxiliary power unit (APU)
(d) external ground power

(e) battery power
(f) standby power.

AC power supply

In a typical system the units and control modules are as follows:

(a) Engine constant speed driven (CSD) generators. The number of generators will depend on how many engines are fitted.

(b) Generator control and protection panel. This panel provides the generator with protection against frequency, voltage, phase and stability malfunctions during operation.

(c) Electrical fault and monitor panel. This panel displays visual light warnings if a defect in the system occurs.

(d) Generator field relay and field switch.

(e) Generator breaker and light. This breaker serves to connect the generator to its load. It is designed so that it can be closed only when all circuits are operating correctly. The light indicates its operating status.

(f) Power meter. Kilowatt output is displayed on this meter.

(g) Bus-tie breaker. This breaker is a device which connects feeder cables to busbars and it is also used to tie different system busbars together.

(h) Frequency control rheostats.

(i) Synchronising lights. The lights illuminate when a phase, frequency or voltage difference takes place.

(j) Essential power selector and power failure warning light. This indicates defects in the aircraft essential to alternating current and battery systems.

(k) Load control circuit breakers. Load controllers keep the electrical load evenly distributed between generators.

DC power supply

The components used are:

(a) transformer rectifiers
(b) reverse current contactor
(c) DC meter selector and indicators
(d) battery, battery switch and charger (the typical battery is a nickel-cadmium 20-cell, 24 volt, 22 ampere hour type; a 35 ampere pulse-type charger is employed to keep it charged).

External power system

Ground power can be supplied through a connector receptacle normally mounted on the right lower side of the nose area (see fig. 20–1). The ground power is connected through a heavy duty cable from power outlets located on hangar floors and wall outlets. When the aircraft is parked at the terminal building, power is supplied in a similar manner. It can also be supplied through its own auxiliary power supply or a ground electric power cart. The cart is a mobile source of generated ground power. Ground power cannot be operated when the engine-driven generators are running.

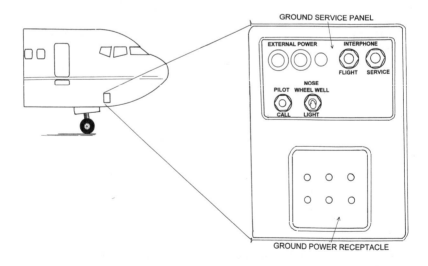

Figure 20–1   Ground Service Panel

Auxiliary power unit (APU)

In a situation where no ground- or engine-driven generators are available this unit can be started and it will supply power for most needs. Its main functions are to supply power on the ground and in flight if required. It also supplies compressed air for the air conditioning and engine-starting operations.

Standby power supply

A standby power system supplies 115 volts AC when all other electric power systems have failed. Protective electronic circuits will automatically switch in standby power if the main sources of power should fail during a flight. A static inverter unit converts direct current from the battery and produces 115 volts AC at 400 hertz.

Power distribution and protection

Electrical power generated by the engine generators is carried through aluminium cable to the electronic equipment bay. Aluminium cable is utilised to save weight. In other areas of the installation copper wire or cable serves to conduct electrical power. Different types of conducting wire are used for specific functions. Protective insulating material made from polyvinyl-chloride (PVC) and polyester and silicon cover the power conducting wire. Other protective materials such as metal braiding cover the cable depending on where the installation is being fitted. Devices called busbars, which are rectangular copper bars, serve for connecting the wires. Each generator on the aircraft has its own busbar distribution network. It is also possible to remove a generator from the system if the situation calls for such action. The remaining generators are designed to supply extra power if needed.

Routing and fitting of wire and cable looms are done in a specific way on aircraft. Care is taken to make the looms secure and protected. When being passed through pressure bulkheads (dividing wall sections separating a pressurised area from a non-pressurised area), special components and sealing material serve to protect and secure the wire looms. Wax twin plastic tie-raps and insulated metal clip materials are utilised to make a wire loom secure and safe.

In areas of high temperatures or hot exhaust gas around engines special types of cable are used. Earth studs are located at different points for earthing purposes. Crimped terminals are the preferred method of terminating connecting wires and cables to prevent a loose connection causing a malfunction or interference in avionic systems. Screening of wires and cables to prevent interference in the radio and navigation systems is essential. Other electrical equipment such as motors, generators and ignition systems are a big source of interference. In the electronic equipment bay most units are enclosed in protective metal cases.

Many protection circuits are put to work in the power system. The protection circuits will automatically operate when a defective generator reduces the total generated power to the aircraft. Other circuits serve to sense any change in line current. Overload protection circuits include load-shedding, which is a means of switching off unnecessary electric loads during a malfunction in the system. For instance, galley power could be offloaded when power is needed for more essential systems. Another method of protection is using bus-tie breakers (BTB) to trip off at certain levels. A generator control relay (GCR) operates if a serious problem arises in the power system. Load controllers use devices called current transformers to sense any change in the current load of each generator. When all generators are sharing, the aircraft demands that the current signal output from the transformers be zero. When a difference occurs the transformers generate an output. Fault alert lights are mounted on an indicator panel which is normally located on the flight engineer's instrument panel.

Circuit breakers, marked to indicate the system and unit each protects, are located in the cockpit. For example, the high frequency and very high frequency systems are marked HF 1, HF 2, VHF 1 and VHF 2. This method of marking and dividing the system makes it easy to locate a circuit breaker when needed by flight and maintenance crews. The reader might be interested to note a Boeing 737 uses thirty miles of wire on the aircraft.

Before an engine is started, the fire protection procedure is carried out. A fire protection control panel is normally located on the pedestal which is a dividing component between the flight crew in the cockpit. Mounted on the control panel are the engine overheat lights, the fire test switch, engine fire test switches and fire bottle discharge switches. All fire protection systems are tested and checked before any major engine system is operated. If a fire occurs on an engine or the auxiliary power unit, the flight or maintenance crews can discharge the fire bottles manually from the cockpit. When discharged the bottles release chemical fire extinguisher substances over the affected areas. Regular checks are made of all fire protective devices, fire bottles and systems to make sure they are operational.

CHAPTER TWENTY-ONE

GROUND PROXIMITY WARNING SYSTEM (GPWS)

The ground proximity warning system (GPWS) was first used on a large scale in the United States from 1975. After a number of aircraft accidents occurred the aviation authorities issued a notice making it mandatory by law that all aircraft above a certain weight install a ground proximity warning system.

Many aviation safety experts have stated that this system has helped to reduce aircraft collision-with-terrain. Flying conditions can change to the extent that a flight crew have to descend quickly into unknown mountainous or rough rising ground. This could happen as visual observation was becoming more difficult. In a situation like the one described a GPWS will alert the flight crew to the existence of rising or high ground. The system also provides a visual and audio warning if an aircraft is flying too low below the glideslope when on an instrument landing approach. Another situation which would cause a warning to be given to a flight crew would be if the aircraft was descending too fast. It also warns a pilot if he unsuspectingly flies too close to rising ground (see fig. 22–1).

The system receives input signals from many aircraft systems to give it the information to operate as a warning system. Signal inputs are received from the instrument landing system (ILS), indicated airspeed system, altitude, barometric altitude rate and the radio altimeter system. Information is received from the aircraft's flying controls. The status of the aircraft's flap and landing gear positions is passed to the system computer.

Aircraft equipment

A typical system on a civil transport aircraft would comprise:

161

(a) a ground proximity warning system computer
(b) warning lamps
(c) a control panel
(d) a master GPWS test switch
(e) a warning loudspeaker.

GPWS computer

A typical computer weighs about eight pounds and is about sixteen inches long, two and a half inches wide and eight inches high. The computer electronic circuits are enclosed and protected by a rectangular metal case. It is normally situated and secured on a radio rack in the electronic equipment bay. Inside the computer are microprocessors and integrated electronic components needed to create numerous different audio warning messages. The circuits used in the computer have the ability to provide priority status to each warning message. This priority comes into operation when more than one message is received by the computer at the same time. The priority

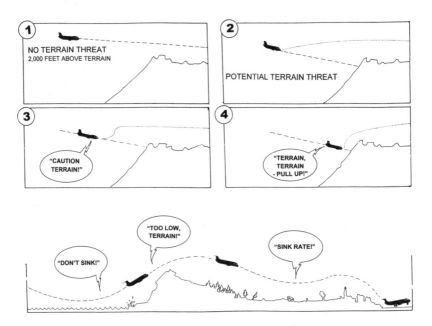

Figure 21–1   GPWS Rising Terrain Avoidance Operation

warning message pattern in a soft warning ground proximity warning system is as follows:

(1) Whoop Whoop Pull Up
(2) Terrain (Ground)
(3) Too-Low-Terrain
(4) Too-Low-Gear (Landing Gear)
(5) Too-Low-Flaps
(6) Minimums
(7) Sink Rate (descending too fast)
(8) Don't Sink (do not descend)
(9) Glideslope-Glideslope (landing approach on glideslope radio beam is not correct; the aircraft could be below or above the glidepath and if it is the system will give a warning).

The final output warning signals from the computer are audio which the flight crew receive through the GPWS cockpit warning loudspeaker.

An example of a GPWS warning is as follows: When an aircraft descends at a rate which is more than the recommended barometric air pressure descend rates for the terrain clearance altitude for which it is flying, a warning will sound. The audio part of the warning is a voice repeating caution 'Terrain'. Also, depending on the speed of the aircraft and its descending rate, a Sink Rate warning will follow. Another situation which produces a warning is when an aircraft during take-off loses altitude. The GPWS warning from the computer is set to come on at different altitudes on take-off. If, for example, the aircraft lost fifteen feet during take-off the 'Don't Sink' repeated twice would be heard from the loudspeaker. When the aircraft reaches 700 feet it would have to lose about seventy feet in height for the warning to be triggered. A Too-Low-Terrain warning is sounded when an aircraft is flying fast and low with the landing incorrectly positioned.

Too-Low-Flaps warning takes place when the aircraft is flying too close to the ground and the flaps are not in the landing configuration. Another warning from the GPWS a pilot will receive occurs when the aircraft ground clearance is less than 1,000 feet, the landing gear is down and it is below the glideslope radio beam. If the aircraft goes too far below the glideslope beam a higher-priority message will be triggered. This takes the format of a Whoop Whoop Pull Up. Two types of warning alert are provided based on position data and the terrain the aircraft is operating in. One is a 'hard warning', which is a louder audio signal and repeats itself at a much faster rate than normal. The other warning is known as a 'soft warning'. The hard warning broadcast cannot be cancelled if the aircraft has descended below the glideslope radio beam to such an extent that ground clearance is too low. In approach and landing operation when the aircraft passes through at a low-range radio altimeter (LRRA) system minimum descent height setting, the GPWS will give a warning of Minimums, Minimums. All the warning alerts are given with visual flashing lights or a steady glowing light. To prevent nuisance warnings, built-in electronic circuits in the computer monitor the signals and stop unnecessary audio and light warnings. The ground proximity warning system is designed to operate only when abnormal conditions are present.

POWER REQUIREMENTS

A typical GPWS system requires 115 volts AC. The system has its own circuit breaker marked GPWS which is located on the circuit breaker panel in the cockpit.

GPWS SELF-TEST CIRCUITS

The system can be tested on the ground or in flight. To carry out a GPWS self-test on the ground the aircraft has to be in a certain configuration; it must not appear to the computer as if the aircraft is coming in to land or in a take-off operation. In a landing operation the flaps of an aircraft are normally set at more than 15 degrees. To carry out the GPWS ground test, flaps must be less than 15 degrees and landing gear (nose wheel and undercarriage wheels) down on the ground. When this system is being fully checked the aircraft must be in the hangar. During maintenance, when necessary, an aircraft, just like a car, is lifted off the hangar floor by hydraulic jacks. The nose and undercarriage wheels are removed to allow servicing of the wheels and areas they are normally located in. When the nose wheel and undercarriage wheel assemblies are refitted, extensive lowering and retracting tests are undertaken to ensure all is well. Watching these tests is very interesting but a reader who is given the opportunity to see them should be certain to bring ear protectors as the noise level can be high during the operation. A self-test circuit on a GPWS checks most of the electronic circuits, warning lights and audio broadcast messages. It also checks other aircraft systems that feed input signals to the GPWS computer. If a fault is found a warning light will appear in the cockpit, alerting the pilot or maintenance personnel that the system has a defect. The messages heard in the cockpit when the self-test is operated are Glideslope-Glideslope, Whoop Whoop Pull Up. When these are broadcast a red pull up light is illuminated. This system has been very useful in preventing aircraft from colliding with rough, uneven high terrain.

Enhanced Ground Proximity Warning System (EGPWS)

Controlled flights into terrain (CFIT) were once the most likely cause of aviation accidents. In response to that problem the Allied Signal Corporation designed and developed a new advanced avionic system called the enhanced ground proximity warning system (EGPWS), using new computer technology combined with satellite communication and navigation equipment. The safety of aircraft with this new safety avionics system installed was greatly increased. To assist the project the research and development team at Allied Signal had access to previously classified military material from the American and Soviet authorities. Included in the material were digital terrain data files, topographical charting maps and charts of terrain elevation world-wide. The elevation charts gave the details of high ground surrounding airports in many parts of the earth.

A typical EGPWS system provides more advance-warning time when approaching high terrain: the flight crew receive alert warnings almost a full 60 seconds sooner. The system contains new safety features: terrain awareness and display (TAD) and terrain clearance floor (TCF).

The functions of these new features are as follows:

(a) The TAD feature uses the aircraft's geographic position and altitude cross-referenced with a terrain database to predict potential conflicts between the aircraft's flight path and the terrain. It also provides graphic displays of any conflicting terrain.

(b) The terrain awareness alerting algorithms inside the system computer continuously compute terrain clearance envelopes ahead of the moving aircraft. When the boundaries of these envelopes conflict with terrain elevation information stored in the computer terrain database, an alert is issued.

(c) The TCF function provides an element of protection to the basic GPWS modes. It creates an increasing terrain envelope around the prospective airport runway directly related to the distance from the runway. A TCF alert is based on present aircraft location, nearest runway centre point position and radio altitude. A TCF function is active during an aircraft take-off, cruise and final approach. This alert mode completes the existing mode four protections by providing an alert-based insufficient terrain clearance, even when in landing configuration. The basic GPWS mode four generates aural and visual alerts if an aircraft is in a potentially hazardous condition with respect to unsafe terrain clearance.

(d) The visual colour code for this system is based on displaying solid colours for cautions and warnings. For example, if a GPWS message is generated by the enhanced (EGPWS) system for TAD or TCF warnings, a red illuminated light would be displayed. A caution warning alert would result in an amber light illuminating. Aural warnings are broadcast from loudspeakers in the cockpit. Avionic units that supply data are the radio altimeter transceiver, air data/inertial reference unit, navigation receiver, flight management system (FMS), guidance and envelope computer, central maintenance computer, flight control unit and weather radar transceivers. Discrete data inputs are also provided by the slat flap control computer, flight warning computer and landing gear control interface unit.

A typical aircraft system consists of: a line replacement unit (the computer) and mounting tray; aircraft power wiring; signal sensor input and output devices; and a cockpit loudspeaker and warning light display panel. Modification work when fitting new equipment is minimized by using the existing holding tray and wiring already installed for the old system. Extra modification circuits, if installed, would give the pilot the ability to switch between the aircraft weather radar and the EGPWS display panels. The visual alert display from the EGPWS can be displayed on the weather radar indicator or on the electronic flight instrument system display indictors.

EGPWS Simulator Testing

In the simulator environment the EGPWS is used to give flight crews situation awareness training of specific airports with difficult terrain surroundings. Normal and abnormal flight conditions are simulated to show practical examples of how the system can operate as a safety

166

tool. Flight situations such as engine power failure with an extreme climb-out decision are often included.

The search to improve the usefulness of the EGPWS is still being pursued. A data information record on the many man-made high buildings and towers of all shapes and sizes in the world would be useful. A feature is being developed called a cockpit terrain map (CTM), which would provide maximum and minimum terrain elevations when flying over bad terrain not shown on a normal display. That data would be useful when an aircraft has to leave an en-route airway centreline. Another situation in which this function could be of use is an emergency descent because of an engine loss. Knowledge of the height of the terrain when the aircraft is over mountains in excess of 12,500ft would help the pilot.

A built-in circuit using the sensor inputs of geometric altitude will take the place of barometric altitude. The reason for that change is to prevent barometric errors caused by the wrong setting of barometric pressure. It can also stop different altimeter instruments from causing errors during QNE, QNH and QFE procedures.

Within the FMS plan, a GPWS terrain overview will give an opportunity to clear the terrain involved in the proposed flight. In the event of a flight plan change, the terrain data information is made available to the flight crew. The system will also offer a terrain data service, displaying locations in the flight plan of probable terrain-induced turbulence.

When an aircraft has EGPWS fitted the risk of a controlled flight into terrain is reduced. It was the authorities' and industry's response to the problem of controlled flight into terrain, and to date it appears to be working well.

CHAPTER TWENTY-TWO

TRAFFIC COLLISION AND AVOIDANCE SYSTEM (TCAS)

The traffic and collision avoidance system was developed and created to prevent mid-air collisions. This system is also known as traffic alert and collision avoidance system. After a series of unfortunate mid-air collisions in the early 1950s, the aviation authorities began to seek a system which would track other aircraft flying in the immediate area and also alert the pilot to a possible mid-air collision. The effort to find a system was increased when during the five-year period between 1968 and 1972 eleven mid-air collisions occurred in the United States. The aircraft involved in the collisions were of the civil transport type. Early attempts to design a system in the following years failed due to a lack of the necessary technology. The traffic collision and avoidance systems that were developed did not pass the tough practical test the aviation industry and government safety teams gave them. A big problem was the inability of the system to decode or understand interrogation replies from more than one aircraft at a time.

In 1981 it was agreed by all involved in the development of traffic alert and collision avoidance that it was possible to develop a system. The next step undertaken was to formulate regulations governing the type and fitting of the system. The Federal Aviation Administration (FAA), airlines, manufacturers of aircraft equipment and all interested groups set up a minimum operating performance specifications standard for the new system. In early 1989 regulations were issued by the FAA covering the installation and type of new systems which could be fitted to aircraft. The regulations required that aircraft of a certain category with more than thirty seats operating in and into the United States would need to have a traffic alert and collision avoidance system fitted within certain time periods. Civil transport aircraft were allowed until the end of 1991 to comply with the regulations.

During the search for a system which could meet the specifications great use was made of the air traffic control aircraft and ground systems which were working so successfully together. In order to check and evaluate the traffic alert and collision avoidance system Piedmont Airlines in 1982 tested a prototype TCAS for approximately 900 flying hours at high traffic airports. The recorded data and information from the test were analysed. From 1982 to 1987 further tests continued and TCAS 11 was installed in Boeing 727 aircraft serving normal commercial flights. Flight crews' comments and opinions plus recorded data were obtained on the new system. Many hours of airborne operation of the TCAS confirmed the system would be an aid to pilots when flying in heavy traffic areas. The TCAS 11 system at present only issues vertical preventive advisories; future systems will also issue horizontal advisories recommendations to flight crews. The airborne air traffic control transponder system and ground equipment are a good example of aircraft surveillance and control. The modern air traffic control system based on the Second World War identification, friend or foe (IFF) system helped in the development of the new traffic avoidance system.

Due to ever increasing air traffic a constant up-grading and development of air traffic control equipment is given a high priority in the aviation industry. Traffic collision and avoidance systems will help the flight crews to see and avoid aircraft which are potential threats faster than before.

TCAS function

The object of the system is to provide a dependable risk-free separation between aircraft flying near one another. For the safe separation operation to work all other aircraft in the flying zone must have a fully operational air traffic control transponder system, or better still a TCAS system, fitted. On civil transport aircraft only one system is installed. In a typical system the equipment would consist of a TCAS computer, two directional antennae and a control panel. In many installations the air traffic control panel on the aircraft serves the transponder and the traffic alert and collision and avoidance systems. When the system is installed one directional antenna is situated on the top of the fuselage in the forward nose area. Another omnidirectional antenna is fitted on the bottom of the fuselage. The antennae are a special type of device. Both antennae are utilised by the computer to transmit four electronically pointed radio beams in one of four different directions searching for intruder aircraft. No physical movement of the antennae takes place as they operate electronically.

The computer does not use air traffic control stations; instead it monitors other aircraft transponder transmissions. When the computer receives other aircraft transponder transmissions it stores the information, and if that aircraft flies into its airspace an interrogation process will take place. Due to the fact that the traffic alert and collision avoidance system works so closely with an aircraft's transponder, the reader might at this stage welcome a short reminder on air traffic control transponder systems. Each transponder system on commercial transport aircraft at this time have nearly all been converted to Mode S. Before Mode S transponders were fitted many aircraft were operating Mode C or A. The Mode C transponder can give identification plus altitude when it is interrogated by the ground station or an airborne TCAS system. An aircraft using only Mode A can provide only a selected code non-altitude reply when interrogated (aircraft carrying only Mode A transponders are in the non-civil transport category). An aircraft with a Mode S transponder is able to reply to an interrogation from an air traffic control ground station or traffic collision and avoidance system with identification, altitude, range and bearing. Aircraft equipped with a Mode S transponder and a traffic collision and avoidance system are able to co-ordinate avoidance action with each other. An important Mode S aspect is its address, which is a unique binary number assigned to each individual aircraft. This allows traffic collision avoidance system to communicate with specific aircraft. If an aircraft has no transponder, it is invisible to the TCAS-equipped aircraft.

Depending on the aircraft model and type of TCAS system installed, the received information is displayed on the pilot's and co-pilot's indicators which are located on the forward instrument panels. On aircraft with the electronic flight instrument system display (EFIS) installed, indications are displayed on the electronic horizontal situation indicator (EHSI) and electronic attitude director indicator (EADI).The information a flight crew receives from a traffic collision and avoidance system is the altitude, bearing, distance and position of the intruder aircraft. A resolution advisory (RA) is a vertical manoeuvre recommendation that should be performed or avoided by a pilot to ensure safe flight. When the aircraft in the airspace is a hazard or threat, the pilot is given collision avoidance advice in a verbal and visual format on how best to deal with the problem. The pilot is advised of the vertical movement and speed of the intruder aircraft and the positions of other intruders that present potential threats.

When the system is functioning it will select the class of threat the aircraft poses by noting its speed and position. It then calculates what threat that represents to the aircraft. The intruder aircraft is shown to the pilot on his cockpit indicator as a symbol. If a pilot selects the traffic advisory (TA) on the control panel the system will aid him in visually noting the intruder in his airspace. Other information issued if the intruder is equipped with a Mode S transponder is range, bearing and altitude.

TCAS computer unit

This unit is normally located on an electronic equipment rack in the equipment rack bay. It operates with 115 volts AC. The computer

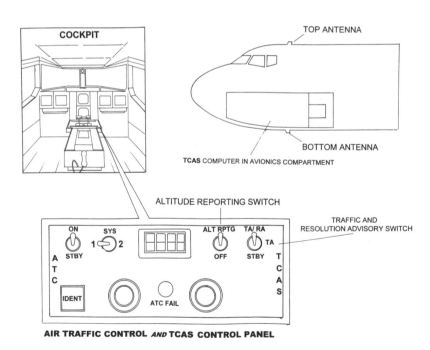

Figure 22–1   TCAS Unit Location

receives the following information from its own aircraft systems and it then stores the data for future use:

(a) Radio altitude (height as determined by the low-range radio altitude transmitter system).
(b) Signal information from the air traffic control transponder system.
(c) Transponder identification code.
(d) Maximum airspeed.
(e) Signal inputs from an air–ground switch circuit. This is an aircraft's weight-on-wheels gear. In other words, is the aircraft on the ground or in the air?
(f) Input signals from the ground proximity warning system.
(g) Heading input signal (this signal input permits the computer to determine the aircraft's flight path).
(h) Normally the computer can monitor up to thirty aircraft at any one time.

Control panel

In a typical system the control is located in the pedestal electronic panel. It can be a dual control used for the onboard air traffic control transponder and traffic collision and avoidance system, or a single-function control panel. Mounted on the front panel are the following operating switches:

(a) STBY (Standby). Transponder warming up but not on duty.
(b) TA (Traffic Advisory) only.
(c) RA/TA (Resolution Advisory/Traffic Advisory).
(d) Test.

Many controllers also have function switches called above and below. The above and below function on a control panel gives the pilot the means to display intruder aircraft at certain separation altitudes above and below the aircraft. Another function switch permits the pilot to choose the display area. A one- to ten-mile airspace display area can be selected. The traffic alert and collision avoidance audio signals can be fed to the cockpit loudspeakers. Finally a display select switch allows the pilot or co-pilot to select traffic advisory or traffic resolution as required. Controllers vary, an average about 2.25 by 5.75 inches and weighing 1.8 lb. Fig. 22–1 shows controller and antenna locations.

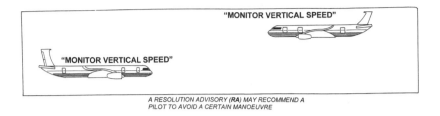

A RESOLUTION ADVISORY *(RA)* MAY RECOMMEND A
PILOT TO AVOID A CERTAIN MANOEUVRE

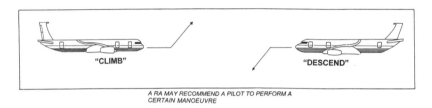

A RA MAY RECOMMEND A PILOT TO PERFORM A
CERTAIN MANOEUVRE

Figure 22–2   Resolution Advisories

System operation

The computer is the heart of the system. Through the directional and omnidirectional antennae the computer transmits and receives information which it then passes to the indicator. Information from the computer includes aircraft proximity, threat or non-threat aircraft and type of threat. It also gives verbal and visual advice to the pilot and co-pilot on the best movement to avoid the intruders. When operational all aircraft in its airspace are interrogated on a continuous basis. The computer measures the time between the interrogation and a reply. Electronic circuits in the computer then work out the range of the aircraft interrogated. If the aircraft being interrogated has a Mode S or C transponder the altitude is also calculated. The computer when operating divides other aircraft into different classes of threat. Most TCAS computers use the classes:

(a) non-threat
(b) proximity threat
(c) traffic alert threat (TA)
(d) resolution advisories threat (RA).

The indicator shows the distance, bearing, range and altitude of the intruder aircraft. The symbols, shape and colour inform the pilot if the aircraft is classed as a non-threat, proximity or traffic advisory (TA) or resolution advisories (RA) (see fig. 22–2). Traffic collision and avoidance systems serve in two modes: one is traffic advisory, and when in this mode the system only tracks aircraft which surround it and will indicate yellow on the indicator; in the second mode traffic advisory/resolution advisories (TA/RA) will track aircraft and issue resolution advisories which can be verbal commands to the pilot to climb, descend, reduce descend, increase climb and other such information. Also visual indications are displayed on the indicator. When the threat is over the computer will give a verbal clear-of-conflict message. Traffic collision and avoidance systems operate at the same frequencies as the air traffic control ground stations.

Operating frequencies for TCAS, air traffic control ground stations and airborne air traffic control transponders are as follows. TCAS transmit frequency is 1,030 megahertz. Receive frequency is 1,090 megahertz. The air traffic control ground stations transmit on a frequency of 1,030 megahertz. The receive frequency is 1,090 megahertz. The aircraft transponder and traffic collision and avoidance systems transmit and receive on opposite frequencies. Airborne transponders transmit at 1,090 megahertz and receive on 1,030 megahertz. When transmitting, the traffic collision avoidance system utilises the top and bottom aircraft antennae to interrogate other aircraft transponders. It receives transponder signals from other aircraft through the top directional antenna and the bottom omnidirectional antenna. During the periods when TCAS is working, signals have to be sent and received through specific antennae. Radio frequency power output is approximately 500 watts.

When the system is in resolution advisories (RA) operation it utilises the maximum airspeed information to calculate the rate at which the two aircraft are approaching each other. The traffic advisory operation will, should an intruder aircraft's flight bring it near enough to be a potential problem, issue a voice command of Traffic, Traffic. In close encounters with other aircraft, corrective resolution advisory voice and visual commands are issued to the flight crew telling them to Climb, Climb, Climb, Reduce Climb, Reduce Climb. Other voice and visual commands are Increase Descend, Increase Descend. When the situation warrants it commands such as Descend, Descend, Descend, Climb Now, Climb Now are also issued.

All the aural announcements just mentioned come under a corrective operation. The preventive operation issues commands of Monitor Vertical Speed, Monitor Vertical Speed. At the completion of the encounter when aircraft separation has been achieved the system would issue a single announcement Clear Of Conflict synthetic voice signal, after which the pilot would return quickly to the previous normal flight pattern. Mode S transponder-equipped aircraft transmit every ten seconds a message informing aircraft which are equipped with TCAS of the proximity and presence of nearby aircraft. A typical time between interrogation of one aircraft and another is one second. In heavy air traffic when radio electric interference could be a problem, the signal strength of each interrogation is increased. This is called the 'Whisper Shout' technique. A traffic alert and collision avoidance system has a built-in test system and monitor system. If a fault develops in the system it will display a TCAS Fail indication on the indicator instrument in the cockpit. Faults which can occur include:

(a) airborne transponder, radio altimeter, EFIS display systems
(b) antenna or coaxial cable fault
(c) incorrect information from the radio altimeter
(d) defective unit in the TCAS system.

The system is equipped with a self-test circuit which can be operated from the control panel. When the self-test is correct, first the indicator shows a visual message TCAS TEST and then TCAS PASS will appear if the test is successful. At the same time as the visual indications an aural message is also heard in the loudspeaker. When a defect is found in the system it will display a visual TCAS FAIL and the problem codes associated with it. A voice message will state TCAS Test Fail.

Traffic display

When a pilot receives a resolution advisories (RA) on his vertical speed indicator (VSI) a green arc area appears which indicates the vertical speed necessary to gain a safe vertical separation from the aircraft threat. At the same time a red arc area displays which vertical speed to avoid in his quest for safe separation. When the TCAS is off the colour white is displayed. A TCAS FAIL is displayed in the colour yellow. Yellow is also the colour used to indicate a situation when it does not know the bearing of an intruder aircraft. When that happens other information is displayed such as distance, altitude, and an arrow showing the movement of the intruder.

(a) An open cyan-coloured diamond means the aircraft are non-threatening and are over six nautical miles away. Altitude separation is more than 1,200 feet.

(b) A filled cyan-coloured diamond tells the pilot non-threatening TCAS aircraft are at around six nautical miles. The altitude is less than 1,200 feet.

(c) A filled amber ring indicates to the pilot that an aircraft is coming closer. The system also gives the pilot a voice warning. The voice warning takes the form of 'Traffic, Traffic'.

(d) A saturated red square alerts the pilot to threatening aircraft coming closer and he must take evasive action. This also triggers a voice command of Climb, Climb or Descend, Descend depending on the signal data received by the traffic alert and collision avoidance system.

Other symbols which serve to give information are:

Down Arrow – intruder aircraft is descending at about 500 feet per minute.

Up Arrow – intruder aircraft is ascending at about 500 feet per minute.

It can also give the altitude of aircraft above and below by displaying a plus or minus sign followed by a distance. For example, if an intruder aircraft is 600 feet above the pilot it will display altitude range (+06).

CHAPTER TWENTY-THREE
AUTOMATIC PILOT

In 1912 an American, Lawrence Sperry, flight tested an autopilot. This test was a success. During the 1930s many improvements to autopilot systems took place. American and European pilots used ground radio wave beams to show an aircraft could be landed with no hands on the controls. At that time a fail-safe system of autopilot did not exist. Automatic systems had also to prove they were fail-operational. If the autopilot failed at a critical stage of a landing approach or at a climb after take-off, how would the system be able to cope? Many questions were being asked by aviation authorities about safety during the early days of autopilot development.

At the start of the 1970s automatic landings began to take place on a regular basis. Since then automatic pilot systems have become very complex and are operating at a high level of safety. Standards of the engineering and electronic circuits involved in an automatic pilot system on a modern aircraft are very high. A system called Triplex in Europe and Triple-Redundant in America is used as a fail-safe method of operating automatic pilot. In other words, installed on an aircraft are three self-contained automatic pilot systems. When a fault occurs in one system, it is automatically disengaged and control of the aircraft continues with the remaining two systems. For the safety of passengers, crew and aircraft the flying controls have a back-up system for the back-up automatic pilot system. Strict regulations govern the use of automatic pilot systems when an aircraft is landing. The regulations are issued by the International Civil Aviation Organisation (ICAO). Not many airports have the quality of instrument landing system, electronic radio-transmitting equipment and runway visual-range high-intensity lights needed for an aircraft to make a fully automatic landing.

A fully automatic pilot landing is called a Category 3a operation. In such an operation the weather situation is another large factor to be considered. When a Category 3a operation is attempted, the regulations state: 'Operation down to decision height of 100 feet with

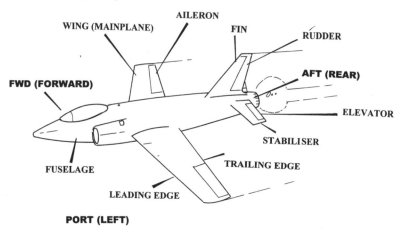

Figure 23–1   Structure of an Aircraft

external visual reference during the final phase of the landing, down to runway visual range minimum of 200 metres.' The pilot must also be sure the landing attempt has a good probability of success. Aircraft are certified for automatic pilot landings according to weather minima categories. Pilots have to take stock of cloud-base height and how good or bad visibility and runway lighting are before attempting an automatic pilot landing. To date no aircraft accident has occurred when an automatic pilot system was used for a landing. When the first automatic pilot systems began to be used on regular passenger flights the safety specifications laid down called for a theoretical failure rate in the range of not more than one per ten million landings.

The aircraft structure

An aircraft consists of the following structural parts:

(a) Fuselage – main body of the airframe. A metal beam known as the main spar supports the wings and engines. This section also serves to hold and support the cockpit and tail unit.

(b) Wings – the port and starboard wings are employed to support the aircraft in flight. They also serve for attaching engines and storing fuel. The front edge of each wing is called the leading edge. The rear is called the trailing edge. A movable control

178

section called an aileron is located at the trailing edges of both wings.

(c) Tail – this structural part consists of the fin, which has a movable control surface called the rudder. The horizontal stabiliser and elevators are also in this area. Fig. 23–1 shows a basic aircraft.

Aerodynamics

When in flight an aircraft is acted on by four forces:

(a) Lift. The shape of a wing has a big influence on how an aircraft flies. A lot of the lift force is created by the wing surface. When a wing is shaped so that the air flowing across the upper part has to travel further than the air passing under it, a very good lift is created. This happens because the air which is passing across the upper part of the wing is travelling further with only the same time to achieve the distance as the air moving under the wing. The result of this is that the air on the upper surface of the wing moves faster, which increases the pressure (force) underneath. Air pressure on the upper part becomes less, as it is driven underneath the wing. The result of this is lift, a greater force pushing up against a lighter force resisting on top.

(b) Drag. This is the opposite to thrust and is the resistance created by the aircraft's shape as it moves through the air. In other words, drag acts as a brake on the aircraft. Drag will resist the aircraft as it moves forward. Depending on the air density, size, shape and speed of the aircraft the amount of drag will vary.

(c) Thrust. This force overcomes drag. It is the force which propels the aircraft forward. Engine power produces thrust.

(d) Gravity (Weight). The gravity, or weight, is the actual weight of the aircraft. Weight is a force which pushes the aircraft down towards the ground. Lift serves to overcome gravity.

An aircraft when it is in the air moves around on three axes:

(a) Lateral. The lateral axis runs from the wing tip edge of the left (port) wing to the edge of the right (starboard) wing.

(b) Longitudinal. This axis runs from the forward nose area to the end of the tail.

(c) Vertical. The vertical axis runs from the bottom centre to the top of the fuselage.

The important factor regarding the three axes of aircraft movement is stability during flight. An aircraft before it can be certified to fly has to prove stability around the three axes. Any instability in one of the axes can cause a dangerous situation.

Pilot flying controls

Primary flying controls

(a) Ailerons

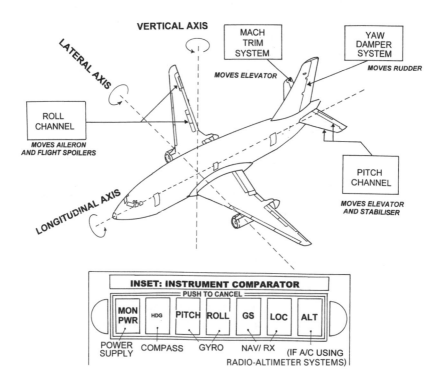

Figure 23–2   Automatic Flight Control Systems

(b) Elevators
(c) Rudder
(d) Stabiliser.

Secondary flying controls

(a) Trailing edge flaps
(b) Leading edge flaps
(c) Leading edge slats
(d) Spoilers
(e) Speed brakes.

To keep the aircraft stable the primary and secondary control surfaces are utilised.

Automatic pilot system

Automatic pilot systems are divided into three different categories. The first one is a single-axis-control autopilot. This type of autopilot is often installed on small aircraft. A single-axis autopilot normally has control over the wing movement; in other words it controls the aircraft roll attitude. It is also supplied with navigation signals from the radio navigation systems. Another type of autopilot used is the two-axis-control unit. This type of autopilot gives two control loops which direct the aircraft ailerons and elevators. Pitch and roll movement of the aircraft is possible with a two-axis autopilot. It also controls the radio and magnetic navigation systems. Finally, the triple-axis autopilot is a very complicated type. On civil transport aircraft this is the type most often installed. With this autopilot system installed a pilot can employ it to control all aspects of flying the aircraft. When autopilot mode is selected the aircraft can be automatically controlled in roll (wings plus ailerons moved and positioned), which is the longitudinal axis. It can also be controlled in the lateral axis (this is the pitch control of the nose, i.e. the nose can be moved up or down by moving the aircraft elevators). The other axis, the vertical or normal axis, governs the directional stability of the aircraft (see fig. 23–2). When the aircraft goes into a yawing motion the rudder is moved to prevent or control it. The autopilot can control the rudder. A famous condition in the yaw movement is called Dutch roll. Dutch roll occurs when the rudder begins oscillating. Control problems arise from this situation, and the autopilot normally takes preventive action by changing a wing position to stop it. If Dutch roll was not prevented it would cause a serious condition to arise. A system called a yaw damper is fitted to aircraft to control it.

Flight control devices

The devices which aid an automatic pilot to control an aircraft's attitude in flight are gyroscopes and accelerometers. These devices are in effect primary references for the autopilot system. Any changes in aircraft attitude create an error feedback signal which is amplified to operate hydraulic power control units and servomotors. Power control units serve to move surface flying controls such as wing flaps by means of control valves and hydraulic actuators. The hydraulic systems installed on wide-body civil transport aircraft are powered to certain pressures by electric and engine-driven pumps. Hydraulic pumps are powerful and on a large wide-body aircraft can move big areas of wing flaps quickly. Aircraft maintenance personnel are very careful when operating hydraulic systems on the ground when an aircraft is in the hangar for checks. The controls for operating the hydraulics are located in the cockpit on the overhead instrument panel. Before switching on the hydraulics, a careful check is carried out to ensure no damage can happen to personnel or equipment. A fluid called Skydrol is used in the hydraulic systems. The Skydrol fluid is supplied at a pressure of 45 psi to the electric-motor-driven pumps. Pump output pressure is about 3,000 psi and normally has a flow of approximately four gallons per minute.

Navigation signal inputs

The navigation signals used by an autopilot system are as follows:

(a) Instrument landing system (ILS) signals; these include the localiser and glideslope radio beam runway approach signals.

(b) Very high frequency omnidirectional radio range (VOR) signals. The signals from the VOR navigation system are used by the autopilot to fly the aircraft on selected radio navigation radials. VOR signals are transmitted from the ground navigation station. Another system which the autopilot uses is the distance measuring equipment system (DME). This system provides the autopilot with the distance in nautical miles the aircraft is from a DME ground station. The distance is known as the slant distance.

(c) The low-range radio altimeter system supplies the autopilot with altitude signals. When making an automatic or instrument landing system runway approach, the radio altimeter provides signals indicating the height the aircraft is from the ground to the autopilot. The radio altitude system measures from zero to 2,500 feet. To make an automatic landing the radio altitude system has to be operating correctly. A Category 3a landing attempt cannot be carried out or attempted if that system is not operating.

(d) During long-haul route flights the Omega navigation system passes navigation signals to the autopilot which allow it to steer the aircraft from way-point to way-point. An Omega system receives navigation signal information from up to 10,000 miles away. It gives the autopilot bearing positions in longitude and latitude.

(e) Compass information is provided to the autopilot by the magnetic heading reference system (MHRS). This allows the aircraft to keep a constant heading or select a new heading.

(f) Another long-range navigation system, called the inertial navi-

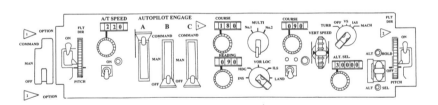

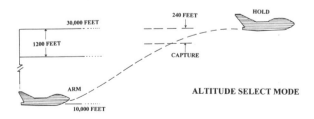

Figure 23–3   Autopilot Control Panel

183

gation system (INS), is used by the autopilot if it is installed on the aircraft. The INS system is a self-contained navigation unit and does not need ground navigation signals to give the autopilot bearings.

(g) Air data from outside the aircraft are passed to the autopilot from the pitot-static system. The air pressure information from this system is used for altitude and air speed information.

Autopilot control panel

An autopilot control panel allows the pilot to bank the aircraft left or right using a turn control. Another control allows the pilot to pitch the aircraft up or down. When the control is dead centre it is in what is called the 'Detent' position. The detent position is where a pilot would start if a gradual movement was needed to bring the aircraft into a new pre-selected heading or course. When the turn was completed the turn control would go back into the detent position. On some aircraft the control column might be employed for pitch and roll operations, and this is known as controlled wheel steering (CWS). Devices called transducers are mounted on the control column and as the column stick moves, the transducers pick up signals which are processed by the autopilot computer and then used as flight pitch or roll commands. Many different types of autopilot control panels are used on civil air transport aircraft (fig. 23–3 illustrates a Boeing 747 control panel). In this example two stages are displayed:

(a) Arm-Select desired altitude, which in this case is 30,000 feet.

(b) Capture – this function allows enough time and altitude for the aircraft to intercept smoothly and level off at the desired altitude. Capture normally takes place in two stages. First the aircraft has to be within 1,200 feet of selected altitude. The capture altitude is the desired altitude plus or minus sixteen times the altitude rate in feet per second for descending or climbing. For example, an aircraft climbing at an altitude rate of 900 feet per minute = 15 feet per second. With an altitude of 30,000 feet selected, the capture altitude = 30,000 feet minus 16 times 15 (16 x 15 = 240 feet). The capture altitude = 30,000 minus 240 feet = 29,760 feet (see fig. 23–3).

Interlock relays

To prevent excessive error signals reaching the autopilot a system of interlock relays are fitted into the system. The interlock relays will disengage the autopilot if the signals being passed to it from other aircraft systems do not meet the specifications allowed by the autopilot computer. Both pilots in the cockpit can disengage the autopilot by pressing an autopilot disconnect button which is mounted on their column control sticks. Before a pilot switches an autopilot system into control of an aircraft, he must ensure the aircraft is receiving all avionic system signals correctly and the aircraft is trimmed to a normal stable condition. Also, the automatic control system has to be synchronised in such a manner that everything continues in a smooth flying manner. No excessive physical pressure or movement on the control column is allowed at the hand-over period from pilot to automatic pilot.

Auto-manual glideslope approach

The G/S AUTO (approach) position on the control panel is utilised to capture and follow a localiser and glideslope radio beam signal path when approaching the runway. Normally in this mode of oper-

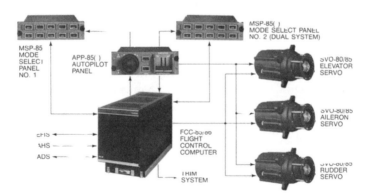

Block Diagram of Autopilot System Units

ation the aircraft would be below the glideslope radio beam.

In the G/S MAN (manual) position the aircraft is normally above the glideslope radio beam. It is normal flying practice for the pilot to approach the localiser radio beam first.

Several control positions are available for selection during autopilot operation. The ALTITUDE HOLD position provides a constant barometric altitude and holds the aircraft at the selected altitude. Another control function is called AS (Airspeed Hold); this is used to ensure a selected airspeed. The Mach Hold is used to maintain the selected Mach.

Autopilot failures

To ensure passenger, crew and aircraft safety, a standard classification of autopilot ability to avoid failure and yet not deviate from the selected aircraft flight path is called Fail-Soft in Europe and Fail-Passive in the United States. A Fail-Operational is a situation where a system has some failures but is still functioning. The system in that case would automatically land an aircraft. An autopilot system can operate the aircraft's flying control surfaces (rudder, ailerons, flaps and elevators); in other words the autopilot can command the control surfaces to operate. In a flight director system the pilot moves the control surfaces. Pilots use both systems to control the aircraft. Normally pilots permit the autopilot to control the aircraft and utilise the flight director system to monitor the autopilot.

The reader can now appreciate something of the complexity within an autopilot system. An autopilot system has to automatically process all signals to and from electromechanical hydraulic fluid powered flight control systems that have the ability to move flying control surfaces. It can move the rudder, ailerons, flaps and elevators. It must at all times keep the aircraft flying in a stable but safe manner. Radio navigation and instrument landing system signals have to be processed and acted on. Altitude signals from the radio and pitot-static systems are received and processed. The autopilot must also keep the aircraft on course and make sure it reaches its destination, and if need be land the aircraft. The autopilot must also assist the pilot who wants to manoeuvre an aircraft in a specific pitch or roll attitude. At present automatic pilot systems are used mostly to assist pilot and co-pilot in the flying of the aircraft, and for the immediate future a human pilot is what most people will insist on.

Chapter Twenty-Four
Flight Director System

The aim of the flight director system is to furnish the pilot and co-pilot with visual commands needed to continue on the correct pre-selected lateral and vertical flight path. To help the flight director carry out this function, input signals are provided from different navigation and attitude systems. It serves in manual flight. When operating, the flight director system does not move any of the control surfaces. Input signals utilised depend on what mode of operation the pilot has selected on the flight director system controller. Aircraft pitch and roll attitude is passed to the system from the vertical gyro. Steering computers serve for various modes of operation; they send signal commands to the different navigation instruments. These commands are displayed by the instrument pointers and symbols to the pilot as an aid to flying the aircraft. In a flight director system the attitude director indicator (ADI) displays the pitch and roll attitude of the aircraft. During an instrument landing approach the pre-capture and capture of the localiser and glideslope radio signals are indicated on a panel called the approach progress display module.

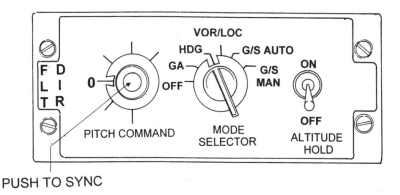

Figure 24–1   Flight Director Control Panel

187

Flight director units

A typical system consists of the following units:

(a) Flight director computer. Normally located on an electronic equipment rack in the equipment bay on the bottom of the fuselage.

(b) Attitude director indicator (ADI). This is located on the pilot's and co-pilot's instrument panels in the cockpit. This instrument contains the aircraft command bars.

(c) Approach progress display (APD). Located on the pilot's and co-pilot's forward instrument panels.

(d) Go-around switch. This is located on the pilot's and co-pilot's engine thrust levers. The thrust levers are situated forward of the pedestal in the cockpit. This go-around switch is used when the flight crew have decided that instead of landing the aircraft they will take it around for another go. In the go-around mode of operation, the roll channel section in the flight director computer will produce signal commands which cause the aircraft wings to level. At the same time a signal from the pitch channel generates a 14 degree pitch-up command. The pilot will also be given a go-around visual green light on the approach progress display module which is located on his forward instrument panel.

(e) Flight director control panel. Location is normally on the pilot's and co-pilot's forward instrument panels.

(f) Instrument amplifier unit. The location is the radio electronic rack in the equipment bay.

(g) Flight instrument accessory unit, which is located on a rack in the equipment bay.

Control panel

On aircraft used for civil transport two controllers are fitted. Each controller controls a self-contained individual system. All electronic components and devices are enclosed in a metal case. The front panel has the following variable selection switch and controls on it (see fig. 24–1):

(a) Off position.

(b) HDG. In this mode the pilot can select a magnetic heading as a command signal input. Signals from the pitch and roll computers are used during this operation.

(c) VOR/LOC. This is a radio mode of operation. The signal input is from the navigation receiver. Input commands to the roll computer are very high frequency omni-range VOR and localiser signals. Pitch command signals come from the vertical gyroscope, or they could also be from the air data computer.

(d) G/S AUTO APP (Automatic approach is used for an instrument landing system (ILS) runway approach). This is also a radio mode of operation. The signal inputs are from the navigation receiver. Other signal inputs are also taken from pitch and roll computers.

(e) GS MAN . This mode of operation is normally employed to force a capture condition of both VOR or localiser radio and glideslope radio beams. It is utilised if a problem exists within the computer radio beam sensors.

(f) A pitch command knob. This knob permits the pilot or co-pilot to direct the aircraft command bars to a specific level as needed on a landing, take-off, cruise and climb.

(g) An on-off altitude switch marked ALTITUDE HOLD. When this switch is selected to on, or altitude hold, it automatically removes all signals except the altitude hold signal from the manual pitch command knob. The flight director computer in this mode of operation generates signal commands to hold the aircraft at the barometric air pressure altitude that it was set at.

Approach progress display (APD)

This unit is divided into two visual displays. It serves to give the flight crew visual indication through green and amber lights of the selected mode conditions. This module shows the aircraft flight director and automatic pilot system flight mode condition. The left half of the display is utilised for the flight director system and the right half is put to work for the autopilot system. The approach progress display annunciator lights indicate to the flight crew what status the flight director is at during approach. When the controller is set on the VOR/Loc or Auto Approach operation mode, a light on the approach progress display module will glow amber before capture, and on capturing the landing radio beams it will change to green. During a landing approach, when the pilot has selected a localiser frequency and is operating in an automatic approach mode, a glideslope light will glow amber before capture and turn to green on capture.

Flight director operation

Assuming the pilot has switched the control switch to off, the system will retract the command bars from the dial of the attitude director indicator (ADI). The command bars are then held out of sight behind a retract shield on the instrument. If the pilot now moves the flight mode switch on the controller to the HDG mode of operation the roll channel in the steering computer is set into a magnetic compass heading operation. Command signals are now passed to the flight director from heading select. In the VOR/Loc operation, radio navigation and instrument landing system (ILS) operation radio beam signals from the navigation radio receiver are used in the flight director system. For the flight director to operate in this mode the pilot must select the proper frequency for the system being selected. When the VOR/Loc position is selected the computer prepares for capturing the radio beam. When the aircraft intercepts the radio beam at a certain signal strength a navigation capture operation is made by the flight director computer. At the capture of the instrument landing system (ILS) radio beams, the signal inputs are from the navigation receiver.

The difference between a flight director system and an autopilot system is the fact of command. A flight director can only direct a pilot which way to fly the aircraft. The autopilot system can operate the aircraft's control surfaces but a flight director can only command the pilot to move the control surfaces. Many pilots make the most of both systems by allowing the autopilot to control the aircraft and then using the flight director system to monitor the autopilot operation.

190

CHAPTER TWENTY-FIVE
AIRCRAFT WALKABOUT

If a comparison list were drawn up between a human body and an aircraft certain similarities could be found. On an aircraft the engines are its heart, producing the powerful beat and thrust needed to lift and push it forward. The fuselage is the body from which limbs called wings and undercarriage wheel assemblies are attached. A rudder and tail complete its rear. The eyes, ears, sensors, nervous system and brains are the avionic computer systems. Using the new nerve system of Fly By Wire, no steel mechanically connected cables are used to move rudder, flaps and other important control surfaces. Commands are sent from the pilot through electronic computer signals. Finally, aircraft come in all different sizes, shapes and colours, just like people.

One big difference between aircraft and people is the cost and space needed to produce them. To build the Boeing aircraft a building which covers 472 million cubic feet (13.37 million cubic metres) is needed. It is the largest building in the world, and is the size of ninety American football fields. A 747-400 is 231 feet 10 inches long (70.66 m) and 211 feet 5 inches (64.44 m) wide. The distance from the ground to the top of the tail is 63 feet 8 inches (19.41m). It weighs 870,000 pounds (394,630 kg) fully loaded. When on a long-haul flight it can carry 44,700 gallons (169,190 litres) of aviation fuel. On such a flight it has the ability to fly 420 passengers plus their luggage over 8,300 miles (13,350 km) without stopping to refuel. It can cruise at approximately 500 miles per hour. Total cost to take a new 747 off the aircraft parking area is about 170,000,000 United States dollars; enough fuel on board is included to get you home. In Seattle at the Boeing Aircraft Company a new 737 aircraft is rolled off the production line every two days. Each 737 needs 328,000 parts to complete. Thirty miles of electric wire is used, made up in 500 wire bundles. The aircraft is assembled in sections and joined together in a very skilful operation which results in all sections dovetailed together in a perfect fit. To paint a 737, fifty-five gallons of paint are used, which adds 300 pounds to the weight of the aircraft. The lifetime of the plane is approximately thirty years. Total cost is 31,000,000 United States dollars. The new 777 aircraft uses two engines with 90,000 lb of thrust each (one and half more times than four engines on an old 707). It cruises at 554 miles per hour and flies at up to 43,100 feet (13,137 m), which is more than eight miles high. The avionics used in the new modern high-speed aircraft have reduced space, weight and maintenance costs and added greatly to the safety of passengers and crew.

At this stage in the book it is time to leave the theory of avionics and visit an aircraft on the ground. During the walkabout a visit will be made to all areas containing avionic instruments, electronic computers and antennae devices. At the end of it the reader will have a reasonable knowledge of where avionic equipment is fitted on a large aircraft.

A pre-flight walkabout is always carried out by maintenance personnel before an aircraft departs on a long-haul flight. During the walkabout they cast a watchful eye over the aircraft's movable and static structural components. A final check takes place of the underbelly hatch doors, engines and wings. In the cockpit before departure another type of check takes place. The flight crew check all avionic and flying control surfaces using the self-test facilities available in the cockpit. All this pre-departure procedure is necessary and results in safer flights for everybody on board.

Avionic walkabout

The aircraft for this walkabout is a wide-body civil transport Boeing 747 modern jet. We begin at the nose of the aircraft. The section of the nose we are interested in is the radome, a hinged section made up of a honeycombed composite material used to protect the weather radar system antennae. Also located under the radome are the glideslope and localiser antennae which are used in the instrument landing system (ILS).

Located in the same area of the nose and situated beneath the port (left) and starboard (right) windows are the air data pitot and static probes. Pitot and static probes are used with airspeed and altitude instruments to indicate the aircraft speed and altitude in flight. Positioned on each side of the nose wheel are large square doors. Recessed inside the nose wheel doors are the glideslope track and capture antennae. Moving a little further to the rear of

192

the nose, a square flush-fitted hatch door comes into view which gives access to the main electronic equipment bay. We will visit the bay later. Continuing the walk to the rear you will notice various V and shark-fin-shaped devices protruding from underneath the aircraft fuselage. The devices are communication and navigation antennae.

First in line, starting from the main electronic equipment bay hatch door, are number one and number two air traffic control antennae. Behind them are the number one and number two

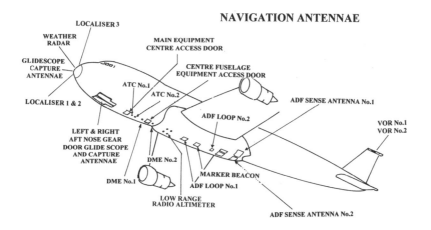

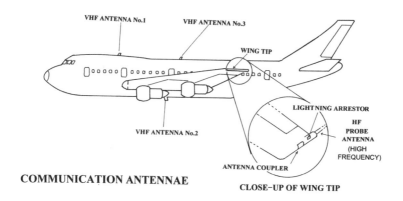

Figure 25–1   Antennae Locations

distance measuring equipment antennae. The four antennae just mentioned are small, V shaped and painted red. Also in the same area is a large shark-fin-shaped antenna which is used for very high frequency (VHF) radio communications. Aft (rear) of the antennae is another flush hatch door giving access to a small avionic equipment bay. The bay contains an electronic equipment rack on which are secured two low-range altimeter transmitter/receivers used to measure radio altitude from zero to 2,500 feet. Also located on the rack are two automatic direction finding (ADF) radio receivers used as navigation aids. Moving further back and still looking at the bottom of the fuselage, six round flush disc-shaped antennae can be seen. These antennae are used by the radio altimeter (RAD-ALT) system to transmit and receive altitude signals. Further back a square flush panel can be seen; underneath the panel is the number one ADF loop antenna. It is a flush-mounted antenna, i.e. it is recessed into the skin of the fuselage. A short square-shaped flush antenna is seen next. This antenna is the marker beacon system antenna. Marker beacon antennae can be shaped in various ways, and normally either a boat or square shape is used. Following the marker is the ADF number two loop antenna.

The next area you meet is the aircraft undercarriage wheel well. This area contains two automatic direction finding (ADF) system couplers, small devices used to couple radio signals from the sense

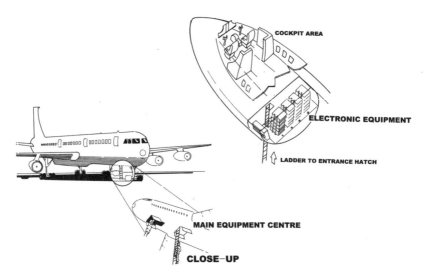

Figure 25–2   Electronic Equipment Component Location

antenna to the radio receivers. Two automatic direction finding sense antennae are located to the rear of the wheel well area. Both sense antennae are part of detachable wheel well area panels. The number one ADF sense antenna is located on the port side and the number two on the starboard side. Each wing tip has a round-shaped pole protruding to the rear which looks like an unpainted barber's pole. The poles are in fact the high frequency (HF) radio system antennae. Beside each antenna are two flush panels behind which are the high frequency radio system's tuner and lightning arrestor (the lightning arrestor protects the radio system during lightning strikes). The tuner is used to match the signals from the transmitter/receiver to the antenna.

Also located on the trailing edges (rear) of the wings are long, round, thin rods with metal needles fitted on the end. The rods are made of carbon and are known as static dischargers. They are fitted on the trailing edges of both wings, tail, rudder and stabiliser. Small static dischargers are fitted at the wing tips. Static dischargers are normally coloured yellow or black, and are used to protect radio communication equipment from noise and interference which is caused by electrically charged air and moisture in the atmosphere. Fitted on the top of the fuselage are two very high frequency radio communication shark-fin-shaped antennae. At the rear, on top of the tail, the very high frequency omnidirectional radio range (VOR) antennae are installed. They are concealed and protected under a round boat-shaped panel. Fig. 25–1 shows communication and navigation antennae locations.

Lower electronic equipment bay

The access hatch door to this area is only accessible by ladder or a high stand. A folding metal ladder is located behind the hatch door. When dropped it provides the means to enter the area (see fig. 25–2). Another means of entrance is through the forward freight door. Also, access is possible from the passenger cabin through a floor-fitted flush hatch door. On entering the main electronic equipment bay you will observe many electronic racks holding black metal cases. This area is the nerve centre of the aircraft. All the computers, amplifiers, power supplies, gyroscopes and synchros are enclosed in the square black metal box cases. Each rack has a quota of standard size air transport radio cases fitted. All radio, navigation, electrical and instrument units are installed on metal trays. The method of securing units to the metal tray is simple but very effective. Metal

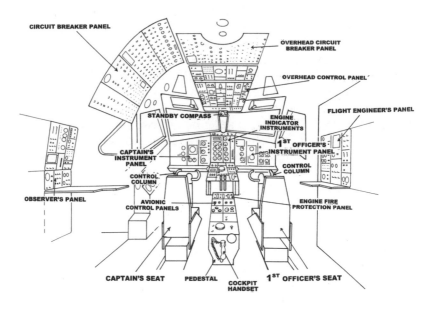

Figure 25–3   Cockpit Interior

holding latches keep each piece of equipment in place. The racks and equipment secured on them are identified by numbers to help maintenance personnel locate avionic equipment when necessary. At the rear of the racks are mating connectors attached to wire looms which are used by the electronic units to receive signals and power of different values. Mounted on metal pillars at the rear of the rack area are power and feed connectors which are joined and interfaced with busbars and circuit breakers.

An example of rack identification marking is as follows: A rack marked E1-1 informs maintenance personnel that it is the first rack of a group. The racks in that group could read E1-1, E1-2, E1-3, and so on. Mounted under each avionic unit on the racks are identification indents: for example the number one very high frequency (VHF) radio communications transmitter/receiver is identified by VHF 1; the number two and three systems are marked VHF 2 and VHF 3. The identification of racks, wire looms, connectors and electronic units is most important for good maintenance and servicing work to be carried out on the aircraft.

Great care is taken by avionic personnel to mark any equipment

196

removed so that if need be it can be replaced correctly.

We continue walking along the metal catwalk until on the left, facing the electronic racks, an entrance leading to a sloping metal crawl-way comes into view. This crawl-way leads to an electronic rack, which holds the two weather radar transmitter/receivers. Attached to the rear of the receivers are metal waveguide sections used to carry the radar radio waves to and from the radar antenna. Also located at the rear of the radar transmitters is a device called a dummy load. A dummy load is used by flight crew and maintenance personnel to test the weather radar system when an aircraft is on the ground, in the hangars or situated in an area where operating the system would be a problem.

Cockpit area

Having completed that part of the walkabout, make your way up the aircraft boarding stairs and enter the port cabin door. On entering you turn left into the cockpit. Inside the cockpit a

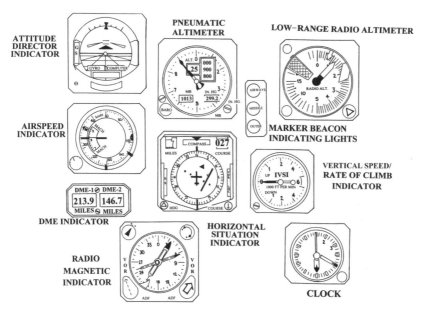

Figure 25–4   Typical Instrument Panel

bewildering array of instruments, control panels, sounds, light modules and circuit breakers confronts your eyes (fig. 25–3 shows cockpit panels). To bring order out of what looks like a confused assortment of equipment we will take each part of the cockpit separately.

It is traditional that the captain, or first pilot, sits in the left cockpit seat and the number two, or co-pilot, sits in the right seat, so all controls and instruments and system circuit breakers on the left half of the cockpit are number one system devices and are used by the captain of the aircraft. There is no reason why the co-pilot should not use an avionic system located on the captain's side, but normally they use the avionic systems, headphones, microphones and navigation instruments located in their own area of operation. Starting at the left, facing the reader is a panel containing many instruments. A normal configuration would include these instruments: the two largest instrument dials are the horizontal situation indicator, and located above it the attitude director indicator (ADI). Both of these instruments are used for aircraft control. The attitude director indicator is used to indicate visually to the pilot the aircraft pitch or roll attitude. It also displays instrument landing system (ILS) information to the pilot. The information includes glideslope, localiser and flight director system commands. On the extreme left on the same panel is a smaller instrument. Normally the radio altimeter indicator is fitted in that position. This instrument displays radio altitude from zero to 2,500 feet. Other instruments on the panel include airspeed indicator and air data altitude indicator, which can indicate up to 50,000 feet.

Also on the panel are the marker beacon indicator lights. A navigation comparison light module assembly is also present. The radio magnetic indicator (RMI) used to display VOR and ADF navigation bearings is located on the panel (fig. 25–4 illustrates a typical instrument panel). Other lights fitted are autopilot warning light and ground proximity warning lights. A small distance measuring equipment (DME) indicator could also be fitted on the instrument panel. The panel also contains a clock. Whatever is on the captain's panel is repeated on the co-pilot's panel. Sometimes an extra system is added, such as, for example, traffic collision and avoidance (TCAS), and an indicator will be installed on the captain's side and on the co-pilot's panel. Each panel is detachable and can be removed individually.

The centre instrument panel contains engine indicating

instruments common to both sides. In a typical cockpit layout a cathode ray tube indicator is located at the right and left bottom section of the forward instrument panels. The indicators are the weather radar indicators. Above the instrument panels is another panel containing the automatic pilot controller panel. Also fitted in that area is the master caution light assembly. On some aircraft the flight director controllers are fitted beside the autopilot control panel. In recent years new electronic flight instrument system (EFIS) equipment has been used. The space on the instrument panels where banks of indicators were located now hold only two or three flat screen cathode ray tubes. In the EFIS system an instrument like an electronic horizontal situation indicator (EHSI) is able to display information from more than one system at the same time. Light emitting diode devices are used to display information on the new equipment.

A very streamlined cockpit instrumentation display is given by the new systems. Many use colour display indicators. At the front of the centre pedestal located between the pilot and co-pilot are the engine thrust levers and flap lever. Located on the captain's side of the thrust lever assembly is a small parking brake lever and parking lever light indicator. The stab trim control is located on the co-pilot side of the assembly. On the lower pedestal panel to the rear of the thrust levers are radio and navigation, air traffic control and weather radar control panels. The engine fire bottle operating panel is also fitted on the pedestal panel.

The overhead panels contain control panels for cabin pressure, voice recorder, inertial navigation, system transfer switches, hydraulic systems control panel and the service-interphone switch. Also overhead, situated behind the control instruments, are the circuit breakers. Each system has individual circuit breakers which are identified for ease of use. At the right side of the cockpit, to the rear of the co-pilot's seat is the flight engineer's panel. On this panel are located the engine electrical generator system switches, the ground power switch, engine generator electrical power systems transfer switches and the auxiliary power switch (APU). Other indicators on the panel include engine pressure, engine total temperature, fuel flow and fuel quantity. The flight recorder control panel is also on the engineer's panel. The engineer has an audio selector box and a microphone and headset.

Another feature of the cockpit area is the provision of a Sarah beacon. This beacon is a safety radio signal beacon to be used if the aircraft crashes. The flight crew would drop it in the vicinity of the crash area and it would help rescue teams to locate the aircraft.

In the cockpit you will notice many thick books. They are the aircraft's library, containing operational manuals for different pur-

A Traffic Collision and Avoidance System (TCAS) Indicator

Units Used in a Collins TCAS System. *(Rockwell/Collins)*

200

poses. Also carried in the cockpit is the aircraft's licence to operate the radio equipment. Another very important document is the certificate of airworthiness; no aircraft can fly without having this certificate on board. It is issued by the government aviation authority. If an aircraft is not maintained to the aviation authority's regulations this certificate can be revoked, which would result in the grounding of the aircraft. Other documents and manuals include the aircraft's technical log. The technical log book is used by the captain after each flight to record all defects, rectifications and other details. When maintenance and other ground personnel carry out the captain's instructions as written in the technical log, the work done is entered and the log is signed by a person authorised to do so. An aircraft also has an operational and maintenance manual in its library. Each pilot and co-pilot is equipped with individual headphones and microphones which are located on the cockpit side walls, and each member of the flight crew has an oxygen mask complete with radio microphone fitted. A supply of oxygen is fitted in the cockpit. A hand microphone or handset is available for captain or co-pilot to make passenger address announcements when necessary. Finally, any member of the flight crew can contact the aircraft cabin crew at any door if need be by using the interphone system.

Leaving the cockpit you enter the passenger cabin. Here, avionic equipment includes cabin attendant control panels containing passenger address and cabin interphone switches. Each position is equipped with a handset, and certain doors, such as, for example, door one left, have a hand microphone. Passenger entertainment control panels are located in the cabin. Also, at designated positions there are megaphones for use in emergencies. Oxygen is supplied through the passenger overhead service units, along with reading lights and air supply. The voice recorder and flight recorder (the famous black boxes) are situated in the ceiling at the rear of the cabin. Another important avionic system is located in the cabin, and that is the emergency floor path lighting. The floor path lighting strips run from the rear to the front of the cabin. In the event of an emergency which results in loss of cabin lighting, the strips guide passengers to the aircraft exits.

That completes the avionic walkabout. Maybe, when you are visiting an airport or taking a flight, you can spend a few minutes locating visually some of the equipment and devices discussed here.

Chapter Twenty-Six
Future Trends

The one constant factor in the field of avionics is change. New technology is shaping the future of airborne and ground navigation, communications, surveillance, safety and inflight passenger entertainment systems. Air traffic is expected to double before the year 2015. An increase like that would exceed the capacity of the present air traffic control systems worldwide. To prepare for the increase aviation authorities in North America and Europe are planning to change the nature of air traffic control. The International Civil Aviation Organisation (ICAO), Federal Aviation Administration (FAA), International Air Transport Association (IATA), National Air Traffic Services (NATS) and other organisations are developing systems to ensure safe and efficient airspace travel. The three systems which when combined make flying safe at any time are communications, navigation and surveillance (CNS). Passenger inflight entertainment is another area which is changing very fast. Already being developed are systems which will provide any number of interactive facilities and services, including video, audio, sophisticated electronic games, information menus, telephone and fax, reservations and shopping.

Future air navigation system (FANS)

Future changes in air traffic control systems in both the airborne and ground equipment will be extensive. Much of the computer hardware and software digital solid state microprocessors are already in place. In space a combination of advanced satellites are supplying a support network which will make it possible for FANS to operate in a safe and efficient manner worldwide. It is planned that FANS over time will evolve into a method of flying airways called Free Flight (unfortunately you will still have to buy a ticket to fly). Free Flight is the concept of giving aircraft greater flexibility of operation while ensuring safety separation distances are adhered to.

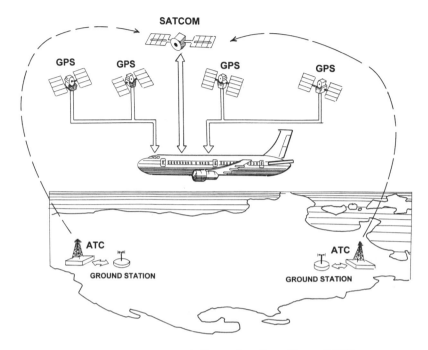

Figure 26–1   Automatic Dependent Surveillance (ADS)

Pilots will be permitted to choose any altitude, heading or flight path best for his aircraft at a given time without prior air traffic control approval. It is expected that aircraft flying at over 29,000 feet will choose their own routes. Air traffic control will monitor all activities through the new all-seeing space satellites and data reporting systems. If an airspace problem arises air traffic control will resolve it.

Wide area augmentation system (WAAS)

This system is being set up in the United States and worldwide expansion is projected at a later date. The major function of WAAS is to remove any error in the global positioning system. Ground monitoring stations combined with a stationary satellite will compensate for natural and man-made errors in the GPS system. The Federal Aviation Administration (FAA) has started to construct twenty-three ground monitoring stations for this purpose.

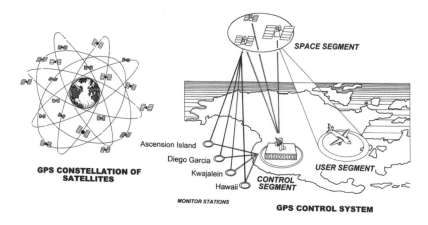

Figure 26–2   Global Positioning System

When the system is fully operational aircraft will be able to approach and land to Category 1 instrument landing system standard using the space satellite system.

Automatic dependent surveillance (ADS)

This system is been developed in Europe. The aim of the system is to provide a datalinked aeronautical communication service. Using satellite communications, the service will permit aircraft to be monitored and controlled when they are outside the range of air traffic control radar. It is planned that anywhere in the world, when flying in airspace over large areas of desert and sea, air traffic control can obtain their current position, intended flight path and other information held in the onboard navigation systems. The United Kingdom's National Air Traffic Services (NATS) is leading this project. (Fig. 26–1 shows the concept of ADS.)

Communications navigation and surveillance air traffic management (CNS/ATM)

This is the system combined with automatic dependent surveillance (ADS) plus an aeronautical telecommunication network (ATN) which the International Civil Aviation Authority (ICAO) is discussing as the system which might be employed for future ground-to-air and air-to-ground communications between flight crews, air traffic control stations and airline operation stations.

Global positioning system (GPS)

This system was developed by the United States for defence purposes. In recent times the United States government has given permission to civilian airlines worldwide to use the system. This permission is subject to a selective availability degradation clause (which means certain levels of navigation accuracy cannot be obtained from the system by civilian users). Originally the system was developed to help soldiers pinpoint where they were in unknown terrain anywhere in the world. Since then the system has been used for a wide variety of functions: overland hikers use it in large land areas; trucking companies operate this system to keep track of their fleet; and many ships utilise it at sea. Future applications include fitting it to cars for navigating in strange cities, and another suggestion is to fit a miniature device on offenders who are on parole and in that way keep tabs on them. The typical system on board an aircraft consists of two global positioning system receivers (this is sometimes called a sensor unit) and two antennae. The global positioning system is normally integrated with the flight management computer system when operating on the aircraft. Fig. 26-2 illustrates the concept of a GPS system.

GPS operation

The system can be looked at as a sort of artificial constellation of stars orbiting on different planes in space. It provides the aircraft that can receive the signals with the information on position, speed, and a twenty-four-hour, worldwide, all-weather operation.

Orbiting the earth there are twenty-four Navstar satellites, twenty-one of which operate at any one time; three are held in reserve on location in space. All the satellites are orbiting the earth at an altitude of 10,900 nautical miles. The orbital planes in which they move are tilted at a 55 degree angle with respect to the Equator. They are also displaced 120 degrees in longitude. When orbiting it takes each satellite a certain time to complete its movement. This orbital configuration was designed to make sure that at least four satellites are always in view and available to users.

Normally from any place on earth at any given time there will be six to ten satellites in view. The satellites must be more than five degrees above the horizon to be available to aircraft GPS receivers. A satellite weighs about 1,700 lb when being launched. It has four atomic clocks on board. These highly accurate clocks keep time to within one second in approximately 70,000 years. Power is supplied by nickel-cadmium batteries and solar energy. A typical satellite measures nineteen feet from tip to tip. The typical operational life-span of a satellite is about eight years. At the end of its lifespan in orbit the satellite will be replaced. Different methods of sending the satellites into space were used: some were launched into orbit from the Space Shuttle, and others by rockets. Each satellite transmits to the aircraft receiver the following information: satellite position, time of transmission and a range signal to fix the distance between satellite and aircraft receiver. When the aircraft receiver has all this information it computes present position, speed and time. The computer in the receiver solves the four unknowns: longitude, latitude, altitude, time.To calculate a precise aircraft position a minimum of four satellites must be in view. The system accuracy is such that the aircraft position to within 100 metres of longitude and latitude of the onboard receiver is possible. Altitude of the aircraft to within 140 metres can be computed. Time can be measured to within nanoseconds.

For an aircraft global positioning system to operate to its full potential, the antenna location needs to be exactly correct, and proper grounding of the antenna to the aircraft skin is essential. Global positioning signals travel in a straight line and arrive from any direction and elevation above the horizon, so it is essential that an antenna be placed on top of the fuselage. Also, to prevent obstruction of signals from wing and tail surface areas, an antenna is positioned as far forward as necessary. On the ground another source of obstruction would be airport buildings and hangars. During installation of a global positioning system cable, great care is taken to secure it from aircraft vibration. Loose connections cause the signals to deteriorate. The type of coaxial cable fitted is also important.

Satellites transmit in the L Band, the only difference being that the frequencies used are a little higher than those that the distance measuring equipment and air traffic control transponders operate with. When orbiting, the satellites transmit radio frequency signals which are modulated with a ranging code and a 50 signal bit per second navigation message. Information contained in the navigation message gives the satellite orbital position, time of message, satellite clock corrections, Navstar constellation status and the operational state of the system (defects or potential defects). A ranging code made up of a signal bit format repeats at regular periods. A typical ranging period transmission happens every millisecond.

Each satellite in the constellation has a unique bit code. Onboard the aircraft the GPS receiver uses the satellite code to identify it. The receiver then tracks the satellite and calculates the range to it. A receiver measures the time delay between transmission and reception of the satellite signal and then by multiplying the time delay by the speed of light in free space calculates the distance travelled.

All Navstar satellite constellations are monitored from ground stations and special antennae which are located in different regions of the world. A stationary satellite is also part of this monitoring system. Information received from the monitors is passed to a master station. In the master control station orbital planes are checked to ensure proper alignment and operation. The orbiting satellites can be updated with new instructions from the ground commanding them to transmit new signals requested by the aircraft operators of the system. To allow the system to serve for a precision landing approach and for take-off operations, greater accuracy is being added to the system. Accuracy is more important in the vertical position than in the lateral position. To improve aircraft accuracy in that respect, differential transmitters and differential receivers based at ground stations are being utilised to make it possible for landing and take-off operations to take place in the future. Already the system is saving aircraft operators' fuel and flight times, opening up preferred routes and making regions of the world which do not have adequate radio navigation facilities more accessible. In time it is expected that airport communications and navigation systems used at present will become redundant when the global positioning system and satellite communications combine together in a fully operational system.

Satellite communications (Satcom)

The advantage of this system compared with other methods of long-range communications is its ability to permit global coverage almost everywhere. Many long-haul aircraft have Satcom installed.

Satellite communications combined with the satellite navigation system are making possible new concepts of aircraft traffic control and operation. The services provided by Satcom are two-way cockpit voice operation, passenger and crew telephone service, aircraft position reporting, facsimile and telex operation, flight plan reports, up-to-date weather reports and engine and fuel information. Other services provided are inflight entertainment, films, music and catalogue shopping, with goods being displayed from downtown stores. The modern technology is giving passengers, while sitting in an aircraft seat at 35,000 feet and travelling at hundreds of miles per hour, telephone, telex and fax facilities to the same standards as on-the-ground facilities. By using the satellite networks already set up in space, aircraft and air traffic control will be in constant contact over vast water and land masses. A typical Satcom system on an aircraft would comprise:

(a) a transmitter receiver
(b) a modem processor
(c) a cabin telephone system
(d) a satcom antenna
(e) a duplexer.

The onboard transmitter transmits on a frequency of 1.5 to 1.7 gigahertz. When the aircraft signals reach the network space satellites they are then re-transmitted in the C Band of frequencies at 4 to 6 gigahertz. When these signals reach the ground communication stations they are processed and then routed to the local ground telephone networks.

Due to passenger demand many airlines are providing a telecommunication service on board their aircraft. To meet this demand some airlines in Europe are using a system called European Terrestrial Flight Telephone System (TFTS). This system is land-based and only operates in Europe. Line-of-sight transmission is used and three different radio ground stations are needed for the system to be operational. Ground stations separated at 500 km distances serve the aircraft flying at cruise level, which can be from 16,000 feet of altitude upwards. Other ground stations operate close to major airports to accept telephone calls before aircraft depart or land. A third ground station handles telephone calls from aircraft flying at up to 15,000 feet. The radio signals used in this system are operated in a method called phase shift keying. When in operation the frequencies employed are 1,670 to 1,675 megahertz when transmitting from ground station to aircraft; from aircraft to ground 1,800 to 1,805 megahertz is used. When a passenger speaks into an aircraft cabin telephone the voice analogue signals are converted into digital data signals for quick transmission. Compared to the present Satcom phone call charges the TFTS system is cheaper. On the other hand, TFTS is restricted in the area it can cover and the number of telephone calls it can handle at any one period.

High frequency long-range communications

At present and for the past forty years high frequency radio systems have been used by aircraft in many regions of the world to communicate with air traffic control and other aircraft. High frequency is affected by the constantly changing ionosphere. This factor makes sending messages by high frequency radio unreliable and can cause delays in aircraft position reporting. To help overcome this problem recent new high frequency systems are using digital tuning and data processing electronic circuits to create a better signal service to ground stations. Digital tuning has reduced the time taken to tune up a high frequency system to less than a second. Also, to prevent defects, new built-in test and monitoring circuits are installed. The weight and space taken up by a high frequency radio system has been greatly reduced. Many airlines utilise high frequency and will continue to do so for some time to come.

Cockpit instrument displays

Another area where new technology has changed methods of presenting information is in cockpit flight instruments. On the new aircraft coming off the production lines at Boeing and Airbus and other manufacturers, liquid crystal display (LCD) technology is being installed. Instrument displays are using a new technology called active matrix liquid crystal display (AMCLD). This new technology provides a flat-panel multi-information instrument colour display which gives clear readability, good reliability, lower weight and reduced maintenance costs. Many electromechanical primary flight instruments like the attitude director indicator (ADI) and the horizontal situation indicator (HSI) are being replaced by active matrix liquid crystal display instruments. Light emitting diode (LED) displays are being used on some aircraft and the new technology is

209

helping to reduce a pilot's workload when viewing instruments in the cockpit. A new technology called field emission display (FED) is also reported to give good results when used to display information. Field emission display gives out plenty of light with good resolution. It is also reported to be uncomplicated and cheap.

Multimode black boxes

Many avionic systems are now being controlled and operated by a combination of electronic circuits housed in a single black metal case. As miniature microprocessors become more powerful less space is needed to enclose them. This is leading to making one black box on aircraft carry out many functions. A recent combined British Aerospace flight recorder and voice recorder which contains all electronic digital circuits and devices to meet the strict specifications of civil aviation authorities is now being installed on aircraft. The new unit saves space and weight without any reduction in efficiency. Another example of this trend is a new navigation receiver which can be used to receive radio signals from three different types of landing system. The receiver is being developed to give aircraft the capability to handle any mixture of the following landing systems:

(a) Instrument Landing System (ILS).
(b) Microwave Landing System (MLS).
(c) Global Positioning System (GPS).

Due to the rapid advance in new technology there will be an interim period before a final changeover to a new worldwide landing system takes place. Not all regions will be ready at the same time. Major avionics aerospace manufacturing companies like Honeywell, GEC-Marconi, Rockwell/Collins and Allied Signal have multimode receivers under development for use in civil transport aircraft. Many military aircraft already use the new receivers successfully. The new data-transaction Mode S transponder has the ability to handle many extra functions. This unit is being used very successfully in air traffic control to transmit and receive a lot more information than transponders normally do. For example, in the advanced safety systems like the Traffic Alert and Collision Avoidance Systems (TCAS) its ability to send and receive information on aircraft bearing, altitude and speed with accuracy and reliability is most important. Once more it is the small, powerful, computer microprocessor which is adding new capabilities to old systems. Honeywell Aerospace is researching new avionics which will provide enhanced vision systems to enable flight crews to see through rain, fog, clouds and darkness, which will make flying safer for all-weather operations.

Avionic safety systems

Since the ground proximity warning system (GPWS) was fitted it has reduced crashes caused by aircraft flying into high ground. To reduce even further the chance of high-ground collision a new GPWS system has been developed by the Allied Signal aerospace company, called Enhanced GPWS. Among the many new features in this system is the ability to 'look ahead'. It means pilots will be given more time to take avoidance action if the aircraft is heading towards high ground. When a situation arises which to the system looks dangerous it will emit an aural warning and a visual warning display in the cockpit; it will also give an aural call-out to the flight crew of what altitude they are flying at. The look-ahead operation will give an audio pre-warning, which will start with Caution-Terrain and then follow with Terrain Ahead. After the pre-warning a full alert GPWS warning is given. During a landing approach the new system automatically monitors the aircraft position on the glideslope radio beam and if a problem arises a warning alert is sounded in the cockpit. If the aircraft goes into an excessive bank angle a warning is sounded.

A recent development, and one which will become more important in the future, is the installation of ground proximity warning systems on helicopters. Onboard tests are being carried out using the new GPWS systems to increase the safety of helicopter flights. Helicopters due to their function spend a lot of time near the ground in small areas of airspace. Pilots of helicopters have a very hard job in circumstances like that and a safety warning system which informs them of ground proximity increases safety during landing and rescue operations.

Windshear radar system

This is a subject which is not generally talked about among non-flying people. To flight crews it is a natural phenomenon nobody wants to meet. Windshear is caused by atmospheric conditions.

During thunderstorms cool air mixing with warm air causes an area of air turbulence. This turbulence has areas of severe downdrafts which are strong enough to make an aircraft lose altitude very fast. Rain-laden thunderclouds have windshear conditions within them. To seek them out and give a pre-warning alert to the aircraft flight crew a windshear radar system has been developed by aerospace avionic manufacturers. The radar scans ahead to locate areas of strong downdrafts which are hidden in the core of thunderclouds. When it locates the windshear it displays its whereabouts on a colour radar indicator in the cockpit. Where windshear occurs strong head-winds are usually present. The headwinds are outflows from the centre of the thunderstorm. The new windshear radar developed by Allied Signal has the ability to measure these winds. When the down-drafts are such that a danger to the aircraft could occur, aural and visual warnings are given to the flight crew. A warning at take-off and landing is most important as that is when the aircraft is at its most vulnerable to windshear. The aural warnings take the following form:

(a) Windshear Ahead, Windshear Ahead (plus a visual warning).
(b) During take-off this warning is given: Go Around, Windshear Ahead.

To gather the necessary information to develop an anti-windshear radar system, research teams from Allied Signal in the United States flew many missions into severe thunderstorms looking for severe downdrafts. They deserve to be commended for their efforts. The result is a system which makes flying safer for everybody. A windshear system on an aircraft consists of a radar receiver/transmitter, colour indicator and an antenna (flat-blade type). On a windshear colour radar indicator the following specific colours are used to display visual information to flight crews:

(a) Blue denotes range marks and numbers.
(b) Green indicates a rainfall 2 situation.
(c) Yellow indicates a rainfall 3 situation.
(d) Red indicates a heavy rainfall 4 situation.
(e) Magenta indicates turbulence ahead.
(f) Red and yellow patches overlying the standard radar indications mean windshear exists.

Traffic collision avoidance system (TCAS)

The crowded flight airspace in which pilots have to work calls for a special type of situation awareness safety system. To help pilots track nearby aircraft electronically, traffic alert and collision avoidance systems were developed. The concept of collision avoidance technology to aid aircraft was first researched by Dr J.S. Morrell of the American company, Bendix Aerospace. Dr Morrell carried out research into the physics of collisions and produced information in an algorithm (a method of problem solving and calculating) which defined the rate of closure between approaching aircraft. From that beginning modern TCAS systems were developed.

New safety systems being created by companies such as Honeywell and Allied Signal have extended the range and reaction time of the system. In the future the system will give very sophisticated surveillance of nearby aircraft up to forty nautical miles away, plus better position and bearing accuracy. It will also give visual and aural recommended evasive action commands in the horizontal plane. A pilot will receive clear audio and visual recommended evasive actions to take when an intruder aircraft is a threat. Warnings will be given to flight crews fifteen to thirty-five seconds before the predicted event occurs; in a high-speed jet aircraft that time can be used to avert a crash. Reliable and proved practical trials involving aircraft closing in on each other at speeds of 1,200 knots and vertical rates of 10,000 feet per minute have shown that the new and future traffic alert and collision avoidance systems are a great asset to safe flight. The combination of good, well motivated and trained flight crews plus safety avionic systems like GPWS, Windshear and TCAS will continue to make flying a safe means of travel now and in the future.

Digital In-Flight Entertainment System (IFE)

Passengers will often make a judgement on the quality of an airline based on their experience with the cabin entertainment system. Some passengers are very self-contained and can travel long distances without the need for external entertainment, whereas others are more reliant on the entertainment system to help them pass the time during long flights.

As such, the in-flight entertainment (IFE) system plays a critical role in the passenger's travel experience and is usually the top priority for the airline's marketing. It follows therefore that all

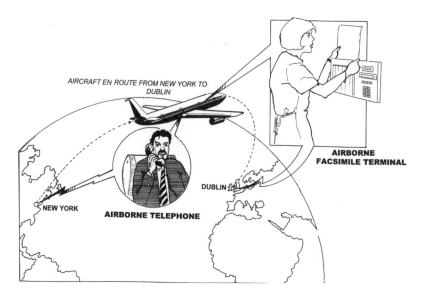

Figure 26–3   Airborne Communications

commercial pilots must know something about the passenger in-flight entertainment system.

Currently, the priority in IFE development is to develop a universal system that will integrate audio, visual, multi-media, data information and communications throughout the aircraft. In other words, to create a single system that has uses and applications simultaneously on the flight deck and in the passenger cabin. New technology makes this system both possible and practical to implement. The first IFE systems proved to be very unpredictable and unreliable, but thankfully today's systems are much more dependable. Fibre-optic conductors combined with smaller terminal boxes have reduced weight and increased stability within the system. In addition, fibre-optic conductors present in the system minimise any noise from electrical interference.

A modern IFE system is interactive and comes with audio and video on demand (AVOD) fully integrated. When using this system, passengers are provided with high-quality audio and video through an in-flight computer system. A typical modern system can handle over ninety different channels of high-fidelity audio. Some systems also feature forty-eight digital audio inputs and over seventy-two analogue audio inputs. More than seven passenger address (PA) inputs are available for aircraft staff use. In addition, typically around twenty video channels from different data inputs are on offer. To view the video programme each passenger has a seat display unit (SDU), typically situated on the back of the seat in front, although sometimes to the side depending on seating arrangements. Access to all audio channels is via a headset that is plugged into a remote jack unit (RJU), usually located on the seat armrest.

The new avionic system of cabin entertainment is very innovative, not only in permitting individual independent choice, but also allowing a passenger to pause or stop the selected programme if they need to temporarily leave their seat for whatever reason.

The system operates on a by-seat basis. The user interface to the system is via the seat handset, which gives access to all the services on offer including volume level, video play/pause and programme selection. The IFE's interactive software also controls each seat's reading and attendant call lights via the handset. When using the system's entertainment controls on the handset, each passenger attains basically the same control as if they were using standard home media equipment such as a CD/DVD or cassette player. The passenger can 'pause', 'fast forward' (preview), 'rewind' or 'stop' the programme selected. Specific audio tracks can be skipped or played again.

Typically, the handset provided for every seat is dual-functional. That means one side of the handset is dedicated to in-flight entertainment and the other side is used for telephone communications: if necessary a passenger could call another seat handset in the aircraft. This is a useful facility when family or friends are separated due to seating arrangements in the cabin. To call an external mobile or terrestrial telephone number the passenger must swipe a credit card as per the instructions given on the handset. The IFE system can relay the instructions through visual and/or aural commands.

Other features provided are video games, shopping services, business services, information services and programme data. The telephone service available includes air-to-ground calls. On many of the new commercial aircraft being built, passengers will benefit from internal connectivity, which will provide high-speed internet data and entertainment services through a broadband connection to the aircraft.

Aircraft Equipment

A typical entertainment system is operated and controlled from the cabin management terminal (CMT), normally located in a video control centre. This centre is normally positioned in the forward cabin area, although it can be located in other areas of the passenger cabin.

Components used by the computer in the CMT include a central processing unit (CPU) and cabin memory expansion unit (CMEU). The enhanced passenger entertainment system controller (EPESC) and the enhanced video system control unit (EVSCU) are sub-systems of the IFE computer system. The computer software can be updated when a reconfiguration of the system is required. Many of the sub-units in the system have their own dedicated software, such as the digital seat electronic box (DSEB), which is fitted on each passenger seat.

Fly-By-Wire (FBW) System

Introduction

Mechanical flight control systems are the most basic way of control-ling flight. The mechanical flight control model was used in all early aircraft but today is only used in small aeroplanes where the aero-dynamic forces are not excessive. This is because as aeroplanes developed and got bigger and faster, the increase in the size and weight of the control surfaces required to control them led to a corresponding large increase in the force needed to be exerted by the pilot to operate them. The first attempt to answer this problem was the hydraulic flight control system. Although hydraulic flight control systems were successful in making the forces required bear-able to the pilots, they proved to be a serious problem in themselves due to their bulk and weight. It was not long, however, before aircraft designers realised the advantages of replacing the complexity, fragility and weight of the hydro-mechanical flight control system with a lighter, more reliable 'fly by wire' (FBW) elec-tronic system.

Fly By Light

During the 1970s, a system was developed in military aircraft of sending electrical signals as pulses of light through fibre-optic conductors to move control surfaces. This system was called 'Fly-By-Light' (FBL). One of the first aircraft to use such a system was the General Dynamic F-16 fighter, which used fibre-optics in a digital flight control system. Some European fighter aircraft also

216

used that system, among them the French Dassault-Breguet Mirage 2000 and a one-off development of the Anglo-French Jaguar aircraft. The FBW Jaguar had a quadruplex digital fly-by-wire system; a quadruplex system allowed fully controlled flight under conditions of less rigid airframe stability.

A typical FBW system uses command inputs from the pilot's force-sensing control stick and rudder pedals; some FBW aircraft use a conventional, centrally mounted control column, but a smaller side-stick, as used on the F-16 for example, is increasingly common. The digital computer-controlled flight system then produces a combination of control-surface movement and deflections to give the required manoeuvre. On the F-16, for example, these manoeuvres are carried out in tune with an automatic aileron-rudder interconnect and yaw-rate limiter.

Fly-by-wire has three advantages. The first is that mechanical linkage is only needed between the control stick and the power control unit (PCU). Secondly, in the cockpit the control column can be removed and a small side-stick control can be fitted, creating extra space in the cockpit. Thirdly, aircraft weight is reduced and crew workload eased.

From the beginning of the 1980s this new technology began to be used in commercial aircraft. Aircraft such as the Boeing 757, 767, the Airbus A310 and the Airbus A300-600 used digital computers to control spoilers, slats and flaps. Further development of this idea took place due to the desire of the Airbus design and research team to create a flight control system (FCW) without the limitations of the mechanical method. The Airbus team also wanted their new system to maintain operational compatibility, no matter what were the handling characteristics of the aircraft type being flown. To meet that objective, the design team had to develop an enhanced flight control system with superior handling characteristics.

They achieved this using by linking the input from the pilot's control stick to a digital computer from which the aircraft received its steering commands. By processing and subtly correcting the pilot's input, the new system allowed the aircraft to fly more stable and in addition allowed better manoeuvrability.

Another objective was to create a fly-by-wire system that would standardise the piloting experience, thus making two different aircraft feel the same to control in all aspects of the flight envelope. In other words, a pilot would have a similar experience both inside and at the extreme boundary of the flight envelope when in different aircraft. Auto-stabilisation on all three axes was provided to give more natural stability to the aircraft. When using the system, if a pilot moves the side stick the computer interprets this and an electrical signal is sent to the primary control unit, which in turn moves the control surfaces. The flying controls respond in a way suitable to the movement of the pilot's control stick. For the operation to take place all other systems associated with that axis command need to agree with what the pilot has done. Some advanced systems will sense a wrong command and automatically correct it. However, these built-in safety features have not got unlimited powers and the pilot remains the final arbiter of what is best for the aircraft safety.

An added safety feature using the fly-by-wire system is that the horizontal stabiliser and rudder have mechanical redundancy built in to prevent loss of control in the event of failure. A major design objective was commonality between all types of aircraft. The pilot's side-stick control is used due to it being more efficient and safer than the older centre control column. An aircraft using the fly-by-wire system has been found to be more stable and better balanced on axis, regardless of which configuration it is in. Flying aircraft in these stable situations permits a pilot more time for flight path monitoring. He also has longer periods for system surveillance. The first subsonic commercial aircraft to have a fly-by-wire system was the Airbus A320. The Airbus designers combined innovative new composite materials with the digital computer flight system to create a more efficient aircraft. Examples of the composite materials are advanced metal alloys, carbon composite material and glass-fibre-reinforced aluminium (Glare). The aircraft first flew in February 1987 and entered regular service in 1988, with Air France.

In a typical fly-by-wire system the digital computers have programs to handle inputs from various sources on the aircraft. This ability allows high-speed control of the aircraft in specific accord with the pilot's intentions. The main computer monitors the whole operation and pilot control is permitted up to the level at which the airframe would become overstressed. To assist flight crew operation the system has a built in artificial 'feel' to the side-stick control when in use. Taking account of aircraft speed and flight conditions, there is a direct relationship between the 'feel' of the side-stick and a surface control turn or change instigated by the pilot. This 'feel' on the side-stick prevents a pilot from over-controlling and over-stressing the fuselage beyond its limits.

An aircraft using the system has the required flying control qualities pre-programmed in the avionics computers. An advantage of this approach is that after test flights and development work the computers can be re-programmed to improve the system. Using hydraulically actuated flight control surfaces that are electronically signalled, control sensitivity is obtained. If necessary both the trimmable horizontal stabilizer and rudder can be mechanically controlled in the FBW system. The computer programs used are very advanced and flexibility is incorporated. They can decide the correct control response in each and every combination of flying factors. All the advantages of advanced computer technology are interfaced with the basic flight instruments – altimeter, airspeed indicator, horizontal situation indicator and attitude indicator. When the system is connected to an inertial navigation system, accurate navigation over long distances is possible.

Passenger welfare is improved on aircraft using the fly-by-wire system as aircraft vibrations can be suppressed. At different locations on an aircraft vibration action takes place in the 2–3.5Hz frequency range, and can reduce passenger comfort. To counteract this problem a device called an accelerometer is positioned to sense vibrations in the frequency range specified. The accelerometer is a spring balance device that measures the vibration forces of the aircraft: it has a centre weight balanced by two springs in a signal feedback circuit. The weight is marked from the centre: left of centre is a negative signal; right of centre is a positive signal. When the weight is displaced from the centre an electric pick-up signal is created. The signal is proportional to the weight movement. The pick-up signal is amplified and returned to the weight to re-centre it. This feedback signal represents the amount of aircraft vibration. The outputs from the accelerometers are passed to the flight primary control computers (FCPC), which then dampen out the vibrations. This function is present even if only one FCPC is operating.

Fibre-optics Data Bus

A typical fly-by-wire system installed on a commercial aircraft has five computers. The electrical signals, which represent data, are pulse modulated in a coder's circuit and then transmitted in a fibre-optics bus into a receiver – normally a photo diode, which converts the incoming infrared signals back into electrical signals. A decoder module then converts the electrical signals into information data. Infrared radiation operating in the area beyond the red visible spectrum is used for transmission of light pulses. Light at the red end of the visible spectrum is used due to it been less attenuated by absorption in transmission through the glass core of the conductor. The conductor used as the data bus has a glass cladding cover that prevents the light signal from going outside the inside glass core boundary.

Avionic data flight control units are used to display pilot side-stick control commands on the ground. The aircraft data is also displayed on the primary flight display (PFD). Another function of the avionic units is to feed the aircraft FBW status into the electronic centralised aircraft monitor (ECAM). Data included in that report is the availability of the five digital computers, servo-systems, and services into the fly-by-wire circuits, failure warnings and system caution warnings. In a typical system, for maintenance purposes the computers interface with the central maintenance system. On the A320 this system is called the central fault display system (CFDS).

The electronic centralised aircraft monitor (ECAM) gives the flight crew the situation of the overall status of the FBW system and its boundary. If and when a failure occurs that has an effect on the FBW system, the flight crew is warned immediately by the ECAM: an alert is given by way of a master warning or caution. Also, information is provided by the ECAM of any problem computers or defective control surfaces. Other information displayed is the operational consequences, including special procedures, precautions and aircraft limitations.

Flying an aircraft with a fly-by-wire system installed has been made easier by the large advances that have been made in cockpit instrument display layout. In the past many instruments, gauges and dials crowded together made it harder for the flight crew to monitor the information on view. Often a selection of switches was combined with the dials and gauges; all of these components increased the complexity of the cockpit display panels. Using large-format displays aircraft designers have been able to remove almost all stand-alone analogue gauges. Many of the multifunction displays in the cockpit are flat-panel liquid crystal displays.

The new cockpit display is reconfigurable to show data on primary flight navigation, engine indication and crew alert system (EICAS), interface control, and maintenance information. Many modern primary flight display panels have different altimeter options – a popular option is aircraft altitude displayed by tape altimeter. Standard round dial display is also offered. The primary flight display takes the place of the well-used electronic attitude direction indicator (EADI).

Computers

The fly-by-wire commercial aircraft is a product of the computer age. To assist those readers who would like a basic review or understanding of a typical computer a brief explanation follows. Those who do not need the review are at liberty to skip it.

The modern-day digital computer is a great tool for aircraft design teams. Present day computers are small, light, reliable and powerful. They only need low electrical power when operating and are relatively cheap. These new computer devices are also very flexible and can be programmed to carry out many different functions. Designers of avionics systems can programme in instructions and commands for all stages of operational aircraft work.

The digital computer manages data, which has been transformed into numbers. For example, the digits zero and one represent high and low voltages. These voltages can then be used to control or command other devices or circuits. A typical digital computer is made up of the following modules:

Central Processing Unit (CPU) This is the thinking or brain section of the computer; the CPU is designed to handle, clarify and obey instructions. The instructions are normally given to it in sets, one of which could be from a specific number to another number. Inside the CPU a sub-module called the arithmetic and logic unit (ALU) is used for performing the calculations and logical operations required. Another section in the CPU contains registers that are used to briefly store data. A major register used is the accumulator, which contains current data being processed at any time.

Also in the CPU is the control unit, which consists of the clock, programme counter, instruction register, instruction decoder and flag circuits. The function of the clock is to generate timing pulses at a certain frequency to synchronise and keep control of operations. For example, one pulse could be used to execute one operation instruction.

A programme counter will count any pulses that are being used. Another duty of the programme counter is to supply a binary digital output in data bits. Within the digital output is provided the address of the next instruction from the program. From the programme counter the next link in the chain is the instruction register, which is used to pass data to the instruction decoder. The instruction decoders decode the data received and will then instruct the arithmetic and logic unit (ALU) to carry out certain functions. The flag

221

function is normally an electronic flip-flop circuit that conducts to show a specific action has been completed.

Memory Digital computers have memory storage ability. Two types of memory exist. First is the permanent data memory, which is known as the read only memory (ROM). This does not change when power is removed from the computer. The information stored permanently contains the fixed CPU instructions, conversion items, measuring constants and calculation tables.

The second memory is a random access memory (RAM). This is used to read data at any address and also to have fresh or new data inserted into any address. Another difference between a RAM and a ROM memory is the storage of information data. When the computer power is switched off the RAM loses the information or data stored within it. The ROM memory does not lose data when computer power is removed. Both types of memory are used for different functions by the computer operator. The storage capacities of the RAM and ROM memories depend on the electronic microchips used by the computer designer.

Peripherals To be complete a computer system needs what are known as peripherals. These include the keyboard, which is used to communicate within and without the system, and the monitor. Also in this group are interface devices and connectors. Input devices and output devices are needed; one such is a light pen, which allows a computer user to draw on the visual display monitor. The familiar 'mouse' is also used during keyboard operations.

Data buses Data buses carry information. Data buses can be fibre-optics or parallel wire conductors. In a typical computer, data buses connect the CPU to other sections with the aid of three sets of parallel wires. (The word 'bus' is simply derived from the common city bus transport system.)

Microprocessor Computers are programmed with instructions on how the CPU must carry out each task given it. The device which makes that possible is known as the microprocessor. This small device is a very flexible part of the computer. The advantage of the microprocessor is that it can be program-controlled. For example, by changing the instruction set it can be used to control lighting, industrial robots and aircraft surface controls. A microprocessor is not a computer – when used in that configuration it would need memory chips and input-output units. The microprocessor can be designed for a specific operation and when several are combined they can, within a microcomputer, be very powerful.

Airbus A380 Flight Control Overview

This aircraft, a super-size passenger commercial model, is already setting new aeronautical design standards. An aircraft with a wingspan of 262ft (80m) and a length nearly the same makes this model different in many ways from those that have come before. The double deck fuselage is similar in size to an Airbus A340 cabin sitting on top of the Boeing 747. Surface controls cover large areas. The vertical stabiliser area is equivalent to the area on an A320 wing. The area on the A380 horizontal stabiliser compares to two A310 wings.

When designing the aircraft the design team rejected a hydraulic-only system of moving and controlling the control surfaces, using instead a combination of hydraulic and electrical power. If the hydraulic-only system was used the disadvantage of heavy feed lines coupled with routing problems would have made it more costly to operate. When electrically powered actuators are used the system is lighter and less bulky, and fluid carrying weight is reduced. Installing the system is easier. Actuators with a large electronic input move the A380 flight control surfaces. The principal features of the aircraft's control surfaces and associated systems are as follows:

(a) The four engines deliver 150kVa each. The auxiliary power unit (APU) is able to supply approximately 120kVa when necessary.

(b) Fuel flow monitoring and operating characteristics are another area which use an avionics input.

(c) The A380 flight control system consists of two elevators each side of the horizontal stabilizer. Each individual elevator has two actuators: one is hydraulic, the other is electro-hydraulic.

(d) Two rudder surfaces are used. Each has two electrical backup hydraulic actuators (EBHAs). When in the normal mode of operation they are powered by hydraulics. In back-up mode electrical power is used to drive rudder surfaces.

223

(e) Located on the tail is a trimmable horizontal stabilizer (THS). A ball-screw actuator powered by the hydraulic motors operates it, and a stand-by-electrical motor is part of that system.

(f) Elevator surfaces have a dual-redundant source of power.

(g) Each wing has three ailerons plus eight spoilers. All spoilers are powered by hydraulics. Some of the spoiler actuators have a back-up electrical power if needed.

(h) Wing flaps and slats use mechanical rotary actuators. Powered control units (PCUs) in the system include hydraulic motors for the flaps and a mix of hydraulic and electrical power for the slats.

It is interesting to note that the joint strike fighter (JSF) being developed in the USA is also pushing the frontier of fly-by-wire further out. What was once beyond the pale is now the very respectable 'power-by-wire' (PBW) concept. As in the commercial field, cost and weight are major factors driving the new technology. A combination of a new technology called electro-hydrostatic and avionics with a computer core interface operation is being used in the PBW system.

The new system being developed by the American Lockheed Martin company utilizes a direct current (DC) electrical power system to provide power to five dual power electronic (PEU) actuator motor and pump operation units. The power monitoring and voltage regulation is provided by the PEU. When the actuator PEU receives a command, a signal is given to the actuator to move it to a selected position. Lockheed Martin intend to use this new integrated electrical system to provide the electrics needed for avionics and other systems on the JSF. PBW uses a 270-volt DC electrical power generation system.

GLOSSARY OF TERMS

AC   Alternating Current – electric current that flows periodically in a positive and a negative direction. Civil transport aircraft alternating current is normally 115 volts, 3 phase at a frequency of 400 hertz.

ADF   Automatic Direction Finding – an aid to navigation. Automatic direction finding permits a pilot to determine the headings or direction of the radio stations being received. Operates on a frequency range of 90 to 1,750 kilohertz. This system can receive radio range stations in the low frequency band and commercial broadcast radio stations.

ADI   Attitude Director Indicator – an instrument that presents the pilot with a visual display of aircraft attitude in flight. Displays pitch and roll commands through command bars. Also shows glideslope and localiser signal information. A slip indicator displays slip and skid indications.

ADS   Automatic Dependent Surveillance – a datalinked aeronautical communication service which will use satellite communication to accurately monitor and control aircraft flying outside the range of air traffic control radar. The system is being developed in Europe.

AFCS   Automatic Flight Control System – a sophisticated electronic method using computers plus hydraulic power to control an aircraft.

AIR TRAFFIC CONTROL   Air traffic control is essential for aircraft to operate safely and with maximum efficiency in the sky and at airports. A pilot can fly under visual flying rules (VFR) or instrument flying rules (IFR). A pilot has to be qualified and the holder of an instrument rated licence to fly under IFR rules. Orderly safe flying takes place due to the work of dedicated air traffic controllers worldwide. Controllers are normally responsible for an area of airspace known as a sector. Aircraft move along in this sector on flight paths. They are then separated vertically and horizontally. Flying routes between airports are called airways. When moving along airways, aircraft keep certain altitudes apart. Normal separation is 1,000 feet (300m), and at very high altitudes 2,000 feet (600m) separates them. At airports airspace is called a control zone. At 45,000 feet and above, a 4,000-foot separation is used. All airways and the control zone are called controlled airspace. During busy periods at airports a system known as stacks is used to hold aircraft waiting to land in a safe queue. Orderly control is essential, as unlike other traffic aircraft in the sky cannot stop and can stay flying for only a limited period. Air traffic controllers do not have an easy job.

AIRWAYS   Airways are fixed routes in the sky used by aircraft in controlled airspace when flying under instrument flight rules (IFR).

AIRWORTHINESS DIRECTIVE   Known as an AD, this aviation notice is sent out by government air safety agencies to alert airlines of a serious defect on aircraft under their control. It also informs them that the defect should be corrected in line with the manufacturer's service bulletin on the matter.

AIS   Audio Integration System – this system is employed to integrate the aircraft radio and navigation systems.

ALTIMETER – PNEUMATIC   An instrument used to indicate pressure altitude in feet. Typical range of operation is minus 1,000 feet to plus 50,000 feet.

ALTITUDE   The height of the aircraft with reference to ground or sea level.

AMLCD   Active Matrix Liquid Crystal Display – a new technology which uses a combination of flat-panel filters, thin-film transistors and liquid crystal. AMLCD is part of the new multifunctional cockpit display systems. Advantages are good readability, improved reliability, less weight and less maintenance.

AMPERE   The unit of electrical current. Named after the French physicist André Ampère, 1775–1836. The ammeter is also named after him.

AMPLIFIER   A device for increasing the voltage, current or power in an electronic circuit.

AMPLITUDE MODULATION   The process of modulating a radio frequency carrier wave by varying its amplitude with an audio signal.

AND GATE   A logic circuit which needs all its inputs to be a logic 1 to produce a logic 1 in the output.

ANTENNA   A device used to transmit and receive electromagnetic radiation radio signal waves.

ANTENNA COUPLER   This unit is used in high frequency radio systems to provide impedance matching between antenna and transmitter. It makes sure that most of the transmitted power from the transmitter is used by the antenna.

APD   Approach Progress Display – a unit used in the cockpit to provide the flight crew with visual illuminated displays on selected flight mode conditions when using the autopilot and flight director systems.

APU   Auxiliary Power Unit – a power unit used to supply electrical power to an aircraft independent of its engine generators and ground electrical power. On a typical transport aircraft, it is located in the tail section.

AREA MICROPHONE   (Area Mic) Name given to the microphone located in the aircraft cockpit. Used in the voice recorder systems to record the last half-hour of general communications from the cockpit.

ARINC   Aeronautical Radio Incorporated – this is an organisation established by airlines to standardise radio equipment and systems for transport-type commercial aircraft.

ATTITUDE   Aircraft physical position in pitch and roll modes of operation when in flight with respect to the earth's surface.

AUDIO ACCESSORY UNIT   A unit on an aircraft providing a communication link between flight crew, cabin crew, ground service crew and the aircraft radio and communication systems.

AUDIO FILTER   A filter designed to select a particular frequency in the audio range of frequencies. Example: in the marker beacon receiver system, the receiver utilises three types of audio filters, a 400 hertz, 1,300 hertz and a 3,000 hertz filter.

AUDIO SELECTOR PANEL   A panel which provides the means for the flight crew to select communication and navigation systems. The system required can be selected by toggle or press to operate switches.

AUDIO SIGNAL   A signal in the audio range of frequencies. Effective audio range is 30 hz to 16,000 hz.

AVIONICS   A contraction of aviation and electronics.

BATTERY   A device manufactured to convert chemical energy to electrical energy. The battery on an aircraft is used for many tasks, including:

(a)   the supply of power for short periods when ground power to the aircraft is not available

(b)   during an emergency situation the battery might be the only source of power to operate essential radio equipment and flight instruments.

A battery can be a lead-acid type or nickel-cadmium. Each of these batteries has advantages and disadvantages. Most aircraft have a separate unit to keep the battery system charged up. The battery or batteries on an aircraft are an important part of the electrical system and are treated as such. Maintenance and inspection of batteries is done on a frequent basis. Most modern aircraft use the nickel-cadmium battery. The 20-cell 40-amp hr nickel-cadmium is used on many modern aircraft.

BEARING   The direction of the aircraft relative to a fixed point, measured in degrees.

BFO   Beat Frequency Oscillator.

BITE   The short version of an avionic method of saying Built-In Test Equipment. Built-In Test Equipment is being used in the new generation of modern aircraft to test electronic equipment and detect failures in avionic systems at the time of occurrence.

BLACK BOX   Name given to electronic equipment units housed in orange metal cases that are located on the aircraft. Also used by the 'media' to describe the aircraft's voice recorder unit and flight data recorder units, both of which are used by civil aviation authorities when investigating flight incidents.

BLADE ANTENNA   A quarter-wave antenna, the shape of which allows transmission and reception of a wide band of radio frequencies.

BONDING   On the aircraft a method of interconnecting metal parts of the main structure with electrical conductors to abolish potential voltage differences.

BOOM MICROPHONE   A microphone which is mounted on an extended arm of headphones or a headset.

BUSBAR   A low-resistance, insulated, electrical power conductor device made of copper or metal strip. Normally located in junction and distribution boxes at different locations on an aircraft. Busbars can be tied together or separated depending on what aircraft system wires are being connected onto them.

CAA   Civil Aviation Authority.

CADC   Central Air Data Computer – a unit used as a single source for airspeed, Mach, temperature and altitude signals. The CADC uses static pressure to calculate the altitude signals. Airspeed outputs are calculated by using pitot and static pressure. Mach signals are calculated by using altitude and airspeed.

CAPACITANCE   The storage of a charge in a container which has a positive charge on one side and a negative charge on the other. Charge measured in coulombs, unit farad. Capacitance is used in aircraft radio receivers and other units for coupling signals from one part of a circuit to another. They are also used as filters.

CDI   Course Deviation Indicator – an instrument used to display navigation steering signals which if acted on cause the aircraft to pursue a definite flight path.

CHIME AMPLIFIER   A unit used on an aircraft to alert cabin crew. It consists of a module containing solid state logic circuits operated by pulses when a passenger or a passenger sign operates the circuit. For example, a 'No Smoking' sign causes the chime to be heard in the aircraft cabin.

CIRCUIT BREAKER   An electronic and electrical aircraft system protection device. It is used to isolate problem circuits and equipment. When excessive current flows due to a component failure the circuit breaker 'pops' or trips. The trip is operated by the heating of a bi-metallic element located in the circuit breaker. An excessive flow of current causes the temperature to rise; on reaching a certain temperature level the circuit breaker trips open, thus protecting equipment and wiring. Circuit breakers can be reset after the defect that caused the problem is rectified. Circuit breakers are manufactured to different current capacity and are only used for tasks within that current-carrying capacity.

COAXIAL   A cable used as a transmission or receiving radio signal line. The coaxial cable used on an aircraft is different from normal coaxial used for domestic television. Coaxial cable utilised in avionic systems is shielded by an inner metal braid to prevent the cable picking up interference from other electrical wire or equipment.

CONE OF CONFUSION   A term used to describe the area near a very high frequency omnidirectional radio range (VOR) ground station. As the aircraft moves closer to the VOR transmitter station, the VOR aircraft indicator needle becomes very sensitive. Due to this sensitivity the indicator needle oscillates from side to side. Another effect in the VOR indicator is that the TO-FROM pointer acts in an unstable manner. The TO-FROM pointer is used in the instrument to indicate the aircraft's situation with regard to its approach FROM or away TO or towards the VOR ground navigation station. The time an aircraft remains in the cone depends on its speed and altitude. Once the aircraft moves away from the confusion zone, all erratic indications cease.

CRT Cathode Ray Tube – a tube used to display visually signals from aircraft navigation and weather radar systems. Cathode ray tubes are divided into three types:

(a) Electrostatic, which uses electrostatic focusing and deflection components.

(b) Electromagnetic, which uses electromagnetic focusing and deflection.

(c) The combined CRT, which has electrostatic focusing and electromagnetic deflection.

CRYSTAL A component used in audio sound reproduction, also used to maintain a fixed frequency in an oscillator circuit. Crystal is found in a substance called Rochelle salt.

CSU Central Switching Unit – a unit used on large passenger aircraft in the cabin interphone system to provide multichannel interphone operation. It acts as a miniature telephone switchboard.

DAA Digital Analogue Adaptor – a unit used to convert digital signal inputs to analogue.

DB (DECIBEL) A unit of relative power. Deci is one tenth of a bel.

DC Direct Current.

DDM Difference in Depth of Modulation – used to compare the modulation depths of 90 hz and 150 hz tones. The aircraft system in which DDM is used is the instrument landing system (ILS).

DECCA Decca, like the Loran navigation system, is an area coverage aid. Area navigation is not a direct line aid and allows pilots to fly aircraft off airways. A Decca ground navigation system consists of a master station and three slave transmitting stations. The Decca system is used by ships and aircraft worldwide. A Decca navigation system is normally set up in transmitting chains which use a fundamental frequency of 14 to 14.33 kHz.

DETECTOR A circuit that demodulates or recovers an audio signal from a radio frequency carrier wave. Also used to detect pulse modulated waveforms.

DIODE A device that allows current to flow through it in one direction only. The material a diode is manufactured from is silicone, germanium and crystal.

DH Decision Height – the height when the runway should be in view.

DME Distance Measuring Equipment – electronic equipment which makes it possible for a pilot to determine the distance of his aircraft from a particular DME station. The equipment is a navigation aid. It uses secondary radar principles of operation. Distance measuring equipment is operated in the frequency range of 960 to 1,215 Megahertz.

DOPPLER An aircraft system that provides the flight crew with ground speed and drift angle. It is used with the aircraft compass system to furnish navigation information.

DUAL CONTROL BOX   An electronic box designed to allow two avionic systems to be operated from the same box. Example: in a typical ATC transponder system on a large aircraft the two ATC systems would be operated from a dual control box.

DUMMY LOAD   A device used in a weather radar system. During a test of a radar system the transmitted radio pulses are sent to the dummy load instead of being directed towards an external target. This means of testing the system prevents any harm or damage being caused to personnel and aircraft during the transmission period.

DUPLEXER   A device used in aircraft electronic units to permit sharing of the same antenna and electronic circuits in the one module.

EADI   Electronic Attitude Director Indicator – an instrument which displays flight information in analogue and digital form on a cathode ray tube (CRT). Indicates aircraft pitch and roll attitude with flight command bars. Also displays radio altitude and glideslope–localiser radio beam information.

EFIS   Electronic Flight Instrument System – a system that uses electronic display indicators to provide aircraft navigation information. The information is shown in colour. A unit called a symbol generator delivers a video signal to the cathode ray tubes (CRTs) located on the electronic instrument panel on the aircraft flight deck.

EHSI   Electronic Horizontal Situation Indicator – an instrument which displays visual lateral and vertical navigation guidance data. It also displays weather radar information, compass and very high frequency omnidirectional range (VOR) data.

EHT   Extra-High Tension – high voltage used to supply a cathode ray tube or high powered radio amplifier tubes used in radio transmitters. Extra-high voltages are used in the power amplifier output stages of aircraft high frequency transmitters. Radar transmitter receivers use very high voltages in the magnetron circuit.

EICAS   Engine Indication and Crew Alerting Systems. A system which uses a computer and indicating devices to alert crew on the operational status of the aircraft engines.

ELECTROLYSIS   This process takes place when two dissimilar metals are brought together and a flow of electrical current is applied through the metal. The result of this can cause the metal to weaken and become damaged. On aircraft it is a situation to be avoided.

ELT   Emergency Locator Transmitter – this transmitter is sometimes called a locator beacon. In the event of a forced landing in remote areas the emergency locator transmitter transmits an international distress signal on the frequency 121.5 megahertz. This frequency is monitored by the civil aviation authorities.

EM WAVES   Radio and Light Electromagnetic Waves.

FAN MARKER   A navigation aid used by an aircraft marker receiver system when approaching a runway.

FANS   Future Air Navigation System – a system in which aircraft movement and airspace separation distances will be carried out over large areas of land and sea with satellites. New avionics technology in the fields of communications, navigation and radar systems is being developed to make it possible. At present the global positioning system (GPS) is already using Navstar satellites located in space to help aircraft navigate over vast distances to an accuracy of 100 metres (300 feet).

FCC   Flight Control Computer – a control computer used in the autopilot, flight director, Mach trim, speed trim and altitude alert systems.

FDI   Flight Director Indicator – which may also be named an ADI. The FDI instrument displays to the pilot many important items of information pertaining to the operation and flight of the aircraft. Examples: pitch and roll attitude, speed command, glideslope and localiser instrument landing system information, decision height, rate of turn, slip and skid. This instrument displays a red warning flag to alert flight crews to any defects in the system.

FET   A field effect transistor which has a high input resistance.

FILTER   A circuit used to stop unneeded frequencies and select a wanted frequency. Example: the high frequency radio transmitter receiver system uses upper side band (USB) and lower side band (LSB) filters to prevent the frequency band not selected from disrupting the required radio frequency.

FLAG   A signal used in avionic systems to denote a failure. Example: when a flag appears in an instrument and permanently stays in view the system involved has a fault which needs investigation. Warning flags are normally coloured red.

FLIGHT INTERPHONE   This system permits the pilot and co-pilot to communicate with each other or if needed with the ground service crews.

FLIGHT LEVEL   Flight level (FL) is an altitude term related to a standard altimeter setting of 1013.2 millibars (a new name has been assigned to millibars; they are now known as hectopascals), no matter what the actual barometric pressure is. All aircraft above a certain transition level synchronise their altimeters to this setting. This keeps all aircraft operating on the same reference. Flight levels are normally quoted in hundreds of feet. FL 20 is 2,000 feet and FL 260 is 26,000 feet.

FLIGHT RECORDER   A unit used in the flight recorder system to record specific navigation, communication, flight command and aircraft flying control data. This unit is one of the celebrated 'black boxes' of media fame.

FM   Frequency Modulation – a method of impressing audio or data signals on a radio frequency signal by varying the frequency of the carrier signal at an audio rate.

FMC   Flight Management Computer – this unit is used in navigation and performance systems. It also operates as an input–output signal processor. Built-in test equipment (BITE) circuits store system fault and defect information.

FMS   Flight Management System – this avionic system consists of five major sub-systems:

(a)   Electronic flight instrument system (EFIS).

(b)   Flight management computer system (FMCS).

(c)   Digital flight control system (DFCS).

(d)   Autothrottle system (A/T).

(e)   Inertial reference system (IRS).

FREQUENCY   Frequency is the rate of oscillation of a signal. Example: electric power supplied to homes in Britain and Ireland is supplied at a frequency of 50 Hz; in the United States and Canada the frequency is set at 60 Hz. One hertz or one cycle of alternating current (AC) goes from positive to negative in less than a second. The rate of change is the frequency in cycles per second. 1,000 cycles per second is expressed as one kilohertz (1 kHz).

FUSELAGE   Main body of the aircraft.

GA   Go-Around – a mode of operation that is carried out when a landing approach is cancelled.

GIGAHERTZ (GHz)   A unit of frequency equal to 1,000,000,000 Hz, which appears in the 'Super-High' or 'Extremely High' frequency range. The frequencies used in the weather radar, low-range radio altimeter and Doppler systems are in the gigahertz band.

GLIDEPATH   Vertical radio beam approach path to a runway.

GLIDESLOPE   A part of the instrument landing system (ILS) – frequency range 329.3 MHz to 335 MHz.

GPS   Global Positioning System – a satellite-based radio-positioning navigation and time system. This system uses the twenty-four Navstar satellites launched into space by the United States. It is a very accurate system and can provide position, speed and time with twenty-four-hour worldwide all-weather capability over land or sea. Global positioning systems give a lot of information to pilots. In the near future air traffic control will use them to manage aircraft traffic at altitudes, distances and speeds never done before. Miniature hand-held GPS computers which provide worldwide coverage and very accurate position, plus navigation information, are being used by pilots who fly small aircraft. Accuracy to 100 metres (300 feet) is available to pilots using GPS. It could be much more accurate but due to a selective availability system operated at present, civilian operators are restricted to certain limits. Only twenty-one of the twenty-four Navstar satellites are used; the other three are back-up spares (on location).

GPWS   Ground Proximity Warning System – a safety avionic system used to alert the flight crew to the existence of dangerous conditions due to ground proximity.

GYROSCOPE   A device consisting of a spinning metal mass known as the rotor supported by metal frames called gimbals. Directional rate and vertical gyroscopes are the types used on aircraft. Gyroscopes are involved in navigation and also in the attitude systems on the aircraft. The vertical gyroscope is used for aircraft pitch and roll attitude during a flight. Directional gyroscopes are used in the compass navigation system. A rate gyroscope measures the rate an aircraft turns on its axis; it is used in the yaw damper and autopilot systems.

HERTZ   The unit of frequency named after German physicist Heinrich Hertz. One hertz equals one cycle per second. Symbol Hz.

HF   High Frequency – a radio system frequency band used for long-distance communications. Operates in the frequency band 2 megahertz to 30 megahertz.

HSI   Horizontal Situation Indicator – an instrument which displays compass and very high frequency navigation information. It indicates in a visual display course deviation signals from the very high frequency omnidirectional range system (VOR) station. Instrument landing system (ILS) and distance measuring equipment (DME) information is also shown on the horizontal situation indicator.

HUD   Head-Up Display – this is a method of using the cockpit screen to display cockpit instrument readings such as airspeed, instrument landing system (ILS) and altitude.

HUNTING NEEDLE   An instrument needle which will not remain steady on a correct bearing. For example, if a radio magnetic indicator (RMI) is receiving a weak automatic direction finding (ADF) station, the ADF needle will wander or drift from a correct bearing. Should this hunting needle effect happen when a strong ADF signal is being received, then the aircraft ADF receiving system is defective.

IC   Integrated Circuit – a circuit produced on a silicon wafer. It can have many components, such as diodes, transistors, field effect transistors and resistors, deposited or built into the silicon wafer. A silicon wafer can contain many complete integrated circuits.

ICAO   International Civil Aviation Organisation.

IDENT   The transmitting by a transponder of an extra pulse along with its identification code when requested by an air traffic controller.

IF   Intermediate Frequency – the result of an incoming radio carrier frequency from a transmitter mixing with a receiver local oscillator band of frequencies.

ILS   Instrument Landing System – a system providing the standard ICAO approach aid to the airport runway. The system uses glideslope and localiser radio wave beams to guide an aircraft during a landing approach. The glideslope radio beam gives vertical and the localiser beam gives lateral (horizontal) guidance.

IMPEDANCE   The total opposition in a circuit, comprising of reactance and resistive elements. Z is the symbol. It is measured in ohms.

INS   Inertial Navigation System – a navigation system using sensitive gyros and accelerometers to develop signals from which navigation information is calculated. This is a non-radio navigation system.

ICS   Instrument Comparator Annunciator – a navigational warning module located in the cockpit. It is used to alert the flight crew to a defect in the navigation systems. The flight crew are alerted to a defective system via warning lights appearing on the instrument warning comparator unit. This unit warns of failures in the instrument landing system (ILS), compass heading system, aircraft pitch and roll systems.

IFR   Instrument Flight Rules. Aircraft flying at a certain height and during weather which restricts vision must fly under IFR rules. The aircraft must also have on board certain avionic equipment and a pilot certified to fly instrument flight rules. When a pilot is flying IFR rules he has to file a flight plan. Air traffic control (ATC) then gives him instructions where and how to fly in controlled airspace. In controlled airspace fixed air routes, called airways, are used. Airways are marked on special aviation charts and are numbered for identification.

INTERROGATOR   A unit used in air traffic control systems as part of the secondary radar system. Also used in distance measuring equipment (DME) on the aircraft.

IRU   Inertial Reference Unit – this unit uses computer circuits and laser gyroscope devices to provide position, attitude and heading information. Acceleration information is also provided.

JITTER   A method of random transmission of pulse pairs transmitted intermittently to the ground station. The ground station retransmits the pulses and the aircraft DME system determines its own unique pulse pair and rejects unwanted signals.

KEY   A word used in radio communications when tuning in a radio very high frequency (VHF) or high frequency (HF) transmitter. Keying a transmitter is the act when the pilot presses the microphone switch to send a message.

KILOHERTZ   Unit of radio frequency measurement. One kilohertz (1 kHz) = 1000 hertz.

KNOT   A unit of speed used in aviation and naval navigation. One knot equals one nautical mile per hour.

L BAND   A radio frequency band from 390 to 1,550 megahertz.

LCD   Liquid Crystal Display – a method which uses the light polarising characteristics of liquid crystal molecules. Liquid crystal displays depend on external sources of light; in most operations normal ambient light is adequate. In dark areas external lighting is needed. The lighting can be applied from the front or rear of the display.

LED   Light Emitting Diode – a diode which gives out light when forward biased in an electronic circuit.

Lightning Arrestor   A device located between the high frequency antenna and tuner. It is used to isolate the radio system from the antenna during lightning strikes. It is enclosed in a glass container, for protection and to facilitate inspection.

LO   Local Oscillator. An electronic circuit used in radio receivers to produce a frequency which is then mixed with an incoming radio frequency. The result of the mixing is an intermediate frequency (IF).

LOCALISER   The horizontal part of the instrument landing system (ILS) which is used for landing guidance. Frequency range 108.1 to 111.95 mHz.

LOGIC CIRCUIT   Electronic circuits used to process binary signals. The format used is based on Boolean algebra. Logic circuits are used in digital systems. The three main logic elements are: And gate, Or gate and Inverter.

LOOP ANTENNA   An antenna used in the aircraft ADF system. In the system the loop antenna is connected via a synchro system to the ADF receiver. When the loop is rotated the pointer of the radio magnetic indicator also rotates.

LORAN   Long-Range Navigation. Loran, like the Decca navigation system, is an area coverage aid. Loran C is the system used on aircraft. It operates on a frequency of 100 kHz. The ground Loran system comprises a master transmitter and three slave transmitters.

LRRA   Low-Range Radio Altimeter – this system is used to measure the vertical distance from the aircraft to ground. Operating frequency 4,200–4,400 megahertz. Radio altimeter measures from minus 20 feet to plus 2,500 feet. This system is utilised during aircraft landing approach procedure.

LSB   Lower Side Band – a sideband of a radio transmission which is of a lower frequency than the carrier frequency. Example: used in high frequency radio communication on the aircraft if needed. In high frequency radio upper side band (USB) is the preferred operating band.

MACH   Mach number is the ratio of true airspeed to the local speed of sound. Mach number is also proportional to dynamic pressure and ambient static pressure. At high altitudes starting at about 24,000 feet the air becomes thinner and expressing speed in units of knots becomes a problem. To overcome this, speed is referenced to the local speed of sound. This is known as the Mach number. The Concorde, a supersonic aircraft, cruises at Mach 2 which is twice the speed of sound. Non-supersonic aircraft cruise at about Mach 0.8. Mach is named after Ernst Mach, the Austrian physicist (1838–1916).

MADGE   Microwave Automatic Digital Guidance Equipment – developed for military use. Sometimes used by offshore oil rig platforms as a navigation aid.

MAGNETRON   A valve where electrons, when placed in the field of a powerful magnet, take a circular path. This gives it the ability to oscillate at microwave frequencies, allowing it to generate high power output for short periods. The magnetron was discovered on 21 February 1940, and was a very important part of the development of radar.

MARKER BEACON   Marker beacons are located on the ground and are used when a pilot is on the final approach to a runway. Three markers are used: an outer, inner and airways. They are all transmitted at 75 megahertz and modulated with 400, 1,300 and 3,000 hertz audio signals respectively. The pilot receives visual and audio alert signals in the cockpit when passing over the beacons.

MEGAHERTZ   Unit of radio frequency measurement. One megahertz (1 MHz) = 1,000,000 Hz.

MEGGER   A test instrument that gives fast and accurate measurement of insulation resistance and continuity resistance. A typical megger would operate in ranges from 100 volts, 250 volts, 500 volts and 1,000 volts. It can be a manual or automatic type. A DC generator produces the voltage.

MICROPHONE   A transducer used to convert audio waves into electrical signals. Normally aircraft microphones are of two types: the boom microphone, which is part of a headset, and a hand-held press-to-talk with a built-in amplifier. They can be called mic/mike.

MICROPROCESSOR   A computer central processor device manufactured using large methods of integration so that all computer central processor operations are fitted into a single integrated circuit.

MIXER   A circuit that combines the output of the local oscillator with that of the received radio signal to produce an intermediate frequency.

MLS   Microwave Landing System – this system operates at higher radio frequencies than the instrument landing system (ILS). It is mostly used by the military. By operating at higher frequencies interference is reduced. It also allows aircraft to make landings from a curved flight path. Instrument landing systems only permit a direct line approach when landing.

MO   Master Oscillator – a circuit used to provide the master frequency in a radio transmitter.

MODE A   A pulse format for an identification code interrogation.

MODE C   A pulse format for an altitude information interrogation.

MODE S   Mode Select. Mode S type transponders are being used in conjunction with traffic and collision avoidance systems to prevent mid-air collisions.

MODULATOR   A circuit used in many transmitter receivers to generate pulses. The pulses are normally of a certain width and shape.

MORSE CODE   A method of sending signals by combinations of dots and dashes giving letters of the alphabet. See page 247.

MOSFET   Metal Oxide Semiconductor Field Effect Transistor.

MOUNTAIN EFFECT   An ADF system error which is caused by the signal from the transmitted (ADF) ground station reflecting off the sides of mountains. This results in many signals coming from different directions depending on which side of the mountain the 'real' signal is reflected from.

MULTIMETER   A meter able to measure voltage, current and resistance.

MULTI-PATH PROPAGATION   This is a situation where a signal transmitted from a ground station is reflected off a building, mountain, or thick clouds and is received in front of another radio signal from the same or another transmitter. The effect of this is image frequencies, interference and ghosts. An example on a television receiver is the presence of an image beside the one you are viewing.

MULTIPLEXING   A method of sending many signals over a single wire. Example: on a typical large aircraft the passenger entertainment system would use a multiplexer unit to transmit over ten channels of music and audio to every passenger.

MEC   Main Equipment Centre – an area on a modern commercial aircraft where electronic equipment is secured.

NAND GATE   A logic circuit which is a combination of an And gate and an inverter logic element.

NAV-RX   A radio unit used in navigation that contains both a very high frequency omnidirectional (VOR) and a glideslope receiver. It also contains electronic circuitry for VOR and localiser operation. The frequency band used in glideslope is 329.00 to 335.00 megahertz; frequency band in the VOR localiser is from 108.00 to 117.95 megahertz. The localiser frequencies are restricted to the range 108.10 to 111.95 megahertz with selection spaced on odd tenths of a megahertz. When in use the navigation receiver provides an aircraft with localiser glideslope radio approach beam information, and VOR navigation course position.

NDB   Non-Directional Beacon – a radio beacon used by an aircraft ADF system as a navigation aid. The NDB beacons are situated on the coast and at inland sites.

NIGHT EFFECT   An ADF error which is caused by changes in the ionosphere at sunrise and sunset.

NOR GATE   A logic element which is a combination of an inverter and an Or gate logic element.

OMEGA   A navigation system providing stable very low frequency (VLF) radio wave signals during unstable conditions. It operates in the frequency band 9 to 14 kilohertz. Omega is a worldwide navigation aid.

OMNIDIRECTIONAL ANTENNA   An antenna which can transmit and receive in all directions. Example: on an aircraft an antenna meeting that specification is the very high frequency (VHF) radio system type.

OR GATE   This logic element is a Nor gate followed by a Not gate.

PA   Passenger Address Amplifier – used on an aircraft by the flight and cabin crew to speak to the passengers.

PITOT PRESSURE   This is static pressure increased by air pressure resulting from the forward motion of the aircraft through the air. It is sometimes called total pressure = static pressure + dynamic pressure.

PITOT-STATIC SYSTEM   This system on an aircraft provides a source of pitot (dynamic) and static (ambient) pressure to the aircraft systems. The pressure inputs are transferred into altitude and airspeed information signals.

PPI   Planned Position Indicator – a radar indicator which shows the position of radar targets at different horizontal bearings.

PRIMARY RADAR   This is a reflection-type radar. It depends on reflected radio pulse signals from the target aimed at. It is the type of radar used on aircraft to monitor weather conditions in front of the nose. It is also used by ground air traffic control stations.

Q   A term used to express the multiplication factor or gain in a radio tuned circuit. It is also used to describe the selectivity of a tuned circuit.

Q-CODE   A signal code set up to standardise commonly used radio transmissions. Q-codes can be used when flight crews are requesting or receiving messages. For example, QTE means 'What is the true bearing from the ground station?' They are also used when flight crews set up barometric air pressure altimeters. To maintain proper aircraft separation all altimeter settings must be set to the local barometric pressure at different flight levels and airports. This weather and barometric air pressure is transmitted from the local ground station to the aircraft.

Q-FACTOR   A measure of how selective a radio tuned circuit is.

QUADRANTAL ERROR   An error found in ADF systems due to the radio navigation signal being re-radiated from the aircraft airframe.

RADAR   Radar is used to detect moving and static objects like storms, aircraft, ships, mountains, clouds and, as we are all aware of, motor cars. It works by transmitting high frequency radio electromagnetic pulse waves at a target. The reflected signals from the target are then received by the aircraft radar receiver and processed and displayed on a radar indicator in the cockpit.

RADAR FREQUENCIES   Radar equipment operates on different frequencies. L Band frequency is normally around 1,000 megahertz, S Band frequency about 3,000 megahertz; the third band is X Band at 10,000 megahertz, and there is also a Q Band at 3,500 megahertz.

RADAR TEST PATTERN   This pattern is displayed on the radar indicator to show for certain if the system is operating correctly. The pattern displays range marks for the different distances the crew can select. The range marks are zero to 30 miles, zero to 180 and zero to 300 miles. Radar video bands are also displayed.

RADIAL   A line indicating a radio bearing to and from a VOR station.

RADIO ALTIMETER   An instrument used in a low-range radio altimeter (LRRA) system. It operates from zero to 2,500 feet. Frequency range used in the low-range radio altimeter system is from 4,200 to 4,400 mHz.

RADIO FREQUENCY   The number of waves or cycles per second in a radio selected frequency. Unit Hertz. Radio frequencies extend from very low frequency 3 to 30 kilohertz to extremely high frequency 30 to 300 gigahertz.

RADIO FREQUENCY AMPLIFIER   An amplifier circuit designed to increase the signal strength of incoming radio frequencies.

RADIO WAVE   A radio wave consists of an electric field plus a magnetic field. The combination of both fields is called an electromagnetic field. The electromagnetic radio wave fields are at right angles to each other. Radio wave propagation or transmission can be polarised.

RADOME   An aircraft nose cone made of dielectric material which can be removed when access is needed for maintenance. On a typical large transport aircraft the radar, glideslope and localiser antennae are positioned under the radome.

REACTANCE   The opposition of inductance or capacitance in an AC circuit to current flow.

RELAY   A device used for electromagnetic switching in electronic and electrical circuits. Relays are found in many electronic circuits on an aircraft. The two main parts of a relay are the solenoid and the armature.

In addition to these, contacts are used to make or break the current or voltage within the relay. Relays can function in circuits and applications needing micro-current or micro-voltage to control an aircraft task. Also, heavy duty relays can carry large amounts of current. For example, a motor might need a starting current of hundreds of amperes; a relay employed in control operations in an aircraft circuit of this nature would be a heavy duty type of relay. Another function for relays is to provide 28 volts DC when required in radio transmitter/receiver units.

RESONANCE   A condition in an AC circuit when the power factor is unity, phase angle zero and voltage and current in phase.

RESONANT CIRCUIT   A circuit used in radio receivers.

RHEOSTAT   A component of resistance the value of which can be varied. The varying of the resistance changes the current in the circuit. On an aircraft sometimes used to vary pedestal and instrument panel lighting in the cockpit.

RHO-RHO-RHO   A navigation position fixing system which depends on measuring the distance and bearings of fixed points. This method of position fixing is sometimes used in the aircraft Omega navigation system circuits.

RMI   Radio Magnetic Indicator – used to indicate relative bearings from the ADF system. It is also used as an indicator by the very high frequency omnidirectional (VOR) navigation system.

RX   Abbreviation for 'receiver'.

SATCOM   Satellite Communications – a method using satellites which provides reliable global communications. This includes full-time voice and data link communications for passengers, flight crew and cabin crew. It can also provide facsimile message transmission and reception. This system combined with global position system is expected to make possible many changes in airborne and ground methods of navigation and communications.

SCR   Silicon Control Rectifier – a diode which unlike a normal diode has three terminals. The extra terminal is called the 'GATE' and functions like a valve grid. A SCR diode is employed in power rectification and also as an on–off switch in aircraft circuits.

SCU   Seat Control Unit – a control used in aircraft passenger entertainment systems. Located in a typical large aircraft on the arm rest of a passenger seat. The SCU contains music channel select switches, light switch and hostess call switch.

SELCAL   A method called 'selective calling' used to contact a particular aircraft by means of high frequency or very high frequency radio. The aircraft has on board a Selcal unit with a code; when air traffic control transmits that code from the ground it causes an aural warning to be heard in the cockpit.

SENSE ANTENNA   An antenna used in the ADF navigation system.

SENSITIVITY   The measure of signal-to-noise ratio in a receiver. It means the ability of the receiver to give a good audio output from a small received signal at the antenna.

SERVICE INTERPHONE   An aircraft audio communication system which permits ground service crews to talk with each other and with the flight crew in the cockpit. A typical transport aircraft would have service-interphone headphone and mike (MIC) jack sockets positioned at important points around the aircraft. For example: nose wheel point and refuelling point. You might have noticed an aircraft engineer with headset on, stationed at the nose of an aircraft when it was leaving or arriving at an airport terminal building.

SIDETONE   The audio signal portion of a communication transmission used by the flight crew to monitor their radio transmissions.

SIMULATOR   A unit used to train pilots. The overall effect in a simulator is very lifelike. Visual, motion and aural effects are excellent. The original Link flight simulator was invented by an American, Edwin Link, in the 1920s. It became known when the United States Army Air Corps started using it after they lost twelve pilots in air crashes during air mail carrying operations. It is said that half a million pilots received training in the Link simulator during the Second World War. Modern simulators are now so good simulator training is counted as actual flying time.

SKIN EFFECT   Skin effect is a phenomenon which occurs at high radio frequencies. The current flow leaves the centre of the conductor wire and flows on the outside of the conductor.

SQUELCH   A circuit used in the very high frequency radio transmitter/ receiver to prevent continuous signal noise entering the headphones (headsets) of the flight crew. The squelch is adjusted through a variable resistor to allow only radio signals of a certain value to be received in the headphones. Flight crews only want to receive signals bearing information and data needed for flight operation.

SQUITTER   Squitter is the name given to the radio frequency pulse pairs transmitted at random by a DME ground beacon. DME ground beacons transmit at different rates of pulse pairs during operation cycles. When transmitting distance and bearing squitter pulse pairs would be sent out at approximately 2,700 pulse pairs per second.

SSR   Secondary Surveillance Radar – the method of using a unit on the aircraft called a transponder to reply to air traffic control ground radar station transmitters called 'Interrogators'. The transmissions and reply from ground stations and aircraft are in the form of pulses. A big advantage of this radar over primary radar is that it can be operated on low power and it also gives air traffic control more information about the aircraft.

STATIC DISCHARGER   A high resistance rod with a tungsten tip located on its tail. The rod provides a low discharge path for any static charges which build up on the airframe of the aircraft. The rods minimise noise interference in radio communication receivers.

STC   Sensitivity Time Control – an electronic circuit used in a weather radar system. This circuit stops the receiver overloading from signals returning from large radar targets close to the aircraft weather radar transmissions.

STEERING COMPUTER   A computer utilised in an aircraft flight director system to provide pitch commands and bank commands.

SUB-MULTIPLEXER(SUBMUX)   This unit is part of the passenger entertainment system on large aircraft. It is used to supply multiplexed music programmes via coaxial connectors to the seat electronic boxes. The submux is

240

supplied from the main multiplexer and can operate alone if the main multiplexer fails. It can handle up to fifteen channels of signals.

SUPER-HETERODYNE RECEIVER   This radio receiver is used in many avionic systems. It receives the incoming radio frequency, then mixes it with an internal generated frequency from an oscillator circuit; the product of this process is an intermediate frequency. Examples of aircraft systems using this radio receiver are: automatic direction finding radio receiver, very high frequency radio receiver.

SYMBOL GENERATOR   This unit is used to compute signal inputs from the different aircraft systems before the signals are displayed on the electronic flight instrument system (EFIS) cockpit instruments such as EADI and EHSI.

SYNTHESISER   An electronic circuit used in navigation and communication equipment. A synthesiser can generate frequencies electronically. It uses as a reference one master crystal. This means only one crystal is needed. In the past each individual frequency had to have its own crystal.

SYNCHRO   An electromagnetic device which is used to transfer angular-position information or signals from one circuit to another. The transfer can take place within the same area or to another location. Many avionic navigation systems use synchros. A synchro can be compared to a transformer, except that its coils are wound differently.

TCAS   Traffic Alert and Collision Avoidance System – a system installed on aircraft to warn pilots of impending collisions. It uses aural and visual methods to alert pilots to possible danger from other aircraft.

TEST NOISE   A means of testing a weather radar receiver. The radio frequency noise is allowed into the receiver, amplified and shown on the aircraft radar indicator. When displayed it confirms a working receiver.

TRANSDUCER   A device which transmits energy by electrical, mechanical or acoustic means from one system to another. Transducers are used in many systems on an aircraft. An example is the use of a loudspeaker in a communication system. The loudspeaker transfers electrical energy through mechanical means to audio energy.

TRANSPONDER   This unit is used as part of air traffic control. It is an automatic transmitter and receiver. On receiving a signal from air traffic control called an interrogation, the transponder replies with the information required. Operating frequencies are: transmitting – 1,090 megahertz, receiving – 1,030 megahertz.

TVOR   A terminal VOR ground station. Normally located at airports. The power transmitted from this type of station is weaker than a normal VOR station.

TWO FROM FIVE CODE   This code is used in aircraft radio systems. It is based on a system whereby any two from five wires may be earthed. This allows ten possible combinations of choice (one for each digit in a zero to 9 combination). Radio frequency selector boxes can be wired to make use of this system.

TX   Abbreviation for transmitter.

UNDERWATER LOCATION BEACON   This beacon device is used by search and rescue teams to locate aircraft submerged in fresh or salt water. It can transmit a signal of 37 kilohertz in water up to 20,000 feet deep. The signal will be transmitted for up to thirty days.

VISUAL FLIGHT RULES   A method of flying at certain heights using only visual means to navigate the aircraft. To fly under visual flight rules visibility must be good. Most of the early flights over long sea and land distances were attempted under VFR rules.

VOLT   The unit of voltage named after the Italian physicist, Alessandro Volta. He also invented the voltaic pile, which was the first battery.

VSWR   Voltage Standing Wave Ratio – the ratio of forward power and reflected power on a transmission line.

WAVEFORM   A means of describing or showing voltage by graphs how current varies with time. The most common types of waveforms are square, sawtooth, sine and pulse. All waveforms have different frequencies within them.

WAVEGUIDE   A means of conducting radar radio frequency power into the antenna. It is manufactured in rigid and flexible pieces.

WAVEGUIDE SWITCH   A switch used in a radar system to transfer the radar transmitted signal into the weather radar antenna or the dummy load as required.

WATT   A unit of power named after the Scottish engineer, James Watt.

ZENER DIODE   The Zener diode is a silicon junction diode used in many circuits as a voltage stabiliser.

ABBREVIATIONS

ACARS	Airborne Communication Addressing and Release Systems
ACFT	Aircraft
ACP	Audio Control Panel
ACSII	American Standard Code for Information Interchange
a/d	Analogue-to-Digital
a/dc	Analogue-to-Digital Converter
ADC	Air Data Computer
ADF	Automatic Direction Finder
ADI	Attitude Director Indicator
ADS	Automatic Dependent Surveillance
AFCS	Automatic Flight Control System
AFDS	Autopilot Flight Director System
AIP	Aeronautical Information Publication
AIS	Audio Integration System
alt	Altitude
ampl	Amplifier
ant	Antenna
A/P	Autopilot
APD	Approach Progress Display
APU	Auxiliary Power Unit
ARINC	Aeronautical Radio Incorporated
a/s	Airspeed
ASP	Audio Selector Panel
A/T	Autothrottle
ATA	Air Transport Association
ATC	Air Traffic Control
ATE	Automatic Test Equipment
ATLAS	Abbreviated Test Language for All Systems
ATT	Attitude
BCAR	British Civil Airworthiness Requirements
BCD	Binary Coded Decimal
BFO	Beat Frequency Oscillator
BITE	Built-In Test (Equipment)
BTB	Bus Tie Breaker
CAA	Civil Airworthiness Authority
CAPT	Captain
CAS	Computed Airspeed
CB	Circuit Breaker

243

CCW	Counter Clockwise
CDI	Course Deviation Indicator
CDU	Control Display Unit
CDX	Control Differential transmitter
COAX	Coaxial
cplr	Coupler
CPU	Central Processing Unit
CT	Control Transformer
crt	Cathode Ray Tube
CTD	Column Timer Decoder
CX	Control Transmitter
d/a	Digital-to-Analogue
DAA	Digital Analogue Adaptor
d/ac	Digital-to-Analogue Converter
DADC	Digital Air Data Computer
deg	Degree
DFCS	Digital Flight Control System
DFDR	Digital Flight Data Recorder
DFDAU	Digital Flight Data Acquisition Unit
DGPS	Differential Global Position System
dh	Decision Height
DME	Distance Measuring Equipment
EADI	Electronic Attitude Director Indicator
EDSD	Electrostatic Discharge Sensitive Device
EFIS	Electronic Flight Instrument System
EHSI	Electronic Horizontal Situation Indicator
elex	Electronics
ENT	Entertainment
EPR	Engine Pressure Ratio
EPROM	Eraseable Programmable Read Only Memory
ESD	Electrostatic Discharge
ESDS	Electrostatic Discharge Sensitive
ETA	Estimated Time of Arrival
FAA	Federal Aviation Administration
FANS	Future Air Navigation System
FAR	Federal Air Regulatons
FCC	Flight Control Computer
FDAU	Flight Data Acquisition Unit
FDI	Flight Director Indicator
FDR	Flight Data Recorder
FL	Flight Level
FMC	Flight Management Computer
FMCS	Flight Management Computer System
FMS	Flight Management System
F/O	First Officer
GA	Go Around

ABBREVIATIONS

GCA	Ground Controlled Approach
GCB	Generator Circuit Breaker
GCU	Generator Control Unit
Glonass	Global Orbiting Navigation Satellite System
GMT	Greenwich Mean Time
GNSS	Global Navigation Satellite Systems
GPU	Ground Power Unit
GPWC	Ground Proximity Warning Computer
GPWS	Ground Proximity Warning System
G/S	Glideslope
hdg	Heading
hf	High Frequency
HSI	Horizontal Situation Indicator
Hz	Hertz
IAS	Indicated Airspeed
ident	Identification
ILS	Instrument Landing System
inop	Inoperative
intph	Interphone
IRS	Inertial Reference System
IRU	Inertial Reference Unit
IVSI	Instantaneous Vertical Speed Indicator
Kt	Knots
kVA	Kilovolt-ampere
LCD	Liquid Crystal Display
LED	Light Emitting Diode
loc	Localiser
Loran	Long-range air navigation system
LRRA	Low-Range Radio Altimeter system
mec	Main Equipment Centre
MEL	Minimum Equipment List
mHz	MegaHertz
mkr bcn	Marker Beacon
msg	Message
MSU	Mode Selector Unit
mux	Multiplex
NAV	Navigation
nc	Normally Closed
NCD	No Computed Data
norm	Normal
OBS	Observer
ONS	Omega Navigation System
OSC	Oscillator

outbd	Outboard
ovrd	Override
PA	Passenger Address
PAR	Precision Approach Radar
PCU	Power Control Unit
PES	Passenger Entertainment System
PPI	Plan Position Indicator
PRF	Pulse-Recurrence Frequency
PROM	Programmable Read Only Memory
PRR	Pulse-Repetition Rate
PSU	Passenger Service Unit
PTT	Push (or Press) To Talk
pwr	Power
RA	Radio Altimeter
RAM	Random Access Memory
rcdr	Recorder
rcvr	Receiver
rcvr/xmtr	Receiver/Transmitter
RF	Radio Frequency
rly	Relay
RMI	Radio Magnetic Indicator
ROM	Read Only Memory
SCR	Silicon Controlled Rectifier
SEB	Seat Electronics Box
SENS	Sensitivity
SMO	Stabilised Master Operator
SPKR	Speaker
SQL	Squelch
SSR	Secondary Surveillance Radar
stby	Standby
TAS	True Airspeed
TAT	Total Air Temperature
TCAS	Traffic Collision and Avoidance System
TDR	Torque Differential Receiver
TDX	Torque Differential
temp	Temperature
TFEL	Thin-Film Electro-Luminescent
TOGA	Take-Off Go-Around
TRF	Transfer
trk	Track
TR	Torque Receiver Synchro
TRU	Transformer Rectifier Unit
ULD	Underwater Locating Device
USB	Upper Side Band

VHF	Very High Frequency
vol	Volume
VOR	VHF Omni Range
V/S	Vertical Speed
VSI	Vertical Speed Indicator
WAAS	Wide Area Augmentation System
WBL	Wing Buttock Line
WPT	Waypoint
WXR	Weather Radar
xcvr	Transceiver
xdcr	Transducer
xfr	Transfer
xmit	Transmit
xmtr	Transmitter
xpndr	Transponder

TABLE ONE
RADIO COMMUNICATION
PHONETIC ALPHABET

Letter	Word	Pronunciation	Letter	Word	Pronunciation
A	Alpha	ALF AH	N	November	NO VEM BER
B	Bravo	BRA VO	O	Oscar	OS CAR
C	Charlie	CHAR LEE	P	Papa	PAP AH
D	Delta	DEL TA	Q	Quebec	QUE BEK
E	Echo	EK O	R	Romeo	ROM E OH
F	Foxtrot	FOX TROT	S	Sierra	SEA AIR AH
G	Golf	GOLF	T	Tango	TAN G O
H	Hotel	HO TEL	U	Uniform	U NE FORM
I	India	IN DIA	V	Victor	VIC TOR
J	Juliet	JULI ET	W	Whiskey	WHIS KEY
K	Kilo	KILO	X	X-ray	X RAY
L	Lima	LEE MAH	Y	Yankee	YAN KEY
M	Mike	MIKE	Z	Zulu	ZOO LUE

TABLE TWO
MORSE CODE

A	dit dah	J	dit dah dah dah	S	dit dit dit
B	dah dit dit dit	K	dah dit dah	T	dah
C	dah dit dah dit	L	dit dah dit dit	U	dit dit dah
D	dah dit dit	M	dah dah	V	dit dit dit dah
E	dit	N	dah dit	W	dit dah dah
F	dit dit dah dit	O	dah dah dah	X	dah dit dit dah
G	dah dah dit	P	dit dah dah dit	Y	dah dit dah dah
H	dit dit dit dit	Q	dah dah dit dah	Z	dah dah dit dit
I	dit dit	R	dit dah dit		

Example: SOS = dit dit dit   dah dah dah   dit dit dit

BIBLIOGRAPHY

Bose, Keith, *Aviation Electronics*, Howard W. Sams Co., Inc., Indianapolis, Indiana, USA. Third Edition, 1977.

Brinkman, David, *Jane's Avionics*, Jane's Information Group, Brighton Road, Coulsdon, Surrey, England. Eleventh Edition, 1992–3.

Pallett, E.H.J., *Aircraft Instruments*, Pitman Publishing Limited, Long Acre, London, England. Second Edition 1981, reprinted 1982–4 and 1985.

Pallett, E.H.J., *Aircraft Electrical Systems*, Longman Group UK Limited, Burnt Mill, Essex, England. Third Edition, 1986.

Powell, J., *Aircraft Radio Systems*, Pitman Publishing Limited, Long Acre, London, England. First Edition 1981, reprinted 1984–5.

Ramsden, J.M., *The Safe Airline*, Macdonald and Jane's Publishers Ltd, Shepherdess Walk, London, England.

United Airlines Maintenance Operations Training Staff, *Avionics Fundamentals*, IAP Inc., 7383 6WN Road, Casper, Wyoming 82604-1835, USA. First Edition 1974, revised 1987.

Magazines

Avionics Magazine. Editor David W. Robb. Publishers Phillips Business Information Inc., Seven Locks Road, Potomac MD 20852, USA. Published monthly.

Flight International. Publishers Reed Business Publishing, East 42nd Street, New York, USA. Published weekly.

The Boeing Aerospace Company training manuals. The training manuals are very informative and interesting. They are always laid out in a neat manner for aircraft professionals and interested enthusiasts.

Aviation Electronics. The author, Keith Bose, has written a good book on avionics systems. It is written in a practical vein and is suitable for anybody interested in increasing their knowledge of avionics.

Avionics Fundamentals. This book by the maintenance operations training staff of United Airlines gives the reader a good explanation of avionics principles. It also has many illustrations and pictures. This book is useful to anybody wishing to learn more about avionics.

BIBLIOGRAPHY

Aircraft Radio Systems. J. Powell has created a book aimed at the maintenance engineer. It contains much of interest to the non-technical reader. This is a good book for anybody needing more information on radio and navigation systems.

Aircraft Instruments and *Aircraft Electrical Systems.* Both of these books are by E.H.J. Pallett. They give clear explanations of their subject. Each book has many illustrations which help the reader to follow the well-written text. Good books for anybody seeking further knowledge of electrical and instrument systems.

Jane's Avionics, edited by David Brinkman, is an excellent book which contains specific information on civil, military and research avionics. All systems and equipment are discussed and explained. It is a book full of interesting material for the professional and enthusiast. The material is presented in clear non-technical language.

The Safe Airline by J.M. Ramsden is a book which explains in a plain style how the airline industry operates. It also gives information on how a high level of safety is maintained in the industry. A good read for anybody interested in the aviation industry.

The magazines listed are both excellent reading and always publish up-to-date articles on avionics and general aircraft news. *Flight International* is a magazine by professionals in aviation for people interested in all sectors of the aerospace industry. *Avionics Magazine* is also written by professionals and always has very interesting articles on present, future and past avionics systems.

INDEX